Contributing editor, Norman T. Adler

ASSISTANT PROFESSOR, UNIVERSITY OF PENNSYLVANIA

Readings in
Experimental Psychology Today

CRM BOOKS
Del Mar, California

Contents

Introduction

The goals of psychology are scientific and intuitive understanding, accurate prediction, and, where necessary and wise, effective control of the behavior of men and animals. Although much can be done to achieve these goals without resorting to experiment, there is no question of the central role of experimentation in modern psychology.

A psychological experiment, after all, is no more than the careful and explicit manipulation of some condition and the equally careful and explicit measurement of the effects of the manipulation on some aspect of behavior. To be sure, we always have to be careful that we have manipulated what we intended to manipulate—experiments must be controlled. Moreover, our measurements must be repeatable and meaningful—good experiments are both reliable and valid. The core of experimentation, then, comprises manipulation and measurement.

Experiments further our understanding of behavior; some would argue that no firm knowledge can be based on thinking and theory alone but must include experiment. Understanding becomes surer and expands in direct proportion to its actual demonstration with the real behavior of real organisms. If we understand a man's motivation to be material greed, there is no better confirmation of our understanding than to manipulate his greed with large sums of money and observe, if we are correct, corresponding changes in his behavior.

In the same manner, prediction is both verified and enhanced by experimentation. Predictions in isolation share only the not inconsiderable interest of the soothsayer and the clairvoyant. Scientific knowledge advances when predictions are confirmed by measurements of events, and perhaps even more when measurements fail to confirm predictions. For example, the history of public opinion polling records steady advances in predicting the voting behavior of large groups of people. These advances have been as much, or more, advanced by the failures—such as in the Truman-Dewey election in 1948 or the Yorty-Bradley mayoralty election in Los Angeles in 1969—as by the many successes. In each case, real measurement of real events has served to

confirm or deny the predictions of man about men.

Experimentation is crucial in the field of behavioral control. Here, as nowhere else in the history of psychology, there has evolved an effective, experimentally based technology for the wise and effective use of psychological principles. It started in the laboratory with animals. As principles developed, they were systematically and experimentally applied to the behavior of people. The results of experiments with people have been fed back and have affected the conduct of laboratory experiments into basic psychological principles.

Experimental psychology was born toward the end of the nineteenth century in Europe. The concerns of the first experimentalists were, of course, with people, their simple reactions and particularly their sensory impressions. Sensory psychology, in a more sophisticated form, continues to be central to experimental psychology today, as Part II of these readings indicates in depth.

When experimental psychology moved to the United States, around the start of this century, it was preponderantly concerned with animals, their learning and motivation; these concerns are reflected in two broad trends in modern psychology: the work in learning and behavior modification (Part III) and the study of motivational and biological factors (Part IV).

But people cannot be kept from studying people, intrinsically the most fascinating of animals. Experimentally, this concern has expressed itself in studies of communication and thought (Part II), although it also pervades sensory experimentation, as well as the educational and therapeutic applications of principles of learning.

Modern experimental psychology is thus a blend of the European and historical and the American and modern. Psychologists today use scientific experimentation to further their understanding of man—his behavior, his motivation, his hereditary hangups or gifts, his sensory mechanisms, his cognitive abilities or disabilities, his drives. The information they gain is scientifically grounded, permitting prediction; it also can be applied by other psychologists to guide therapy and for beneficent control of behavior.

I
Philosophical and
Historical Basis of Psychology

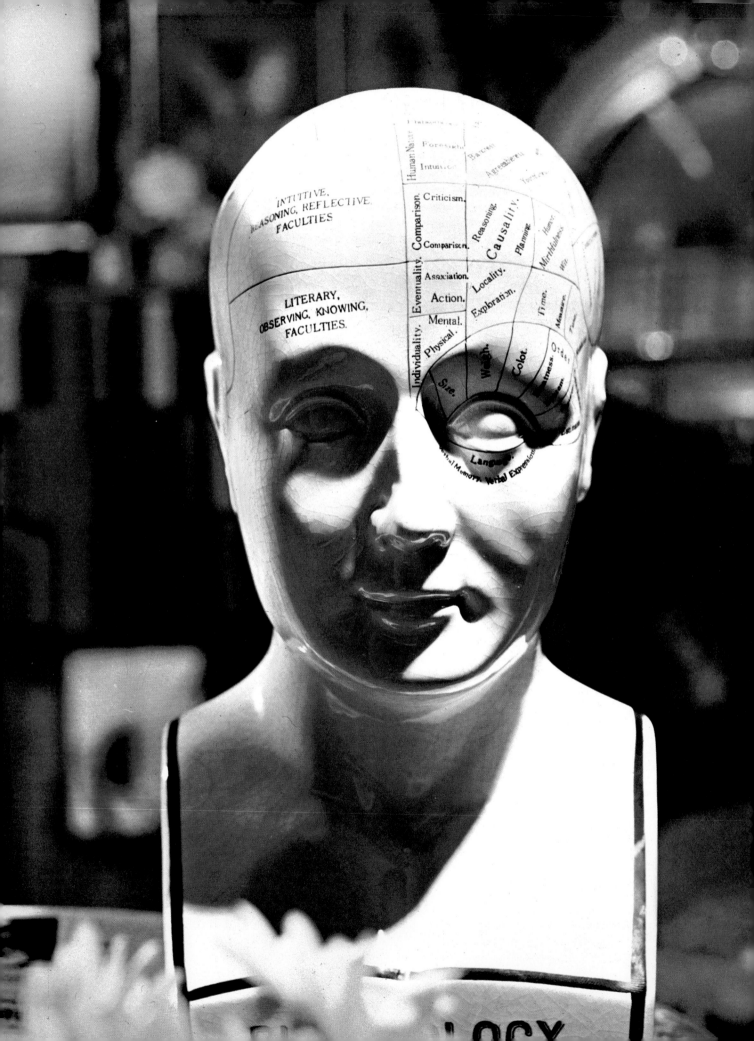

Is Phrenology Foolish?
David Bakan

Psychology today is more than the study of behavior. It is an intellectual tradition based upon historical and philosophical precedents. David Bakan explores the devious and fascinating history of phrenology. Considered a hoax in modern times, phrenology, as the author points out, was developed by some of the great physiologists of the eighteenth and nineteenth centuries. Although phrenology in its character-analysis function was a fad, its emphasis on individual differences and the possibilities for self-improvement was the start of a tradition still influencing American educational practices and a source of scientific problems. Currently relevant topics like localization of function in the brain and the role of the nervous system in behavior emerge from this movement.

There is a shop like it everywhere. It's a narrow, dim little thing, crammed with the oddments of half a dozen times and cultures. It looks dusty but really isn't; it should contain valuable "curiosities," but one is at a loss to say what their value might be. For the most part, the contents of such a shop are unintelligible. Those square brown bottles look as if they once were used; there is a painted cast-iron dog that clearly was a toy; there are tons of old prints, swords, and walking sticks. That's an astrolabe, perhaps, and that the visor from a suit of armor. The rest is yesterday's nameless junk become today's *bizarrerie*. Sometimes a passerby may glimpse, through a ship's wheel or behind a row of campy Perseuses, a smallish porcelain bust.

This bust usually has thin, sensitive, slightly smirking lips and a high, poetic-looking forehead. Beginning under the eyes is a network of lines that wriggle up over the brow and spread out over the skull, forming a series of contiguous patches reminiscent of a picture puzzle, or of a well-cracked hard-boiled egg. In each patch or puzzle-piece there is a neatly lettered word: Combativeness, Ideality, Reverence, Self-Esteem, Language, and some thirty more, all nouns and all capitalized, abstract, and long—the lexicon of some stone-dead philosophy.

"What's *that*, for heaven's sake?"

"Oh, that's something they used in phrenology," a friend might chuckle. "You know, that thing about reading the bumps on your head? Some sort of parlor game, like table tipping, automatic writing, palm reading, and that kind of thing."

The bemused citizen won't get much more from a good desk dictionary, where he will find something like this:

The doctrine or belief that the outer configurations of the skull indicate the position and the strength or intensity of various mental faculties and characteristics. [From Greek *phren*, *phrenos*, mind + -logy, science or study of]—phren. o. log' ic or i. cal *adj*—phre. nol' o. gist *n*

In other words, there is little readily available within the store of popular or current academic knowledge that would connect our porcelain bust with some of the most prestigious names in early nineteenth-century American culture, and nothing to suggest that phrenology may have had an important influence on the development of twentieth-century American psychology.

Well, what was phrenology? Examined historically, phrenology appears to have two parts: the *-logy* or science part, and the hoopla or country-fair part, each of which made its contribution to nineteenth-century American culture—that same culture within which twentieth-century psychology developed certain peculiarly American features.

Phrenology as Science

The *-logy* part of phrenology was, at least in terms of the *theory* of scientific inquiry, neither pre-science nor pseudo-science; it was science pure and simple, indeed the better of its day. The science part of phrenology grew from the researches of two men, Franz Joseph Gall (1758–1828) and Johann Kaspar Spurzheim (1776–1832). Both men were Germans and physicians, and both are accorded respect by the historians of science as pioneer neurologists. Spurzheim modified Gall's theories in certain particulars, but together they laid down and publicized the three broad hypotheses within which phrenology conducted itself.

If I say that phrenology, as it was understood by Gall and Spurzheim, postulated and studied *the influence of physiological and anatomical characteristics upon mental behavior*, and, in particular, asserted and studied *the cortical localization of function*, it doesn't sound too terribly quaint or pre-scientific, and that is precisely the larger framework in which phrenology should be viewed. In accordance with these two overarching hypotheses ("laws" or "facts" we are perhaps unwisely tempted to call them now), the phrenologists conceived of a human brain having some thirty-seven independent powers or functions.

About fourteen of these functions were considered "intellective" and the remainder were "affective," like Amativeness (the various sexual urges or "passions"), Adhesiveness (the ability to form and maintain attachments to persons), Ideality (the power or faculty of imagination), Self-Esteem (a favorable term meaning self-respect or even self-understanding), Reverence, Benevolence, and so on. These powers were located in different regions or "organs" of the brain, the organs or physical sites being named after their respective powers or functions.

Deriving from the relationship of function and cerebral region was the famous doctrine of the skull, now the only feature by which phrenology is remembered. The doctrine of the skull held that *the development of the cerebral regions affected the size and contour of the cranium,* so that a well-developed part of the skull would indicate a correspondingly well-developed organ or mental faculty.

These three hypotheses formed a lamp of theory under which Gall and Spurzheim proceeded with painstaking caution. Their labors may be described in such

terms as "empiricism," "observation," and "testing of propositions." The phrenologists were extremely and scientifically self-conscious, and particularly crusty about what they called "metaphysical authors and mystical psychologists." The latter speculated in their armchairs and did not go out and observe as Lord Bacon had advised. By metaphysical authors they meant, for example, John Locke, an ancestor in the direct line of Titchener and the structuralists, whom American functionalists were later to attack so keenly. The early phrenologists used the word "metaphysical" as a term of utter opprobrium; indeed, their tone on the whole subject of armchair speculation and untestable propositions reminds one of the behaviorist Max Meyer, who posted a sign over the entrance to the laboratory of the University of Missouri that said "No metaphysicians or dogs allowed," or of John B. Watson, who snapped at misty-eyed souls that there was no such thing as mind. In an address to the Boston Phrenological Society in 1832, a speaker delivered the following positivistic blast:

Enemies [of phrenology] have said that it is an *irreligious* science—that it leads to *materialism.* My objection to this argument is, that it is entirely senseless. My allegation is, not that it is false, but unintelligible. The question, *whether the brain thinks,* is merely logomachy; the words, however correct in grammatical construction, have not any correspondent ideas, and cannot have . . .

Shades of Ludwig Wittgenstein, and words that should delight anyone favorable to modern positivistic thought. James Shannon, president of Bacon College in Kentucky, an advocate of phrenology, put the *-logy* part of phrenology quite unexceptionably:

Whoever maintains that the brain is the organ by which the mind acts, and that the mind performs different functions by different parts of the brain, is a phrenologist. This is the broad basis upon which the science of phrenology rests. All beyond this are merely the details of the science, and subjects of enquiry and observation.

What caused difficulties for scientific phrenology were the limitations of the means of inquiry and the emergence of data that were less than wholly confirmatory. Gall, Spurzheim, and other phrenologists were attempting to account for the obvious fact that some men had mental gifts or powers that enabled them or compelled them to perform in ways different from others. They succeeded in approaching this scientifically, in the sense that they imposed a reasonably comprehensive, reasonably noncontradictory organization or order upon the data *available to them.* Prior to the advent of phrenology there was a relative chaos of unconnected observations: some men clearly had a capacity for friendship, others equally clearly had not; some had lofty or fertile imaginations; some had great gifts of logical analysis; some had an intense interest in sex, while others were more sluggish.

The aim of the phrenologists in assigning human

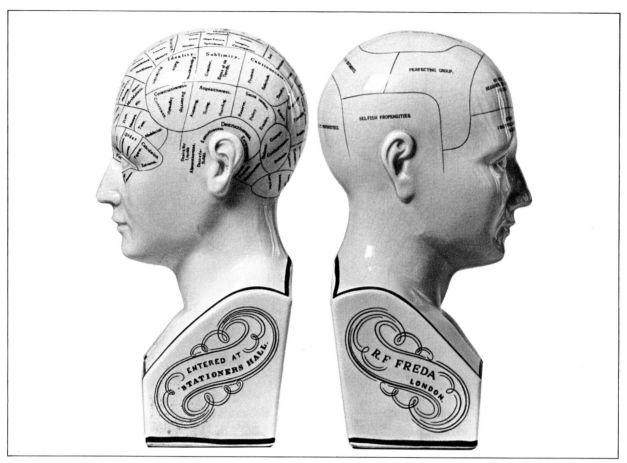

functioning to these particular thirty-seven-odd categories was in no way different from the aim of modern psychologists interested in assessing human functioning. It was to find variables on which people differed from each other of such a nature that manifestations of the variables would correlate highly among themselves but the correlations among the variables would be low.

It will be noted that I have just formulated the problem of the categories for human assessment in terms of correlation. Indeed, it was the absence of appropriate correlational devices, including techniques of factor analysis, that turned out to be a major reason for the failure of scientific phrenology to thrive.

What the early phrenologists needed was a statistical tool enabling them to study relatively large samples in terms of correlation among personality and intellectual manifestations in behavior. Such a tool hadn't been invented yet, and so they applied instead cruder sorts of correlational analyses. Yet their efforts at collecting data, tabulating them, and categorizing measurements by types of personality as they could assess them are very obvious harbingers of the methods of personality assessment in use today.

Even an experimental orientation is distinctly evident in Pierre Flourens' experiments with pigeons' brains, in the course of which the French physiologist demon-

strated (in 1845) that the excision of the cerebellum—the phrenologists' organ of Amativeness—did *not* impair the urge or ability to reproduce. In 1861 the French surgeon and anthropologist Paul Broca demonstrated that the faculty of speech was *not* seated behind the eyes, but in another part of the brain entirely. Although these two experiments were plainly sponsored by the phrenological movement, they constituted a double-barreled *coup de grâce* in the eyes of an already highly skeptical scientific community.

The empirical orientation of the phrenological movement was itself associated with the movement's becoming the object of skepticism. The empirical conscience of Spurzheim and other responsible phrenologists was expressing grave doubts about the so-called doctrine of the skull, which was giving way under the weight of observations that skull characteristics and behavioral manifestations were not as highly correlated as had been believed (even without the help of correlation coefficients). By the mid-1830s serious phrenologists were at pains to dissociate themselves from it.

Yet by this time the word phrenology was so firmly bonded to the doctrine of the skull, which was always conceived of as only a part of phrenology, that the refutation of that doctrine could only be interpreted as the failure of the whole movement. Meanwhile another kind of phrenology, more popular but much less scientifically meticulous, had seized upon the doctrine of the skull and made it its central feature. By the late 1840s the scientific and intellectual community had accepted the identification of phrenology with its vulgar expression and shrank from the slightest contact with it, to the extent of repressing its connection with the scientific research that continued to be done in both Europe and America.

Phrenology as Hooplah

Johann Spurzheim arrived in Boston on August 24, 1832. He gave many lectures and demonstrations, including a series of lectures at Harvard, with a special series for the medical faculty. As one contemporary observer put it, "the professors were in love with him." Some six frenzied weeks after his arrival Spurzheim died, mostly it would seem of exhaustion, his brains having been thoroughly picked by the Brahminical professors. There was a widely attended funeral, with most of intellectual Boston in attendance. A specially formed committee, headed by Josiah Quincy, the president of Harvard, expressed "a sense of the public loss sustained by the death of this distinguished man," and the Boston Phrenological Society was formed as a memorial to him.

In September of 1832, George Combe, a Scottish lawyer, came to America. Combe, though not a physician, had thoroughly studied the work of Gall and Spurzheim, and he could demonstrate Spurzheim's new dissecting techniques as well as all the extremely minute craniological measuring procedures. (Combe made important technical contributions to the methodology of Dr. Samuel G. Morton, whose works in physical anthropology are considered seminal.) This polished and witty man very favorably impressed Daniel Webster, William Emery Channing, Horace Mann, Dr. Samuel Gridley Howe, and many other leading New Englanders. He became the darling of that lecture-loving age and spoke to large, enthusiastic audiences in Boston, New York, Albany, Philadelphia, Baltimore, Washington, and other eastern cities.

The initial enthusiasm for phrenological lectures was the property of that same fairly large, relatively homogeneous class of cultivated persons who were responsible for the burst of intellectual activity often referred to as the New England Renaissance, having Boston-Cambridge-Concord as its hub. As this first vociferous enthusiasm on the part of the lyceum crowd began to wane—partly because phrenology ceased to be as novel as, say, mesmerism—the popularists saw a good thing and moved in.

The belief that science was a particularly direct and efficacious instrument for improving human life had been expressed and put into practice by Franklin and Jefferson; this belief had spread rapidly and taken deep roots, nurtured by the ripples of material prosperity re-

sulting from the nation's first major industrial expansion. The ordinary citizen became increasingly receptive to anything that was "scientific." Phrenology was touted as scientific, promising to analyze a person thoroughly, quickly, and sympathetically (that is, "democratically"). It guaranteed to show him, scientifically, the way to personal improvement and personal happiness.

The energetic tutelage to the nation by the firm of Fowler and Wells spread phrenology and enriched them. The huckstering mind is essentially the same in all times and climates, whether speaking from the back of a painted wagon or in front of a TV camera. And the vast majority of men have always wondered with varying degrees of intensity who they are and who their neighbors are, and how they can perfect themselves; just as surely they have welcomed anyone or anything that promises unambiguously to tell them. Thus phrenology came to enjoy an extraordinary popularity in mid-nineteenth-century America. Fowler and Wells turned it into a national industry. They had "parlors" in New York, Boston, and Philadelphia. They booked lecture tours for traveling phrenologists in every corner of the nation. The list of their publications on phrenology was virtually endless. They published all the classical literature, and they themselves were tremendously prolific; their *Phrenological Self-Instructor* was a best seller. They sold all sorts of paraphernalia to be used in connection with examinations and demonstrations: busts, pointers, charts, skulls, casts of famous heads. As the vogue spread from the salons of the East, popular phrenology became increasingly cluttered with these paraphernalia, each itinerant phrenologist adding, according to his genius, some additional gimmick. In the space of a few decades, popular phrenology became a rural entertainment whose charlatanry was a source of embarrassment to any thoughtful man.

But before popular phrenology got quite out of hand, it put into wide circulation one of the major devices associated with all psychometric movements, the printed rating-scale specifying clear alternatives. On each of these rating-scales or "test forms" the phrenologist would indicate the magnitude of each of the thirty-seven-odd functions or organs. The ratings varied from "small-medium-large" to nine-point values, sometimes further qualified by pluses and minuses. The scales were accompanied by complete explanations, so that the person phrenologized could read about himself in detail and gain a clear "mental daguerreotype," as a Fowler and Wells advertisement put it, of himself. It was a fundamental assumption of popular phrenology that one could infer the nature of mental functioning on the basis of information collected in an hour or so. This assumption met almost no resistance and is still retained in most modern psychometric methods.

The Cultural Interweave

The science of any period is a rich source of what are essentially images or metaphors that illustrate, if not shape, that period's view of itself. After a certain time lag, these images or metaphors become the skeleton on which the articulate members of a culture unwittingly drape their various arguments and propositions. The influence of evolution and natural selection as Victorian metaphors has been widely discussed; "relativity," however vaguely understood, has impressed itself deeply on twentieth-century culture as a metaphorical equivalent of "discontinuity," "isolation," or "loneliness." (It is only a short symbolic step from trains passing each other in the daylight to ships passing in the night.) As the most widely discussed science of its period, phrenology also provided a set of images or metaphors or formulaic ideas that could be applied to widely varying problems and situations.

The wide acceptance of phrenology as a valid science and as an exciting entertainment meant that its assumptions were assimilated on a large scale. You simply couldn't talk about phrenology intelligently and sympathetically unless you first accepted its fundamental

lunatic had been taken back, divinely withdrawn in retribution for some secret sin or crime, and the devil(s) had moved into the vacuum. It was very difficult to square this idea with alternations of lunacy and lucidity without raising theological questions about a divine Indian-giving; treatment sometimes consisted in quite literally beating the devil out of the temporarily afflicted. Phrenology's simple assertion that only part of the brain was afflicted was accepted *because it worked;* it enabled people to argue quite sensibly for conditions in which a particular weakened faculty could in some way be modified by "exercise." You could no longer exile or punish people for insanity, any more than you could punish them for more physical forms of weakness.

This image or metaphor of brain exercise applied equally well to criminals. Reformers armed with phrenological arguments objected to capital punishment or physical punishment of any sort, and advocated instead proper conditions for exercise and thus, interestingly enough, for the indeterminate sentence. In all cases

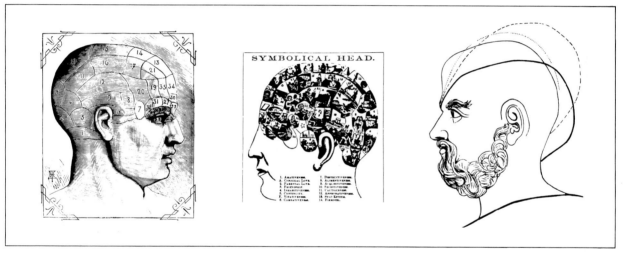

premise that man himself could be studied scientifically and that the phenomena of mind could be studied objectively and explained in terms of natural causes. On a less articulate level, millions of people absorbed such a premise as they lined up to have the bumps on their skulls read.

From its beginnings in Gall and Spurzheim to its brassiest moments in the sideshow, phrenology expressed the notion that the different parts of the brain could be altered, trained, or flexed as the different parts of the body or musculature could be. Perceived as a sort of mental flash or headline—THE MIND IS A SET OF MUSCLES—this notion became a metaphor that was of immense practical use to all sorts of people.

Humane men and women were, for instance, desperately concerned with the plight of the insane. So long as the mind or brain was conceived of as a unitary, nonmaterial entity—a disembodied bit of the Godhead —treatment of the insane could only take the form of horrified neglect or active punishment. The mind of the

they urged the modification of treatment with respect to the phrenological or mental characteristics of the individual criminal.

A more specific though less significant event might be chosen to illustrate the genuine *practicality* of phrenology in its time. Blind deaf-mutes were considered utterly beyond the reach of human aid. Dr. Samuel Gridley Howe, who became the head of the Perkins School for the Blind in Boston, had Laura Bridgman examined phrenologically. The analysis of her skull "proved" that she had an active, intelligent brain. Work was then begun that enabled Laura Bridgman to become the first systematically educated blind deaf-mute, work that continued long after the doctrine of the skull had dropped into the scientific limbo.

Phrenologists took a deep interest in the psychology of learning and were well represented in the avant-garde of educational reformers. Horace Mann, who as the first secretary of the Massachusetts Board of Education revolutionized public instruction, was steeped in phrenological thought. (He had been so impressed by George Combe that he named a son after him.) Phrenologists urged a short school day, together with physical training and a good deal of free play; they were opposed to drill and the use of punishment; they advocated "learning by doing"; they objected to training in the classics exclusively and urged the training of all the mental faculties—always with the metaphorical model before them that learning was simply the proper exercise of the muscles. (In connection with their belief that environment influenced mental behavior, they argued that infants should be exposed to as many "sensations" or stimuli as possible. Recent studies in the cheerless wards of municipal hospitals have drawn much the same conclusions.)

In its role as a vehicle for cultural values, popular phrenology was intensely democratic, in the Jefferson-Jackson tradition. It confirmed every man's notion that he had individual talents that needed only to be discovered and exploited. These talents could be scientifically identified and a vocation chosen—they (and not, for example, social background) constituted a sufficient and legitimate entrée to whatever career was indicated. That individual potential could be identified speedily and scientifically became an acceptable *fact*. Horace Greeley advocated editorially that phrenology be used in the selection of trainmen, as a way of reducing accidents. Want ads like this one, which appeared in the *New York Sun*, became fairly common:

Apprentice wanted.—A stout boy not over 15 years of age, of German or Scotch parents, to learn a good but difficult trade. N.B.—it will be necessary to bring a recommendation to his abilities from Messrs. Fowler and Wells, Phrenologists, Nassau Street. Apply corner of West and Franklin Streets.

Fowler and Wells did a booming business in such recommendations, and it is difficult to dismiss them as just another exhibit in the vast museum of suckerdom. Computerized matchmaking firms are doing a profitable business today, and their printed forms are remarkably similar in mode to the phrenological test forms with which stout boys trotted down to the corner of Franklin Street. It has become apparent that a goodly percentage of the aptitude and achievement tests widely adopted by school systems and by industry test only the ability to read or verbalize on certain middle-class wavelengths. The interesting thing here is not that it's easy to sling phrenological mud at modern psychometrics, but rather that *all* forms of psychometric assessment have been very generously received by American culture.

Even literature was informed by the phrenological movement. Poe based his entire theory of poetry on the faculty of Ideality, and his Roderick Usher types are cast in phrenological molds. Whitman salted his poetry and prose with phrenological names. He particularly loved Adhesiveness because he was told that he had a large dose of that "comradely" virtue, and was so taken by the rating-scale done for him by Fowler and Wells that he had it bound into the early editions of *Leaves of Grass*.

In its role as a discipline, phrenology performed importantly in the front lines of the virulent war between science and religion. Phrenology was bitterly attacked by conservative church groups for its radical implications for the life of society. It was regarded as inevitably leading to atheism and, because it made moral or immoral behavior dependent on the nature of the body, to immorality. Some observed with considerable outrage that things like soul, spirit, and faith had to be squeezed into the organ of Reverence, just one among thirty-seven, and rather smaller than that of Amativeness, for instance. In short, there was a good deal of preliminary skirmishing, to be followed by the great battles between religion and science that were to be occasioned by the publication of *On the Origin of Species* in 1859.

In his introduction to that work, Darwin mentions a book called *Vestiges of the Natural History of Creation*. The *Vestiges* was published (anonymously) in 1844 and had gone through ten editions and revisions by 1853.

It had caused a frightful stink, having advanced a theory of the evolution of the species, which, however, lacked the theory of natural selection to be added by Darwin. The author of the *Vestiges* was Robert Chambers, a Scotsman and close friend of George Combe and his brother Andrew, physician to Queen Victoria, and also a leading spokesman of the phrenological movement. Darwin praised the *Vestiges* in the following terms: "In my opinion it has done excellent service in this country in calling attention to the subject [evolution], in removing prejudice, and in thus preparing the ground for the reception of analogous views."

Cannot the same thing be said for phrenology as a whole? That it prepared the ground by introducing into the arena of public discussion many of the same issues and in many of the same terms? The phrenological movement displayed a perhaps inordinate optimism about the possibilities of change through education and modification of the environment, an optimism very like John B. Watson's. To mention an even more striking parallel, the "atmosphere" of phrenology is most congenial to many of the social and scientific assumptions that stand behind B. F. Skinner's *Walden Two* utopianism.

Man, and man's mind, could be studied objectively. Radical changes could be effected in the mind by altering the relationships among the various cerebral functions and by modifying the environment in which those relationships are formed. These radical changes in mental behavior were, for the most part, necessary and desirable. These are the conclusions that American functionalists drew from the Darwinian theories. And they are for the most part central to phrenological thought. The *Vestiges* drew heavily upon phrenological thought; phrenological thought got a thorough airing in the United States in the 1830s and 1840s; and Darwin drew heavily on the *Vestiges*. That is to say, there seems to be a discernible underlying continuity or tradition of psychological theory and practice stretching from the early 1830s into the twentieth century, and it seems reasonable to suggest that the general terms in which phrenologists articulated their optimistic science sank into American culture and remained there, to be re-aroused with the advent of the self-consciously scientific psychology of the late nineteenth and twentieth centuries.

Now is perhaps the time to underscore a point that must seem obvious; namely, that phrenology was a science of *individual differences*. It was grounded in the belief that every man had a different "cerebral musculature" and that conditions could and should be individually tailored to innate differences and with respect to the flexibility allowed by the analogy to the musculature. Gall and Spurzheim wanted to know *why* some men made good bankers or poets or murderers, and phrenology was the system they constructed as an answer. Popular phrenology quickly appropriated this system and bent it to intensely practical uses—aptitude testing, vocational guidance, marriage counseling, and the patching up of the sore spots of a man's life wherever they might lie.

"Ganz Amerikanisch"

Within psychology as a whole, there are two major approaches to psychological phenomena. One is the effort to obtain general propositions that hold for the generalized human organism. The other is a study of individual differences, the measurement and assessment of those individual capacities that enable a given person to adjust to and manipulate his environment. The study of individual differences lies at the center of the functionalism that began with William James and with John Dewey and J. R. Angell. Historically, such functionalism exists in a prior or telegonic relationship with industrial psychology, with the social psychology of William McDougall, and with certain applications of behaviorist doctrines, all of which form a strand or cluster of emphasis felt to be characteristically American.

Psychology is usually considered to have been born as an independent discipline in the last quarter of the nineteenth century. At this time, young American scholars went to Germany to learn the "new" psychology, largely from Wilhelm Wundt, who in 1879 had set up the first important laboratory for experimental psychology. His laboratory was designed to generate and test propositions that would be true for all persons, for a human mind assumed for the purposes of research to be generalized and nonunique. The American students returned to their colleges and universities to set up laboratories, do research, and teach in the new ways they had acquired in Germany. However, almost immediately they began to use their new methods to study individual differences. They seemed to consider this radical change of target hardly worthy of comment, but Wundt referred to it as *ganz amerikanisch*—entirely and typically American.

Historians of psychology account for this seemingly instinctive shift of emphasis by speaking of pressures soundlessly exerted by the cultural environment, and they point to the confluence of Darwinian theories and the general competitiveness of American society as a major source of those pressures. But a case can be made, perhaps, for the following plot summary: the widespread familiarity with phrenological theories; the repression of these theories on the part of the scientific community both because of the failure of the doctrine of the skull and because of the excesses of popular vulgarized phrenology; the advent of the Darwinian argument, informed by many of the same theories; the enthusiastic and perhaps even uncritical reception by the scientific community of Darwin's theories; the ready seizure by American functionalists of certain Darwinian motifs, especially those relating to organic structure and function as the products of successful adaptation; the remarriage of these motifs with a bias toward individual differences that had been lurking in the context of scientific psychology since Spurzheim talked to the Boston doctors.

The Psychology of Robots

Henry David Block and Herbert Ginsburg

When Descartes put forth his mind-body dualism, he initiated one of the most enduring traditions in psychology, man as machine. With the advent of robots, computers, and cybernetic theory, psychology entered the latest phase of the man-as-machine tradition. In the present article Block and Ginsburg discuss the building of behaving and perhaps thinking automata. After explaining the kinds of learning and perception of which robots are capable, the authors discuss the future potential of these devices. They also speculate on the "ethics" of man-machine relations.

Robots have begun to teach children, explore the moon, sort mail, launch spaceships, watch bank accounts, carry out previously impossible scientific experiments, check income tax returns—and a computer may even make the decision to initiate our next war. We have already entered into the first phase of the Age of Robots. This is a time in the affairs of men when machines operate with almost human intelligence and perform functions that once only man could do.

Besides sharing his labor, machines also literally have become *parts* of man. For example, many people owe their lives to an artificial kidney, to a pacemaker that keeps the heart beating regularly, or to an artificial lung. The result is a living organism, part human, part machine, that can be considered a *cyborg*, a term coined for a cybernetic organism by science writer Daniel S. Halacy, Jr.

To many psychologists, robots offer a way to simulate psychological processes. We reason that if we can understand a psychological process, we ought to be able to build a machine that puts that process into action. For example, if we propose a model for letter recognition, then we should be able to construct a robot that recognizes letters. If we are successful, our model is at least an adequate solution. If our machine does not recognize letters, clearly something is lacking in the theory.

Psychologists are interested in robots for other reasons. One of these is a theoretical concern with the basic mechanisms underlying a robot's performance. The argument runs like this. Often robots are designed to replace people at some job. Robots calculate; they teach; they do chemical analyses. In fact, much of robot performance could be termed "intelligent." Robots get information from the world and manipulate this knowledge in different ways. Since robots seem to perform intelligently, the psychologist is interested in studying the processes enabling them to do so. The psychologist has a strong desire to peer into the proverbial "black box" to see the ways in which the innards of the machine operate. For the psychologist, the robot is a dream fulfilled; one can look into this machine, hoping to see more there than one's imaginings. Does the black box contain stimulus-response connections, cognitive maps, learning networks, or something else? Of course, having fathomed the contents of the box, the psychologist has no guarantee that people function just as robots do. But at least he has discovered one possible process underlying a given psychological function.

Critics often disparage the idea that machines exhibit intelligent behavior, dismissing the concept with a curt, "They'll do only what you tell them to do." This simply is not true of "learning machines," particularly those that are capable of making random—therefore undirected—choices. Nor is it true for analog computers.

Recent developments in engineering point the way to new directions in the design of robots. It is already possible to perceive the general outlines of robots of the future, although the details of their implementation remain hazy. In the next twenty years robots will perform increasingly sophisticated tasks. They will imitate humans, navigate about the landscape, understand a language, and recognize objects. What will be the nature of these machines? How will robots of the future get information from the environment and make use of what they have learned? Perhaps a comparative psychology of modern robots will answer some of these questions.

Sensation

In some ways the sensory abilities of machines are far more acute than those of man. Robots are not limited to the range and type of physical energies to which man's sensory system is attuned. Robots can detect and respond to the entire electromagnetic spectrum, including radio waves, infrared, ultraviolet, x rays, and gamma rays. When so designed they are much more sensitive to sonar, temperatures, humidity and to the presence of many chemicals. The robot sidewinder missile, for example, like the sidewinder snake, senses the heat emanating from its intended victim. The missile's sensors can detect the heat from a jet aircraft engine at a great distance and direct the missile on a path to intercept that heat source. Similar arrangements can be made from an ICBM to seek out the center of a city, which is distinctly warmer than the surrounding countryside. The gyro platforms of spacecraft maintain their bearings with an accuracy that makes the motion sensitivity of our inner ear seem very crude.

Helicopter pilots complain that engine noise prevents them from hearing bullets hitting the craft. A computer, analyzing the ambient noise of the engine, can detect the signal added by the sound of impacting bullets. The sonar cane and the laser cane, currently being developed to help the blind navigate, detect the presence of obstacles by sound or laser beams respectively.

Perception

While the robot generally excels in sensation, he encounters difficulties in perceptual functioning. It is hard for a robot to recognize an object that is in its natural surroundings. This, of course, is an easy task for even a small child. A three-year-old can walk into a room and correctly identify a toy contained in a box. He can do this even though the amount of light reflected from the toy, its shape, its color, and so on, are all different from what he has experienced before. In fact, the child can recognize the toy even when only part of it is visible. And if the toy moves, the child can usually track it, and considers that it is the same toy despite the many perceptual changes that have taken place. Of course, many perceptual skills underlie the child's recognition of the toy. The child must isolate figure from ground; he must perceive constancies of form, brightness, distance, and color; he must follow a moving object and attribute to it a constant identity; and he must infer the whole object from a visible part.

Robots cannot yet perform at this level. The three-year-old (and perhaps even the six-month-old) is generally superior as far as perception is concerned.

Today's robots can "read" the magnetic printing on bank checks by matching each specially designed character against standard templates. Clearly these are highly artificial conditions. Within the past year robots have been given a limited ability to read printed writing (zip codes on mail and certain business office forms). "Learning" procedures, instead of mere template matching, are sometimes utilized in the design of these machines. More sophisticated techniques employ feature recognizers, which involve the detection of only certain critical characteristics, thereby reducing the amount of stored data required for "reading." In spite of this it probably will be some time before a machine can understand handwriting because recognition of irregularly formed letters so often relies on context and meaning. For example, most people can easily read a half-blurred word on the printed page. We use such contextual cues as the sequential probabilities of the letters (if the first letter is q, the second is almost certainly u) and the meaning of the sentence ("he used a bucket to draw———from the well"). Current research on pattern recognition is developing methods so robots can use as information not only the frequency-of-letter combinations but also grammatical context.

Speech recognition also is difficult for machines, again because context and meaning are involved. A step in this direction is the auditory pattern recognition machine, "Tobermory," currently being built at Cornell University under the direction of Frank Rosenblatt. Successful development of robots that can recognize a spoken human language will require some radically new strategies in processing the incoming information. New ideas will emerge from the collaborative efforts of both psychologists and engineers.

Global or generalized decision, another type of visual perception problem, appears to be beyond the ability of current machines. Consider the problems: Does the object have a hole in it? Is the boy in front of the table? How many pirates can you find hiding in the tree? The superiority of humans in these and similar perceptual problems probably is related to extensive experience and manipulation of the environment. By contrast, current robots are "creatures of instinct"; their design provides them with a fixed computational procedure for the solution of these problems. Robots of the future will have a greater capability to "learn" and to adapt themselves to their environment.

Getting Information

Today most robots are passive creatures. The computer, the pattern recognizer, and many other machines not only lack the means to leave their homes but would meet disaster if they did. Also, the current robot must be spoon-fed. It requires highly structured and specific formats of inputs and outputs, like punch cards or magnetic tape, in order to operate effectively. In the future, however, robots will explore their environment; they will actively seek out experiences and information.

A prototype for robots of this sort is currently being developed at Stanford Research Institute by Nils Nilsson, Charles Rosen, and others. This machine, which we will call for now the "Wanderer," can explore a limited environment, such as a large room (see Figure 1). The Wanderer's "brain" is a computer, which divides the room into imaginary regions, like a checkerboard (see Figure 2). In our approximate version of its program-

Figure 1. The Wanderer, a robot developed at Stanford Research Institute.

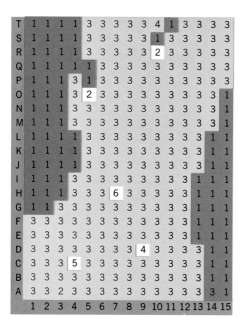

Figure 2. The Wanderer is a self-navigating robot that explores a strange room by dividing it into imaginary regions and registering in each region what it has perceived. This image then becomes the robot's cognitive "world map."

ming, we can say that the computer initially assigns the symbol "1" to each square, indicating to the machine that it does not know the contents of the corresponding region of the room. The robot has "eyes" (a range finder) so that it can look around the room. If it sees something occupying a particular region, it changes the symbol in the corresponding memory square to "2," whereas if it sees that the region is empty it changes the corresponding square to read "3." For regions that the machine can't see, the symbols are left unchanged. The robot wanders around the room under the control of the computer. If it touches an object in a certain region in the room, the computer changes its entry in the corresponding square to "4" if the object is movable and to "5" if the object is immovable. The square corresponding to the position of the robot itself is labeled "6" and this figure moves around the memory as the robot moves around the room.

Such a robot, after being left for a while to familiarize itself with the contents of the room, can execute the following instructions: "Proceed from where you are at H-7 to location A-3 being sure not to hit any object and all the while remaining unobservable from location T-10. This is to be done by the shortest path possible subject to these conditions." After figuring out the desired path, the robot proceeds at once to take it without overt trial and error.

The contents of Wanderer's computer memory we call the robot's "world map" for this room. (For a different room it might keep a different world map.) The computer could also have a copy of the world map whose symbols could be manipulated without changing the original world map. Thus, by performing the operations on the copy, it could answer questions like "If you moved three squares to your left and if the objects at D-9 and O-5 were moved to P-10 and Q-10, could you then see what is at R-10? How long would it take you to get to R-10?" Manipulations performed on the copy of the world map permit the machine to indulge in "contemplative speculation" or "fantasy" without destroying its view of reality (the original map). Also, with this model we can assign a precise meaning to the concept "the machine comprehends the meaning of a certain sentence." For example, if we tell the machine that "An immovable object has been placed in region J-9" and the machine responds by changing the symbol in J-9 to "5," we know that it understood the meaning of the sentence. The sentence "Region J-9 now has an immovable object in it" would have the same meaning if again the machine changed the symbol in memory square J-9 to "5." This gives a concrete and specific meaning to the notion of "comprehension."

The robot could conceivably need a rest period or at least a coffee break. For example, if the input of new information is so rapid that the world map cannot be kept updated at the same rate, the robot could hold the data in a buffer memory bank (short-term memory) until it could make the appropriate changes in its world map during its rest period.

In terms of current psychological theory, the navigating robot is very much a cognitive creature. Through perceptual learning it acquires information about the environment; no reinforcement is necessary. It establishes a cognitive map of its surroundings and a symbolic copy of this map that the robot can manipulate.

A robot with a world map may have the capability to deal with a number of perceptual or cognitive problems that current robots find difficult. It may be able to track objects that not only move, but disappear behind obstacles for periods of time. On its copy of the world map, the robot infers where the object is, based on its estimated velocity, and tests this expectancy against a direct observation whenever possible. If the difference between the expected and the observed is small, the estimate is adjusted. If, on the other hand, the discrepancies are large, the robot takes more drastic action, going into a new routine to locate the missing object. In this way, the "cognitive dissonance" causes a redirection of the robot's attention.

Learning

Some robots learn in ways that some psychologists think are conventional. That is, the robot learns to make a response by means of positive and negative reinforcement. For example, a mechanical mouse developed by Claude Shannon at Bell Telephone Laboratories (see Figure 4) learned to find its way through a maze when it was "rewarded" for successful runs and "punished" for the unsuccessful runs. Even very simple machines can be made to learn, using a variety of reinforcement procedures. But despite the predilections of some psychologists, it seems obvious that learning involves more than the two Rs (responses and reinforcements). One way people learn is by watching a task performed by a skilled person. For example, it is difficult to learn to build a model airplane by hearing a lecture on the subject, or even by doing it yourself; but the learning is easier when you watch someone build a model. Robots already exist that learn by watching. For example, Bernard Widrow's broom balancer at Stanford University consists of an electric car on which a broomstick is to be balanced. When the car is moved back and forth on its track it is possible to keep the broom balanced in a near vertical position (see Figure 3). A human soon learns by trial-and-error how fast to move the car to keep the broomstick from falling. Widrow's machine has an "eye" that observes the angular displacement from the vertical of the broomstick and how fast it falls (angular velocity). The machine correlates these observations with the force that the man applies to the car when he successfully balances the broom. Gradually the machine builds up an "operating function" and can balance the broom by itself. This robot does not simply copy the model's successful responses. Instead, the broom balancer analyzes the performance and extracts an idealized strategy for its task. The broom balancer does not have to go through a process of trial and error before it achieves success. Just as you learned to build the model, this robot learns by watching humans perform the task.

Robots of the future will find some types of learning very difficult. One of these is concept formation. We usually say that a person has a concept when he responds in the same way to a number of different things or events. For example, having the concept of "a good neighbor" involves perceiving common qualities in Mr. Jones and Mr. Smith, even though they have different appearances and do quite different things. (Perhaps Mr. Jones helped to plant the concept learner's lawn, while Mr. Smith helped to weed the new lawn.) Even young children learn concepts of this kind. Can a robot?

In relatively simple situations, robots already have achieved some success in learning concepts. If letter recognition is considered a case of concept-formation (despite discriminable variations in the letter's form), then robots can learn concepts with some skill. We also saw how by use of the world map a machine might learn the "meaning" of certain sentences. But what of the more complicated cases? Can the robot learn the concept of "shoe," "reality," "beauty"? Clearly this presents formidable difficulties. Before a solution can be achieved we must come to grips with such problems as the multiple and shared meanings of words, levels of abstraction, extracting common features from large quantities of unstructured data, and testing concepts against experience. Exactly how this may be accomplished is far from evident.

Memory

In the area of rote recall, the robot already has a memory far superior to man's. The computer can store millions of bits of information and recall any of it on demand. But this is only one of several forms of memory. For example, people can recall *sequences* of events ("After you entered the door, Jack rose from his seat and handed you the letter he had been reading. You took it to the table, and so on"), and they can remember the meaning of events ("Secretary Rusk said yesterday essentially, although I don't remember his exact words, that we are bombing to avoid war.").

A robot of the future may be capable of recognizing instantly whether it previously has seen a certain pattern, and if it did, of then recalling the sequence of patterns that followed it.

The pattern may consist not only of inputs from various sensors but also of signals generated inside the machine. In theory, such a system has been shown to be possible.

The logistic problems of handling enormous amounts of information necessary for a really intelligent robot will force us to develop semantic memory. However, the

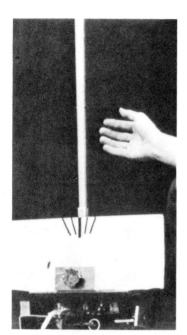

Figure 3. A broom-balancing machine at Stanford learns by watching humans. The humans move an electric car back and forth to keep the broom balanced, and the machine's "eye" observes and correlates the angular displacement from the vertical, how fast it falls, and the force the human applies to the car.

Figure 4. A mechanical mouse created by Claude Shannon of Bell Telephone Laboratories learned to find its way through a maze when it was rewarded for successful runs and punished for failures.

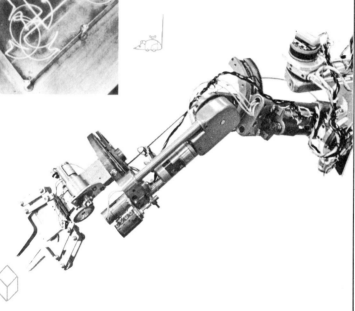

Figure 5. A step in providing the computer with a humanlike ability to observe and manipulate its environment is the hand-eye project at Stanford. The eye of the computer is an ordinary television camera. The outline of a cube is perceived by the computer, which then gives directions to the artificial arm and hand for the picking up and stacking of the cubes to duplicate the outline perceived.

difficulties encountered in current research indicate that, in the near future at least, robots will be limited largely to rote memory.

Language

Robots already can understand certain simple and artificial languages. Computers are fluent in various dialects of Fortran, Algol, Cobol, Basic, PL/1, and the like. A machine like the Wanderer conceivably could understand some very simple commands in a restricted version of English. In this restricted English each word has a unique meaning. In addition, unlike natural English where a given word may serve as noun, verb, or adjective, here it can be used in only one grammatical capacity. Furthermore, only a few forms of sentence structure can be used. Will the robot of the future be able to understand a natural language?

Many workers in this field are privately and very publicly discouraged. Bemoaning the difficulties of designing a machine that can translate human languages, say German into English, has now become an orthodox activity. But the history of technology is replete with examples of unexpected circumventions of the "impossible," and we should be prepared for surprises in this area. Considering the difficulties that robots have had with natural language, it now seems inconceivable that they will be able to understand the finer forms of literary expression, like proverbs or sarcasm. How could a robot decipher "Strike while the iron is hot" or "Hitch your wagon to a star" or the Turkish proverb, "Before you love, learn to run through snow leaving no footprints"?

Logical Thinking

Everyone knows that the computer far surpasses humans in its speed and accuracy of computation. This is the characteristic that endears it to the "computerniks," those starry-eyed young men who may be found loitering at computer installations at all hours of the day and night. It is less well known that computers can function on a more formal and creative level in mathematics. Hao Wang, for instance, demonstrated that a computer could prove over 350 theorems from Alfred North Whitehead and Bertrand Russell's *Principia Mathematica* in a few minutes. Another computer, given basic axioms and operations, can invent theorems and prove them too. While it is sometimes inventive and always correct, this computer's weakness is the absence of taste. Many of its theorems and proofs are not only inelegant, but just plain dull. What we need for the future is a mathematical robot with some sense of what is interesting. A start in this direction has been made by Allen Newell, J. C. Shaw, and Herbert Simon of Carnegie Tech, who have worked on a "logic theorist." They studied human problem-solvers with the hope of finding how they formed their strategies, subgoals, conjectures, heuristic reasoning, and guesses. They then attempted to develop computer programs to operate in similar ways. The advantage of heuristic, or approximate rough-and-ready, reasoning stems from the economics of machine capacity. In principle, complete enumeration of all possibilities will reveal the solutions; but in practice, the number of alternatives rapidly exceeds the capacity of any computer. Heuristic reasoning reduces substantially the number of alternatives that must be investigated to find a solution. But despite some initial encouragement, progress in this area seems to be slow.

Game Playing

In addition to exploiting the skills of robots, we should also allow them to have some fun, even occasionally at our expense. It is in this spirit that a number of researchers have developed chess-playing computers, some of which have been very successful. These computers are usually "learning" machines that are based on heuristic rather than logically correct strategies, and that improve their game as the result of experience. Since, in principle, they could practice against each other at very high speed, as well as against the "book games" of the masters, it is conceivable that in twenty years the World Chess Champion might be a computer program.

Mikhail Botvinnik, the famous Russian chess grand master, has suggested that we will require two championship chess tournaments—one restricted to unaided humans and the other to machines. It is doubtful that such an apartheid arrangement can be long maintained. The widespread affection for thinking machines by computerniks indicates that man-machine relations are not free of emotional attachment. (Remember the Freudian interpretation of the American's attitude toward his automobile.) Now that we have the electric shaver, electric toothbrush, electric scalp massager, and electric buttocks vibrator, can man-machine sexual relationships be far behind? Now that our culture is separating the sexual from reproductive functions, we may expect a sharp rise in the demand for the inventions of pleasure machines. This leads to the ethical and moral questions regarding our treatment of these mechanical objects of our affection. A serious inquiry into these questions was made recently by Roland Puccetti in the *British Journal of the Philosophy of Science.*

The conjecture that the machine will vanquish the chess master has been recently the source of a somewhat hostile controversy that seems to be quite analogous to the vitalism controversy in biology a generation ago, and the evolution controversy of two generations ago. Perhaps both sides could find comfort in the words of the mathematician Michael Arbib, "Say not that we are bringing man down to the level of a machine. Say rather that we are bringing the machine up to the level of man."

Motivation

A robot that can wander through its environment must have a set of priorities for its activities. Leonard Friedman of Systems Development Corporation has proposed one set of "instinctive" behavior patterns for robots. In general, each part of his program directs the robot to perform the sequence of actions that constitutes a particular "instinctual activity," such as nest building, food searching, eating, mating, fleeing from danger, fighting, sleeping, exploring, returning home. These programs are triggered by specific stimuli. Only one program can be carried out at a time. If a new stimulus triggers a higher-priority activity, the program for that activity takes over. When the high-priority activity is completed, the robot may return to the interrupted program.

Human behavior, on the other hand, is often motivated internally as well as by external stimuli. Clearly if robots are to be self-sufficient, they will have to possess drives such as ambition, a need for esteem in eyes of other robots, and a superego prohibiting the destruction of other robots, or at least those of its own socioeconomic grouping. Of course, robot-human relationships also will have to be carefully considered. For robots to be self-sufficient as a species, they will have to reproduce themselves. While there is nothing against this in principle as shown by John Von Neumann in his theory of self-reproducing automata, the implementation seems impractical at the present time. Of course, by using reproduction, natural selection, and evolution, we can solve many of our design problems, since the species that will evolve will be the one best adapted to its environment. This probably would take a long time unless the evolutionary process could be simulated on a computer at high speed. Other means for speeding up the evolutionary rate would be the use of tri- or multi-sexual robots. Eventually, psychologists and engineers will have to face these problems head-on.

The Mind's Eye
Donald O. Hebb

Descartes was a dualist, but he and succeeding generations of philosophers and psychologists have tried to reconcile the mental and physical aspects of behavior. In this article Hebb writes from the position of a physiological monist. He analyzes the nature of introspection, at one time a basic technique in experimental psychology, and incorporates it into his theory of brain function. Hebb, one of the most important physiological psychologists of this generation, emerges with a unified theory of neurophysiology, perception, and imagery.

In our culture, we take it for granted that each of us knows his own mind directly and can describe its operations. To doubt this capacity for introspection, this ability of the mind to observe itself, is to invite incredulity. Yet the evidence is clear that this capacity does *not* exist. Our belief in it is of quite recent origin.

Undoubtedly you know much of what goes on in your mind and can report it. Undoubtedly you have private evidence that bears on the current activity of your mind. Thus, in important respects, your knowledge of yourself is more complete and reliable than the knowledge others may have. Yet it is clear that this knowledge must be inferential and theoretical—at least in part. A second person may be better able than you to evaluate your present mental state and predict your behavior. In principle, self-knowledge may depend on the same kinds of inference that knowledge of another depends on.

No one has so far considered the nature of such inference, and it should be done. We should look at the idea of the self, the knower and the perceiver. Objectively, of course, the whole man is the self and the perceiver. I do not mean to suggest anything else. But

there are some fascinating phenomena concerning the hallucinations of an immaterial self. These phenomena constitute an important psychological problem, and they may help to account for the false conviction that the mind can look at itself. The immaterial self is a myth, but myths are psychological realities. They affect behavior as well as beliefs.

Introspection as Hallucination

I propose that introspection is an illusion so strongly established that it amounts to hallucination. To hallucinate is not abnormal. It occurs with normal people in normal conditions in the dream. A severe lack of sleep will induce hallucinations, which we may think of as waking dreams. It is not necessary to take drugs, to suffer mental illness, or to have an addled brain in order to see visions. Isolation will do it, together with monotony—the monotony, for example, of seeing nothing but the white lines on a curving modern highway for mile after mile at night.

Apparently visions and gross misperceptions are quite familiar to people who frequently drive long distances in the western United States. But each driver thinks he is unique and prefers not to talk about what he has seen. This may change when drivers discover that others sometimes see jackrabbits big enough to step over their cars. A. L. Mosely of the Harvard School of Public Health discovered that all of a group of thirty-three long-distance truckdrivers had experienced hallucinations, some of which led to accidents, as when a driver braked suddenly to avoid a stalled car that wasn't there.

Because people are reluctant to report such visions, we do not know how widespread these phenomena are. Solitary sailors have suffered hallucinations. Charles Lindbergh reported that a spirit or spirits accompanied him in his lonely flight across the Atlantic. Significantly for the idea that monotony is involved, these spirits left as soon as he sighted fishing vessels off the Irish coast.

We do not know how many airplane pilots have seen things—or how many unexplained crashes have resulted —but if truckdrivers see imaginary objects, it is not out of the question that a pilot might see another plane on a collision course ahead of him and crash in an attempt to avoid the phantom plane. Solitary pilots at high altitudes may suffer from what Brant Clark and Ashton Graybiel call the *break-off phenomenon*. The pilot feels somehow detached from reality, in a way he finds hard to describe. Clark and Graybiel got no report of hallucinations, but another investigation found a striking one. The pilot reported that he found himself observing his plane from the outside, seeing it like a toy suspended in space with himself placed like a puppet at the controls.

The illusion of introspection may be the same kind of phenomenon. The normal, healthy mind is capable of improbable tricks. And the conviction that we perceive something is not enough to show that we do perceive it. Perception is complex; self-perception may be even more so.

If our minds have the power to observe themselves, they have not had it long. The Greeks did not talk about mind as open to self-inspection, and the Christian philosophy of the Middle Ages, with its demonic conception of mind, is hardly consistent with introspection. Biologists consider that man is still evolving, so it is conceivable that a new mental capacity could have shown up in Western Europe in the late seventeenth century. The alternative is that John Locke did not discover a new capacity in 1690 but invented one. Our problem today is to disinvent it. We must learn to rid ourselves of that fantasy of direct self-knowledge.

We can see what happened to Locke. He knew that a man can report quite accurately things that are going on in his mind—as judged by his subsequent behavior. It must have seemed to Locke that if the mind knows its own activity, the mind must somehow *perceive* that activity.

The mechanics of this perception remained a puzzle, but as Gilbert Ryle pointed out, Locke found a saving analogy in looking in a mirror. The mind, he thought, may somehow *reflect* on itself and its content. This

figure of speech became common property in the next hundred years, losing all technical flavor. Some more impressive word was needed by the philosopher-psychologist to designate what was still not understood, and in the nineteenth century, *introspection* met that need. Introspection, looking inward, is still a figure of speech—if anything, a worse one than *reflection*. It is easier to develop a fantasy of the mind looking inward than a fantasy of the mind using a mirror—and then forget that this *is* fantasy.

The mind does not observe itself. No two trained introspectors could agree in their descriptions of what they found unless they were members of the same school, brought up as supporters of the same theory. This by itself is almost conclusive evidence that they were not observing, but making theoretical inferences. George Humphrey has shown that the trained introspectors of Cornell, dedicated to the proposition that introspection is the description of sensory content, actually described not sensation but the event that gave rise to the sensation. Any conclusions drawn about mental content in such research can only be matters of inference. Clearest of all is the use of inference in the demonstration of *imageless thought* by Oswald Külpe and his colleagues at Würzburg.

The simplest of the Würzburg demonstrations concerns the mental set connected with the performance of simple arithmetical operations. A person is instructed to add pairs of digits briefly projected on a screen and to observe his own mental processes as he adds them. At another time he subtracts, with similar instructions. After the subject is well into either task, he reports that as he sees the pair of numbers, the answer pops into his mind—nothing more. With the stimulus of **6 2** he does

not find himself saying "add" before saying "eight" or "subtract" before saying "four." He is *set* to add or to subtract, but no evidence of the set is found in introspection. Yet something is there, for the same stimulus produces the response "eight" at one time, "four" at another. The conclusion is inescapable: an active mental process exists whose presence is known to the subject only because it *must* be there to account for the difference in the responses he makes at two different times.

From John Locke onward we find reports that introspection finds nothing but sensory content: actual sensations (due to stimulation) and images (sensation aroused—theoretically—by some associative mechanism). This is a far cry from observation of the mind itself, though if we assume that the sensations are *in* the mind, we could consider the mind to be observing itself. But the mechanism of sensation and of imagery is a mechanism of looking outward. In the light of what we know today about spontaneous activity in the nervous system, there is nothing here to justify the notion of self-observation by the mind.

When I describe the imagery I may have in the course of thinking, it is quite common for me to hear some unregenerate subjectivist say, "Aha, so you do introspect!" It does not follow.

Introspection as Imagery

Each of us has private information about the activities within his own skin: imagery, pain from headache, hallucination, and so on. But this information—which is indeed private because it is not available to another observer—is nonetheless provided by the mechanism of perceiving the world around us. It is not the result of introspection.

An excellent example is pain from a phantom limb. After an arm or leg has been amputated, there is still the hallucinatory awareness of the part that has been cut off—so convincing that at first the patient, if he does not see the stump, may not realize that the limb is gone. In a few cases, perhaps 10 or 15 percent, the patient also feels pain in the missing part. Subjectivists might argue: the patient complains of pain in his right hand, but he has no right hand; so the pain is only in his mind; when he describes it, he introspects, describes mental content, not something that really happens to his body. But the argument cannot be sustained. We are still dealing with a sensory mechanism, even if the mechanism has gone awry.

When you burn the skin of your hand, you say "Ouch!" or "My hand hurts!" This is a normal response involving sensory input to the brain, the excitation of the central processes of perception and consciousness, and the motor output determined by the central processes. Human thought processes are never really simple, but in principle we can see this as a typical reaction to the environment. When I burn my hand and say "Ouch!" no question of the mind's looking inward arises and my speech is not dependent on introspection, any more than is a dog's yelp when you tread on his tail.

Now suppose that a man's arm is amputated. The nerve pathway from the hand is of course interrupted. There is no possibility that an excitation will arise in the hand, but the same excitation, in principle, can start higher in the sensory line leading to the brain. Nerve cells are capable of firing spontaneously and do so normally if they are not exposed to external stimulation. If now the man reports that he still feels the presence of the amputated hand, or if he complains of pain from cramped fingers in that hand, we are dealing with the same mechanism that makes us say "Ouch!" when a normal hand is injured.

Consider the memory image. We commonly hear the voice of an absent friend, see a scene from last summer's holiday, or in trying to recall a passage from a book, see where it was on the page. Such experiences can be understood in the same way as the pain from the phantom limb, except that they would not be the product of spontaneous activity of the central circuits. In these cases the circuits may be thought of as excited by associative mechanisms in the brain.

Suppose you stand before the Rockies and say "I can see the mountains." Here we have a visual stimulus, transmission through the brain, and verbal response—all plain sailing for objective psychology. Now we change the conditions a bit. After the vacation trip you are reminded of your experiences (another thought process excites the same central combination of processes that were excited when you actually were looking at the mountains) and you say again, "I can see the mountains." This is visual imagery—called imagery and not perception only because we know that the adequate stimulus is not present. It is the reexcitation of the same or most of the same cell assemblies that were excited during the original perception. No question of introspection arises. In principle the two cases are very similar. In both, a perceptual activity is excited in the absence of the original sensory stimulation.

It is quite respectable for an objective psychologist to have imagery and report it; his virginity is not thereby brought into question. Apart from such mild gibes at us objectivists, there is a point here of some importance, namely that our imagery is a valid and relatively direct source of knowledge of present brain activity.

Now consider a revealing little experiment devised by Alfred Binet, the inventor of intelligence testing, in an attempt to distinguish between people with visual imagery and those with auditory or tactile imagery. (His attempt failed, because visual imagery is not what you might think.) The subject studies a typical letter square:

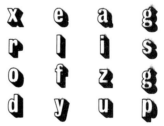

When he has a clear image of it, we cover the letters and ask him to *look at* the image he has formed and repeat the letters. He repeats them readily, but going from left to right in each line, in turn from top to bottom. Now we ask him to look again at his image and repeat the right-hand column of letters from bottom to top, or the letters forming the diagonal from lower right to upper left. He finds, usually to his surprise, that he cannot do so nearly as quickly as before, and that he must rehearse the whole line in order to *see* the letter at the end.

Clearly, he has not formed an image at all, in the sense of something he can look at. If he had, he could easily read off the letters in any order. What he does is reinstate the original perceptual process, which—because of his long habit of reading English—runs from left to right. The imagery turns out to be the recurrence of a *sequence* of individual part perceptions (together with a much vaguer concurrent perception of the whole group of letters).

In the same way, a person who remembers verse by reading from an image of the printed poem might be asked to recite the last word of each line of a stanza, from bottom to top. When he first tries this, he will be surprised to find how much rehearsal he needs in order to see the last word of each line. There is nothing here to suggest an unfettered examination of exhibits in some picture gallery of the soul. What we have instead is a repetition of the same series of perceptual events in their original order—for the image in this case turns out to be a rigidly organized *sequence*.

Our conclusion that reported imagery is not evidence of the mind's self-contemplation applies to other kinds of self-knowledge. Take as example fear and anxiety.

For any person there is a class of situations that can cause fear, with sweating and trembling and interrupted digestion along with strong tendencies to flee. The stimulus situation excites central-nervous-system activity, which in turn produces overt signs of fear. The same central processes are also capable of producing the utterance, "I am afraid." Now suppose we tell our subject that a madman is looking for him with a pistol. Even though the fear-producing situation has not yet occurred, the brain processes are aroused associatively, and the subject sweats and trembles and has an accelerated heartbeat. He may also say "I am afraid," thus reporting on his state of mind, but this is no more evidence of introspection than is his quickened pulse. This mental activity *is* fear and it causes all types of fear behavior, verbal as well as nonverbal.

Now suppose some pathological process causes the brain activity. There is no threat—immediate or remote—but spontaneous firing of disordered neural cells nevertheless results in the words "I am afraid." If we ask "Of what?" the patient with pathological anxiety may have to say "I don't know." Again, the mechanism of response to the environment operates even if the mechanism has gone awry and no longer is adaptive. But it is not an inward-looking mechanism.

There was a time when I could introspect and did so freely, making all sorts of interesting observations. I was well indoctrinated by the common philosophy that said anyone could observe his own mental activities. Later, when I became aware of all the evidence of casting doubt on the existence of introspection, I began to look more critically at the process itself. I found that introspecting included some imagery of looking into the interior of my skull from a point at the back of my head. Unfortunately, this seemed so ridiculous that I rapidly became unable to introspect any longer.

My former introspection involved seeing the world and at the same time seeing myself see it, or recalling some sensory event and watching myself recall it. I then mistook the properties of the perceived or imagined object for properties of the process of perception.

I was *seeing* the perception or image inside my skull, I thought, and I understood perfectly the objection of those who would say that the perception of the evening sky cannot be simply a barrage of nerve impulses reaching the brain, that it is nothing so mechanical, so aggregational and atomistic. Perceiving the sky itself but looking inward at the same time, I took its unity, extendedness, and beauty for properties, not of the sky, but of the *percept* itself, which therefore could not be a flood of individual nerve impulses, no matter how highly organized these impulses might be.

Bicameral Thought

My apparent introspection had two quite unexpected features. There was the hallucinatory element, and there was a doubled mental process, of observing the world from one point in space while simultaneously observing myself from a second point—the back of my head, just inside my skull. I have already made the point that hallucinations can occur in sober, normal people. Now let me go one step farther and show the existence of bicameral thought processes—the capacity to entertain two trains of mental activity at one time. The capacity is quite common and easily demonstrated but has gone unrecognized in the classical literature.

There is a longstanding dogma to the effect that attention is unitary. The dogma is purely a matter of theory and is plainly contradicted by behavioral evidence.

I propose that thought is the activity of cell assemblies that are excited by sense input, as well as by the activity of other assemblies, in a complex network of neural firing. I use the term *phase sequence* to designate a series of these assembly actions (presumably not a series of single actions but a complex flow in which five, ten, twenty, or more assemblies might be active at any one time). Considering the millions of assemblies of which the brain must be capable, it is conceivable that two or more such phase sequences—trains of thought—might occur at the same time.

Common features of human behavior show that two trains of thought do occur simultaneously, but that this bicameral process may be possible only with highly practiced forms of behavior. In addition, one of the processes may have to be sensorily programmed. I interpret this to mean that at least one and probably both phase sequences must be highly organized if they are to exist side by side without interference.

It is quite possible, for example, to carry on an ordinary conversation while driving a car through normal traffic. Both activities involve complex perceptions constantly giving rise to inference, meaning, and adaptive response. Both, that is, require constant, if not elaborate, thought. On the other hand, an unexpected traffic situation abruptly ends the conversation, and it is not possible to adequately argue a difficult point while driving.

On occasion, when reading aloud to a person whose literary tastes were not mine, I have found myself at the bottom of a page with no notion at all of what the heroine had been up to. I had to go back and hastily skim the page in order to keep up with the story. I had thought of something else for the better part of a page, but my audience had not detected any change of pace. Reading aloud requires the mechanisms of verbal thought, and here, without question, two trains of thought were running side by side in my head.

The clinical observations of Wilder Penfield and those of Roger Sperry are relevant to the double train of thought. Penfield elicited thought sequences relating to a patient's earlier experiences by stimulating the temporal lobe while performing brain surgery under local anesthesia. Even though the evoked memories seemed very real to the patient, he was always aware that he remained in the operating room. In Sperry's cases, the corpus callosum—that great bridge connecting the right and left halves of the brain—had been cut. The patient now had two sets of perceptions, thoughts, and intentions, one set in the left hemisphere and another in the right. Because the left half of the brain handles most verbal behavior and the right half deals better with spatial relations, it is conceivable that the normal car driver who can talk and steer at the same time does one with the left half and the other with the right half of his brain.

Self-knowledge, and imagery that has to do with the self, may not always depend on the doubled train of thought. The disturbance of self-concept in the airplane pilot, who had the vivid image of looking at himself and his plane from the outside, must have been a case of doubling. Presumably he was at the same time managing the controls and watching the instrument panel. But there may have been no doubled train of thought in my fantasy of introspection, for it seemed a unified process of simultaneously looking into the interior of my skull and looking at objects in the external world.

Grotesque? Implausible? Inconceivable? Not really. The process is inconceivable only if we have fixed ideas about images and imagery, especially if we think of imagery as the reinstatement of actual sensory experiences—as did most nineteenth-century psychologists.

Imagery in the Absence of Stimuli

Imagery is a much more complex matter. Obviously there is no difficulty about imagining improbable things like Pegasus, unicorns, and thunderbolt-hurling gods. This is creative thought, fantastic or not. But the creativity of memory images may be subtler and unrecognized. Some time ago I discovered to my surprise that my vivid recollection of a certain field, about two acres in extent, involved a visual image of the field as seen from about thirty feet in the air. I had never seen the field from this point. An informal survey of undergraduate students turned up 30 percent or so who found—also with surprise—that they recalled familiar areas in the same manner.

More to the point, however, are certain forms of imagery relating to our own bodies. It is comprehensible, of course, that we can deliberately imagine what we would look like if seen from a distance, but a less complete imagery of the same kind may occur unintentionally and without recognition in other circumstances.

Recall a time when you stood waist-deep in water and stretched out on your back to float. Now ask yourself whether this memory includes a fleeting sight of a face with water lapping about it. Such a visual component of the memory is, of course, fictitious, and we tend to suppress in recall or not to notice the elements that strike us as improbable. Or recall the last time you left the room you are now in, closing the door behind you. See if you detect in the supposed recall some imagery of the body of a person with a hand on the door. But we must look for this type of imagery, for its existence is not suggested in either technical or popular ideas about memory and self-knowledge, and we are likely to extract from the complex imagery of thought only things we *know* are there.

Such imaginal components of thought remain unidentified in part because they are typically incomplete—at least in my own case. My introspection included only the eyes (and perhaps the upper part of the face) gazing into the cavern of my skull. The imagery of myself leaving the room and closing the door is shadowy at best, except for hand, arm, and shoulder.

In these examples of being in one place and seeming to see ourselves in another, the imaginal elements are fleeting and unobtrusive. In some circumstances, however, they may persist and become disturbing because of the inferences we draw from them. If our theory of mind includes a soul that can leave its body, the experience may be acceptable and we may even seek it as a sign of favor from the gods. But if we conceive of a soul firmly attached to the body and not peripatetic (at least until death), and if we assume that only the insane see visions, the experience will be frightening and the circumstances conducive to it will be avoided.

We know something about these circumstances and can make some guesses about how they operate. An essential factor appears to be monotony of sense input. College students were put in experimental isolation, seeing only diffuse light (no pattern vision), hearing only a monotonous buzzing sound (no meaningful sound), lying with covered hands (to prevent tactile perceptions) on a comfortable bed. They remained continuously in this condition of minimal sensory variety except for an hour or two each day for eating and going to the toilet.

After two or three days, those who could endure the monotony began to have hallucinations that were chiefly visual, but that, in a few subjects, included disturbances of the self. Sometimes a student felt that he had two bodies, or that his head was detached from his neck, or that his mind was floating in the air above his body. More commonly students reported seeing complex scenes as vivid as motion pictures.

We know that unchanging or monotonously repeated sensory events lose their power to elicit response or to excite the higher centers of the brain, and this is what appears to have happened. Ordinarily sensation provides a constant guiding influence upon the thought process. This modulation of cortical activity helps both to excite cortical neurons and to maintain organization in their firing. When this influence is decreased or abolished, the spontaneous activity of the cortex must be unorganized much of the time. In fact, the students in the experiment frequently were so lethargic that they were unable even to daydream. But suppose the spontaneously firing neurons happen to include enough of a cell assembly to activate the whole assembly and thus to excite other assemblies, producing an organized pattern of firing. The subject would find himself with vivid imagery: vivid because the sensory output, which we may suppose normally inhibits the processes of imagery, is now decreased or absent. The main content of thought would then consist of imagery, without the usually competitive perceptions of the real environment.

Visual imagery predominated in the isolation experiment, presumably because only vision was completely controlled. And we can understand as primarily of visual origins some of the misperceptions by those students whose minds seemed to leave their bodies. Suppose that as he lay on the bed, the student thought of himself with imagery of his body as seen from above. Because he lacked effective sensation from his body to keep him clearly aware of bodily contact with the bed, he would find himself *looking at*, instead of imagining, his body on the bed.

If you look at something, you must be at a distance from it. The natural inference is that your true self has left your body and is wandering in the void. A person from our culture, not believing in such possibilities, might conclude that he was going mad and leave the situation as quickly as possible. Some experimental subjects did leave the room suddenly and hastily, refusing explanation. Later in the experiment, when it was known that such hallucinations might occur routinely, the students were less disturbed and could report their experiences.

The yogi, however, with his different theory of existence, might infer that he had successfully freed his soul from the husk of his body. He would seek the experi-

ence as often as possible by maintained immobility, quiet, and fixity of gaze—a procedure that is calculated to minimize sensory input and maximize hallucinatory effects.

Conclusions

According to his critics, the objectivist has self-knowledge and yet cannot admit it or make use of that knowledge in his study of man. Such criticism has confused private evidence, one basis of inferential self-knowledge, with introspective evidence and direct self-observation by the mind. I have tried to show that describing my imagery or reporting endogenous pain or saying that I am afraid does not show the existence of introspection.

We can now see that it takes no extraordinary mental agility, no special technical skill, to think of yourself as you would of another person. If your memory of an action includes a momentary sight of yourself doing it, if the doubled train of thought permits you to see yourself doing something while you do it, then there can be no essential impossibility of thinking about yourself as you would about another, making inferences and theorizing about your behavior, with the added advantage of private evidence.

It is true that it is difficult to achieve the perspective of another person when your social behavior over periods of time is in question. But this is not a barrier to seeing segments of your own behavior in objective terms. It means in practice that you must test any theory primarily with others as experimental subjects, no matter how you arrive at the theoretical idea.

Self-observation clearly has much to contribute to our understanding of the human animal. A friend asks a question; an indiscreet answer springs to my lips but is not spoken (I have auditory imagery of words to speak, but the speech is inhibited by other mental processes). In such circumstances I may realize for the first time that someone annoys me or looks ridiculous in my eyes.

However, thought is by no means exclusively verbal. When General X makes a speech and I find my fingertips itching and have imagery of shoving his head in a bucket of water, I know what I think of X and of the speech. When on a hot summer day I see a sheet of smooth water and then feel heretofore unnoticed sweat on my face and back and have visual and somesthetic imagery of immersing myself in the water, I learn something about my previous mental state (unrecognized discomfort). If nothing prevents me from a swim, I can predict my future behavior. But if the imagery of swimming is accompanied by imagery of an impatient wife at the airport, my prediction may take an entirely different shape.

Thought consists of more than imagery, as Külpe showed. Our imagery does not actually control our behavior, but imagery may be the basis of inference in self-knowledge. The cell-assembly activity that is perception, when directly excited by sensation or associatively excited by imagery, is *part* of the thought process. Sensation and imagery are thus very direct sources of self-knowledge. The knowledge is still mediate, however, not immediate: inference, not observation.

Inferences derived from imagery supplement those inferences that I as well as others may make from overt actions. Sometimes the conclusion we draw from imagery may be fantastic instead of factual, as when the yogi concludes that his soul travels through space or when I—early in my career—thought I was directly perceiving my mental processes. But imagery is also the basis of sober, reportable everyday knowledge that we have of our own thoughts and attitudes.

II
Perception and Cognition

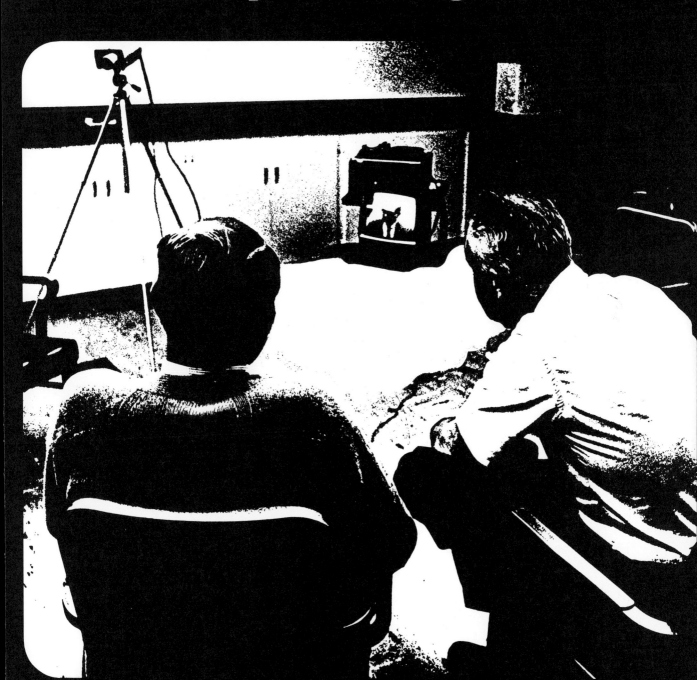

Language and the Mind

Noam Chomsky

Psychology is nurtured by many disciplines; the eminent linguist Noam Chomsky integrates linguistic, behavioral, and philosophical arguments to present a model of human perception, especially that responsible for language. Rejecting classical empiricist notions that knowledge is determined primarily by external factors, Chomsky argues that intrinsic structures are necessary to explain linguistic behavior. He cites psychological experiments and suggests that these linguistic structures have psychological meaning. Finally, he speculates on the biological nature of these mental states.

How does the mind work? To answer this question we must look at some of the work performed by the mind. One of its main functions is the acquisition of knowledge. The two major factors in acquisition of knowledge—perception and learning—have been the subject of study and speculation for centuries. It would not, I think, be misleading to characterize the major positions that have developed as outgrowths of classical rationalism and empiricism. The rationalist theories are marked by the importance they assign to *intrinsic* structures in mental operations—to central processes and organizing principles in perception, and to innate ideas and principles in learning. The empiricist approach, in contrast, has stressed the role of *experience* and control by environmental factors.

The classical empiricist view is that sensory images are transmitted to the brain as impressions. They remain as ideas that will be associated in various ways, depending on the fortuitous character of experience. In this view a language is merely a collection of words, phrases, and sentences, a habit system, acquired accidentally and extrinsically. In the formulation of Williard Quine, knowledge of a language (and, in fact, knowledge in general) can be represented as "a fabric of sentences variously associated to one another and to nonverbal stimuli by the mechanism of conditioned response." Acquisition of knowledge is only a matter of the gradual construction of this fabric. When sensory experience is interpreted, the already established network may be activated in some fashion. In its essentials, this view has been predominant in modern behavioral science, and it has been accepted with little question by many philosophers as well.

The classical rationalist view is quite different. In this view the mind contains a system of "common notions" that enable it to interpret the scattered and incoherent data of sense in terms of objects and their relations, cause and effect, whole and part, symmetry, gestalt properties, functions, and so on. Sensation, providing only fleeting and meaningless images, is degenerate and particular. Knowledge, much of it beyond immediate awareness, is rich in structure, involves universals, and is highly organized. The innate general principles that underlie and organize this knowledge, according to Leibniz, "enter into our thoughts, of which they form the soul and the connection . . . although we do not at all think of them."

This "active" rationalist view of the acquisition of knowledge persisted through the romantic period in its essentials. With respect to language, it achieves its most illuminating expression in the investigations of Wilhelm von Humboldt. His theory of speech perception supposes a generative system of rules that underlies speech production as well as its interpretation. The system is generative in that it makes infinite use of finite means. He regards a language as a structure of forms and concepts based on a system of rules that determine their interrelations, arrangement, and organization. But these finite materials can be combined to make a never-ending product.

Innovative Quality of Language

In the rationalist and romantic tradition of linguistic theory, the normal use of language is regarded as characteristically innovative. We construct sentences that are entirely new to us. There is no substantive notion of analogy or generalization that accounts for this creative aspect of language use. It is equally erroneous to describe language as a habit structure or as a network of associated responses. The innovative element in normal use of language quickly exceeds the bounds of such marginal principles as analogy or generalization (under any substantive interpretation of these notions). It is important to emphasize this fact because the insight has been lost under the impact of the behaviorist assumptions that have dominated speculation and research in the twentieth century.

In Humboldt's view, acquisition of language is largely a matter of maturation of an innate language capacity. The maturation is guided by internal factors, by an innate "form of language" that is sharpened, differentiated, and given its specific realization through experience. Language is thus a kind of latent structure in the human mind, developed and fixed by exposure to specific linguistic experience. Humboldt believes that all languages will be found to be very similar in their grammatical form, similar not on the surface but in their deeper inner structures. The innate organizing principles severely limit the class of possible languages, and these principles determine the properties of the language that is learned in the normal way.

The active and passive views of perception and learning have elaborated with varying degrees of clarity since the seventeenth century. These views can be confronted with empirical evidence in a variety of ways. Some recent work in psychology and neurophysiology is highly suggestive in this regard. There is evidence for the existence of central processes in perception, specifically for control over the functioning of sensory neurons by the brain-stem reticular system. Behavioral counterparts of this central control have been under investigation for several years. Furthermore, there is evidence for innate organization of the perceptual system of a highly specific sort at every level of biological organization. Studies of the visual system of the frog, the discovery of specialized cells responding to angle and motion in the lower cortical centers of cats and rabbits, and the somewhat comparable investigations of the auditory system of frogs—all are relevant to the classical questions of intrinsic structure mentioned earlier. These studies suggest that there are highly organized, innately determined perceptual systems that are adapted closely to the animal's "life space" and that provide the basis for what

we might call acquisition of knowledge. Also relevant are certain behavioral studies of human infants, for example those showing the preference for faces over other complex stimuli.

These and other studies make it reasonable to inquire into the possibility that complex intellectual structures are determined narrowly by innate mental organization. What is perceived may be determined by mental processes of considerable depth. As far as language learning is concerned, it seems to me that a rather convincing argument can be made for the view that certain principles intrinsic to the mind provide invariant structures that are a precondition for linguistic experience. In the course of this article I would like to sketch some of the ways such conclusions might be clarified and firmly established.

Input-Output Models

There are several ways linguistic evidence can be used to reveal properties of human perception and learning. In this section we consider one research strategy that might take us nearer to this goal.

Let us say that in interpreting a certain physical stimulus a person constructs a *percept*. This percept represents some of his conclusions (in general, unconscious) about the stimulus. To the extent that we can characterize such percepts, we can go on to investigate the mechanisms that relate stimulus and percept. Imagine a model of perception that takes stimuli as inputs and arrives at percepts as outputs. The model might contain a system of beliefs, strategies for interpreting stimuli, and other factors, such as the organization of memory. We would then have a perceptual model that might be represented graphically, as in Figure 1.

Consider next the system of beliefs that is a com-

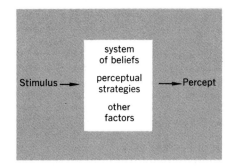

Figure 1. A perceptual model, with the stimulus representing the input and a percept representing the output.

ponent of the perceptual model. How was this acquired? To study this problem, we must investigate a second model, which takes certain data as input and gives as output (again, internally represented) the system of beliefs operating in the perceptual model. This second model, a model of learning, would have its own intrinsic structure, as did the first. This structure might consist of conditions on the nature of the system of beliefs that can be acquired, of innate inductive strategies, and again, of other factors such as the organization of memory (see Figure 2).

Under further conditions we could take these perceptual and learning models as theories of the acquisition of knowledge, rather than of belief. How then would the models apply to language? The input stimulus to the perceptual model is a speech signal, and the percept is a representation of the utterance that the hearer takes the signal to be and of the interpretation he assigns to it. We can think of the percept as the structural description of a linguistic expression that

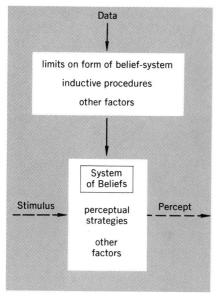

Figure 2. A learning model, with data representing the input and a system of beliefs representing the output.

contains certain phonetic, semantic, and syntactic information. Most interesting is the syntactic information, which best can be discussed by examining a few typical cases.

Surface Structure

The three sentences in Figure 3 seem to have the same syntactic structure. Each contains the subject *I*, and the predicate of each consists of a verb (*told, expected, persuaded*), a noun phrase (*John*), and an embedded predicate phrase (*to leave*). This similarity is only superficial, however—a similarity in what we may call the surface structure of these sentences, which differ in important ways when we consider them with somewhat greater care.

The differences can be seen when the sentences are paraphrased or subjected to certain grammatical operations, such as the conversion from active to passive forms. For example, in normal conversation the sentence *I told John to leave* can be roughly paraphrased as *What I told John was to leave*. But the other two sentences cannot be paraphrased as *What I persuaded*

John was to leave or *What I expected John was to leave*. Sentence 2 can be paraphrased as *It was expected by me that John would leave*. But the other two sentences cannot undergo a corresponding formal operation, yielding *It was persuaded by me that John would leave* or *It was told by me that John should leave*.

Sentences 2 and 3 differ more subtly. In Sentence 3 *John* is the direct object of *persuade*, but in Sentence 2 *John* is not the direct object of *expect*. We can show this by using these verbs in slightly more complex sentences: *I persuaded the doctor to examine John* and *I expected the doctor to examine John*. If we replace the embedded proposition *the doctor to examine John* with its passive form *John to be examined by the doctor*, the change to the passive does not, in itself, change the meaning. We can accept as paraphrases *I expected the doctor to examine John* and *I expected John to be examined by the doctor*. But we cannot accept as paraphrases *I persuaded the doctor to examine John* and *I persuaded John to be examined by the doctor*.

The parts of these sentences differ in their grammatical functions. In *I persuaded John to leave*, *John* is both the object of *persuade* and the subject of *leave*. These facts must be represented in the percept since they are known intuitively to the hearer of the speech signal. No special training or instruction is necessary to enable the native speaker to understand these examples, to know which are wrong and which right, although they may all be quite new to him. They are interpreted by the native speaker instantaneously and uniformly, in accordance with structural principles that are known tacitly, intuitively, and unconsciously.

These examples illustrate two significant points. First, the surface structure of a sentence, its organization into various phrases, may not reveal or immediately reflect its deep syntactic structure. The deep structure is not represented directly in the form of the speech signal; it is abstract. Second, the rules that determine deep and surface structure and their interrelation in particular cases must themselves be highly abstract. They are surely remote from consciousness, and in all likelihood they cannot be brought to consciousness.

Syntactic Structure

A study of such examples, examples characteristic of all human languages that have been carefully studied, constitutes the first stage of the linguistic investigation outlined above, namely the study of the percept. The percept contains phonetic and semantic information related through the medium of *syntactic structure*. There are two aspects to this syntactic structure. It consists of a surface directly related to the phonetic form, and a deep structure that underlies the semantic interpretation. The deep structure is represented in the mind and rarely is indicated directly in the physical signal.

A language, then, involves a set of semantic-phonetic percepts, of sound-meaning correlations, the correlations being determined by the kind of intervening syntactic structure just illustrated. The English language correlates sound and meaning in one way, Japanese in another, and so on. But the general properties of percepts, their forms and mechanisms, are remarkably similar for all languages that have been carefully studied.

Returning to our models of perception and learning, we can now take up the problem of formulating the system of beliefs that is a central component in perceptual processes. In the case of language, the system of beliefs would now be called the *generative grammar*, the system of rules that specifies the sound-meaning correlation and generates the class of structural descriptions (percepts) that constitute the language in question. The generative grammar, then, represents the speaker-hearer's knowledge of his language. We can use the term *grammar of a language* ambiguously, as referring not only to the speaker's internalized, subconscious knowledge but to the professional linguist's representation of this internalized and intuitive system of rules as well.

Theory of Language Acquisition

How is this generative grammar acquired? Or, using our learning model, what is the internal structure of the device that could develop a generative grammar?

We can think of every normal human's internalized grammar as, in effect, a theory of his language. This theory provides a sound-meaning correlation for an infinite number of sentences. It provides an infinite set of structural descriptions; each contains a surface structure that determines phonetic form and a deep structure that determines semantic content.

In formal terms, then, we can describe the child's acquisition of language as a kind of theory construction. The child discovers the theory of his language with only small amounts of data from that language. Not only does his theory of the language have an enormous predictive scope, but it also enables the child to reject a great deal of the very data on which the theory has been constructed. Normal speech consists, in large part, of fragments, false starts, blends, and other distortions of the underlying idealized forms. Nevertheless, as is evident from a study of the mature use of language, what the child learns is the underlying ideal theory. This is a remarkable fact. We must also bear in mind that the child constructs this ideal theory without explicit instruction, that he acquires this knowledge at a time when he is not capable of complex intellectual achievements in many other domains, and that this achievement is relatively independent of intelligence or the particular course of experience. These are facts that a theory of learning must face.

A scientist who approaches phenomena of this sort without prejudice or dogma would conclude that the acquired knowledge must be determined in a rather specific way by intrinsic properties of mental organization. He would then set himself the task of discovering the innate ideas and principles that make such acquisition of knowledge possible.

It is unimaginable that a highly specific, abstract, and tightly organized language comes by accident into the mind of every four-year-old child. If there were not an innate restriction on the form of grammar, then the child could employ innumerable theories to account for his linguistic experience, and no one system, or even small class of systems, would be found exclusively acceptable or even preferable. The child could not possibly acquire knowledge of a language. This restriction on the form of grammar is a precondition for linguistic experience, and it is surely the critical factor in determining the course and result of language learning. The child cannot know at birth which language he is going to learn. But he must "know" that its grammar must be of a predetermined form that excludes many imaginable languages.

The child's task is to select the appropriate hypothesis from this restricted class. Having selected it, he can confirm his choice with the evidence further available to him. But neither the evidence nor any process of induction (in any well-defined sense) could in itself have led to this choice. Once the hypothesis is sufficiently well confirmed, the child knows the language defined by this hypothesis; consequently, his knowledge extends vastly beyond his linguistic experience, and he can reject much of this experience as imperfect, as resulting from the interaction of many factors, only one of which is the ideal grammar that determines a sound-meaning connection for an infinite class of linguistic expressions. Along such lines as these one might outline a theory to explain the acquisition of language.

Sentence Interpretation

As has been pointed out, both the form and meaning of a sentence are determined by syntactic structures that are not represented directly in the signal and that are related to the signal only at a distance, through a long sequence of interpretive rules. This property of abstractness in grammatical structure is of primary importance, and it is on this property that our inferences about mental processes are based. Let us examine this abstractness a little more closely.

Not many years ago, the process of sentence interpretation might have been described approximately along the following lines. A speech signal is received and segmented into successive units (overlapping at the borders). These units are analyzed in terms of their invariant phonetic properties and assigned to *phonemes*. The sequence of phonemes, so constructed, is then segmented into minimal grammatically functioning units (morphemes and words). These are again categorized. Successive operations of segmentation and classification will lead to what I have called surface structure—an analysis of a sentence into phrases, which can be represented as a proper bracketing of the sentence, with the bracketed units assigned to various categories (see Figure 3). Each segment—phonetic, syntactic, or semantic—would be identified in terms of certain invariant properties. This would be an exhaustive analysis of the structure of the sentence.

With such a conception of language structure, it made good sense to look forward hopefully to certain engineering applications of linguistics—for example, to voice-operated typewriters capable of segmenting an expression into its successive phonetic units and identifying these, so that speech could be converted to some form of phonetic writing in a mechanical way; to mechanical analysis of sentence structure by fairly straightforward and well-understood computational techniques; and perhaps even beyond to such projects as machine translation. But these hopes have by now been largely abandoned with the realization that this conception of grammatical structure is inadequate at every level, semantic, phonetic, and syntactic. Most important, at the level of syntactic organization, the surface structure indicates semantically significant relations only in extremely simple cases. In general, the deeper aspects of syntactic organization are representable by labeled bracketing, but of a very different sort from that seen in surface structure.

There is evidence of various sorts, both from phonetics and from experimental psychology, that labeled bracketing is an adequate representation of surface structure. It would go beyond the bounds of this paper to survey the phonetic evidence. A good deal of it is presented in *Sound Pattern of English*, by myself and Morris Halle. Similarly, very interesting experimental work by Jerry Fodor and his colleagues, based on earlier observations by D. E. Broadbent and Peter Ladefoged, has shown that the disruption of a speech signal (for example, by a superimposed click) tends to be perceived at the boundaries of phrases rather than at the point where the disruption actually occurred, and that in many cases the bracketing of surface structure can be read directly from the data on perceptual displacement. I think the evidence is rather good that labeled bracketing serves to represent the surface structure that is related to the perceived form of physical signals.

Grammatical Transformations

Deep structures are related to surface structures by a sequence of certain formal operations, operations now generally called *grammatical transformations*. At the levels of sound, meaning, and syntax, the significant structural features of sentences are highly abstract. For this reason they cannot be recovered by elementary data-processing techniques. This fact lies behind the search for central processes in speech perception and the search for intrinsic, innate structure as the basis for language learning.

How can we represent deep structure? To answer this question we must consider the grammatical transformations that link surface structure to the underlying deep structure, which is not always apparent.

Consider, for example, the operations of passivization and interrogation. In the sentences (1) *John was examined by the doctor*, and (2) *Did the doctor examine John*, both have a deep structure similar to the paraphrase of Sentence 1, (3) *The doctor examined John*. The same network of grammatical relations determines the semantic interpretation in each case. Thus, two of the grammatical transformations of English must be the operations of passivization and interrogation that form such surface structures as Sentences 1 and 2 from a deeper structure, which in its essentials also underlies Sentence 3. Since the transformations ultimately produce surface structures, they must produce labeled

Figure 3. The superficial similarity of surface structures is revealed when sentences are paraphrased or converted to passive form.

```
(1)  I told John to leave
(2)  I expected John to leave
(3)  I persuaded John to leave
```

First Paraphrase:

```
(1a)  What I told John was to leave (ACCEPTABLE)
(2a)  What I expected John was to leave (UNACCEPTABLE)
(3a)  What I persuaded John was to leave (UNACCEPTABLE)
```

Second Paraphrase:

```
(1b)  It was told by me that John would leave (UNACCEPTABLE)
(2b)  It was expected by me that John would leave (ACCEPTABLE)
(3b)  It was persuaded by me that John would leave (UNACCEPTABLE)
```

```
(4)  I expected the doctor to examine John
(5)  I persuaded the doctor to examine John
```

Passive replacement as paraphrase:

```
(4a)  I expected John to be examined by the doctor (MEANING RETAINED)
(5a)  I persuaded John to be examined by the doctor (MEANING CHANGED)
```

bracketings (see Figure 4). But notice that these operations can apply in sequence: we can form the passive question *Was John examined by the doctor?* by passivization followed by interrogation. Since the result of passivization is a labeled bracketing, it follows that the interrogative transformation operates on a labeled bracketing and forms a new labeled bracketing. Thus a transformation such as interrogation maps a labeled bracketing into a labeled bracketing.

By similar argument, we can show that all grammatical transformations are structure-dependent mappings of this sort and that the deep structures that underlie all sentences must themselves be labeled bracketings. Of course, the labeled bracketing that constitutes deep structure will in general be quite different from that representing the surface structure of a sentence. Our argument is somewhat oversimplified, but it is roughly correct. When made precise and fully accurate it strongly supports the view that deep structures, like surface structures, are formally to be taken as labeled bracketings, and that grammatical transformations are mappings of such structures onto other similar structures.

Mental Operations and Grammar

Recent studies have sought to explore the ways in which grammatical structure of the sort just described enters into mental operations. Much of this work has been based on a proposal formulated by George Miller as a first approximation, namely, that the amount of memory used to store a sentence should reflect the number of transformations used in deriving it. For example, H. B. Savin and E. Perchonock investigated this assumption in the following way: they presented to subjects a sentence followed by a sequence of unrelated words.

They then determined the number of these unrelated words recalled when the subject attempted to repeat the sentence and the sequence of words. The more words recalled, the less memory used to store the sentence. The fewer words recalled, the more memory used to store the sentence. The results showed a remarkable correlation of amount of memory and number of transformations in certain simple cases. In fact, in their experimental material, shorter sentences with more transformations took up more space in memory than longer sentences that involved fewer transformations.

Savin has extended this work and has shown that the effects of deep structure and surface structure can be differentiated by a similar technique. He considered paired sentences with approximately the same deep structure but with one of the pair being more complex in surface structure. He showed that, under the experimental conditions just described, the paired sentences were indistinguishable. But if the sequence of unrelated words precedes, rather than follows, the sentence being tested, then the more complex (in surface structure) of the pair is more difficult to repeat correctly than the simpler member. Savin's very plausible inference is that sentences are coded in memory in terms of deep structure. When the unrelated words precede the test sentence, these words use up a certain amount of short-term memory, and the sentence that is more complex in surface structure cannot be analyzed with the amount of memory remaining. But if the test sentence precedes the unrelated words, it is, once understood, stored in terms of deep structure, which is about the same in both cases. Therefore, the same amount of memory remains, in the paired cases, for recall of the following words. This is a beautiful example of the way creative experimental studies can interweave with theoretical

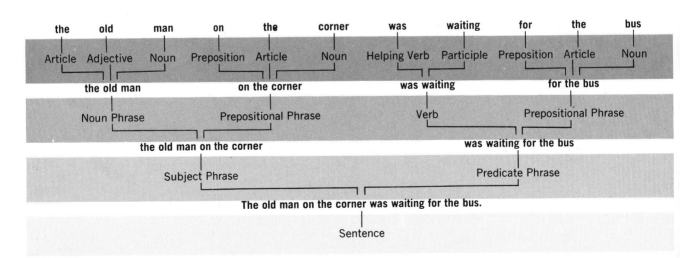

Figure 4. This type of sentence analysis (labeled bracketing) is now considered inadequate; it analyzes the sentence by successive division into larger units, with each unit assigned to its own category.

work in the study of language and of mental processes.

Perceptual Theory

In speaking of mental processes we have returned to our original problem. We can now see why it is reasonable to maintain that the linguistic evidence supports an active theory of acquisition of knowledge. The study of sentences and of speech perception, it seems to me, leads to a perceptual theory of a classical rationalist sort. Representative of this school, among others, were the seventeenth-century Cambridge Platonists, who developed the idea that our perception is guided by notions that originate from the mind and that provide the framework for the interpretation of sensory stimuli. It is not sufficient to suggest that this framework is a store of neural models or *schemata* that are in some manner applied to perception (as is postulated in some current theories of perception). We must go well beyond this assumption and return to the view of Wilhelm von Humboldt, who attributed to the mind a system of rules that generates such models and schemata under the stimulation of the senses. The system of rules itself determines the content of the percept that is formed.

We can offer more than this vague and metaphoric account. A generative grammar and an associated theory of speech perception provide a concrete example of the rules that operate and of the mental objects that they construct and manipulate. Physiology cannot yet explain the physical mechanisms that affect these abstract functions. But neither physiology nor psychology provides evidence that calls this account into question or that suggests an alternative. As mentioned earlier, the most exciting current work in the physiology of perception shows that even the peripheral systems analyze stimuli into the complex properties of objects, and that central processes may significantly affect the information transmitted by the receptor organs.

The study of language, it seems to me, offers strong empirical evidence that empiricist theories of learning are quite inadequate. Serious efforts have been made in recent years to develop principles of induction, generalization, and data analysis that would account for knowledge of a language. These efforts have been a total failure. The methods and principles fail not for any superficial reason such as lack of time or data. They fail because they are intrinsically incapable of giving rise to the system of rules that underlies the normal use of language. What evidence is now available supports the view that all human languages share deep-seated properties of organization and structure. These properties—these linguistic universals—can be plausibly assumed to be an innate mental endowment rather than the result of learning. If this is true, then the study of language sheds light on certain long-standing issues in the theory of knowledge. Once again, I see little reason to doubt that what is true of language is true of other forms of human knowledge as well.

There is one further question that might be raised at this point. How does the human mind come to have the innate properties that underlie acquisition of knowledge? Here linguistic evidence obviously provides no information at all. The process by which the human mind has achieved its present state of complexity and its particular form of innate organization are a complete mystery, as much of a mystery as the analogous questions that can be asked about the processes leading to the physical and mental organization of any other complex organism. It is perfectly safe to attribute this to evolution, so long as we bear in mind that there is no substance to this assertion—it amounts to nothing more than the belief that there is surely some naturalistic explanation for these phenomena.

There are, however, important aspects of the problem of language and mind that can be studied sensibly within the limitations of present understanding and technique. I think that, for the moment, the most productive investigations are those dealing with the nature of particular grammars and with the universal conditions met by all human languages. I have tried to suggest how one can move, in successive steps of increasing abstractness, from the study of percepts to the study of grammar and perceptual mechanisms, and from the study of grammar to the study of universal grammar and the mechanisms of learning.

Communication Without Words
Albert Mehrabian

There is a means of communication about which we are often unaware but that is most "informative." This is nonverbal communication. Even when people communicate with words they give nonverbal cues to their meaning by tonal and facial expressions. For certain kinds of messages the nonverbal content is even more important than the verbal. Albert Mehrabian discusses these issues; he also shows how nonverbal information can be measured and potentially how it can be used to improve our educational practices.

Suppose you are sitting in my office listening to me describe some research I have done on communication. I tell you that feelings are communicated less by the words a person uses than by certain nonverbal means —that, for example, the verbal part of a spoken message has considerably less effect on whether a listener feels liked or disliked than a speaker's facial expression or tone of voice.

So far so good. But suppose I add, "In fact, we've worked out a formula that shows exactly how much each of these components contributes to the effect of the message as a whole. It goes like this: Total Impact = .07 verbal + .38 vocal + .55 facial."

What would you say to *that?* Perhaps you would smile good-naturedly and say, with some feeling, "Baloney!" Or perhaps you would frown and remark acidly, "Isn't science grand." My own response to the first answer would probably be to smile back: the facial part of your message, at least, was positive (55 percent of the total). The second answer might make me uncomfortable: only the verbal part was positive (7 percent).

The point here is not only that my reactions would lend credence to the formula but that most listeners would have mixed feelings about my statement. People like to see science march on, but they tend to resent its intrusion into an "art" like the communication of feelings, just as they find analytical and quantitative approaches to the study of personality cold, mechanistic, and unacceptable.

The psychologist himself is sometimes plagued by the feeling that he is trying to put a rainbow into a bottle. Fascinated by a complicated and emotionally rich human situation, he begins to study it, only to find in the course of his research that he has destroyed part of the mystique that originally intrigued and involved him. But despite a certain nostalgia for earlier, more intuitive approaches, one must acknowledge that concrete experimental data have added a great deal to our understanding of how feelings are communicated. In fact, as I hope to show, analytical and intuitive findings do not so much conflict with as complement each other.

It is indeed difficult to know what another person really feels. He says one thing and does another; he seems to mean something but we have an uneasy feeling it isn't true. The early psychoanalysts, facing this problem of inconsistencies and ambiguities in a person's communications, attempted to resolve it through the concepts of the conscious and the unconsious. They assumed that contradictory messages meant a conflict between superficial, deceitful, or erroneous feelings on the one hand and true attitudes and feelings on the other. Their role, then, was to help the client separate the wheat from the chaff.

The question was, how could this be done? Some analysts insisted that inferring the client's unconscious wishes was a completely intuitive process. Others thought that some nonverbal behavior, such as posture, position, and movement, could be used in a more objective way to discover the client's feelings. A favorite technique of Frieda Fromm-Reichmann, for example, was to imitate a client's posture herself in order to obtain some feeling for what he was experiencing.

Thus began the gradual shift away from the idea that communication is primarily verbal and that the verbal message includes distortions or ambiguities due to unobservable motives that only experts can discover.

Language, though, can be used to communicate almost anything. By comparison, nonverbal behavior is very limited in range. Usually, it is used to communicate feelings, likings, and preferences, and it customarily reinforces or contradicts the feelings that are communicated verbally. Less often, it adds a new dimension of sorts to a verbal message, as when a salesman describes his product to a client and simultaneously conveys, nonverbally, the impression that he likes the client.

A great many forms of nonverbal behavior can communicate feelings: touching, facial expression, tone of voice, spatial distance from the addressee, relaxation of posture, rate of speech, number of errors in speech. Some of these are generally recognized as informative. Untrained adults and children easily infer that they are liked or disliked from certain facial expressions, from whether (and how) someone touches them, and from a speaker's tone of voice. Other behavior, such as posture, has a more subtle effect. A listener may sense how someone feels about him from the way the person sits while talking to him, but he may have trouble identifying precisely what his impression comes from.

Verbal Versus Vocal Information

Correct intuitive judgments of the feelings or attitudes of others are especially difficult when different degrees of feeling, or contradictory kinds of feeling, are expressed simultaneously through different forms of behavior. As I have pointed out, there is a distinction between verbal and vocal information (vocal information being what is lost when speech is written down—intonation, tone, stress, length and frequency of pauses, and so on), and the two kinds of information do not always communicate the same feeling. This distinction, which has been recognized for some time, has shed new light on certain types of communication. Sarcasm, for

example, can be defined as a message in which the information transmitted vocally contradicts the information transmitted verbally. Usually the verbal information is positive and the vocal is negative, as in "Isn't science grand."

Through the use of an electronic filter, it is possible to measure the degree of liking communicated vocally. What the filter does is eliminate the higher frequencies of recorded speech, so that words are unintelligible but most vocal qualities remain. (For women's speech, we eliminate frequencies higher than about 200 cycles per second; for men, frequencies over about 100 cycles per second.) When people are asked to judge the degree of liking conveyed by the filtered speech, they perform the task rather easily and with a significant amount of agreement.

This method allows us to find out, in a given message, just how inconsistent the information communicated in words and the information communicated vocally really are. We ask one group to judge the amount of liking conveyed by a transcription of what was said, the verbal part of the message. A second group judges the vocal component, and a third group judges the impact of the complete recorded message. In one study of this sort we found that, when the verbal and vocal components of a message agree (both positive or both negative), the message as a whole is judged a little more positive or a little more negative than either component by itself. But when vocal information contradicts verbal, vocal wins out. If someone calls you "honey" in a nasty tone of voice, you are likely to feel disliked; it is also possible to say "I hate you" in a way that conveys exactly the opposite feeling.

Other Nonverbal Cues

Besides the verbal and vocal characteristics of speech, there are other, more subtle, signals of meaning in a spoken message. For example, everyone makes mistakes when he talks—unnecessary repetitions, stutterings, the omission of parts of words, incomplete sentences, "ums" and "ahs." In a number of studies of speech errors, George Mahl of Yale University has found that errors become more frequent as the speaker's discomfort or anxiety increases. It might be interesting to apply this index in an attempt to detect deceit (though on some occasions it might be risky: confidence men are notoriously smooth talkers).

| TIMING | Timing is also highly informative. How long does a speaker allow silent periods to last, and how long does he wait before he answers his partner? How long do his utterances tend to be? How often does he interrupt his partner, or wait an inappropriately long time before speaking? Joseph Matarazzo and his colleagues at the University of Oregon have found that each of these speech habits is stable from person to person, and each tells something about the speaker's

personality and about his feelings toward and status in relation to his partner.

| DURATION | Utterance duration, for example, is a very stable quality in a person's speech; about thirty seconds long on the average. But when someone talks to a partner whose status is higher than his own, the more the high-status person nods his head the longer the speaker's utterances become. If the high-status person changes his own customary speech pattern toward longer or shorter utterances, the lower-status person will change his own speech in the same direction. If the high-status person often interrupts the speaker, or creates long silences, the speaker is likely to become quite uncomfortable. These are things that can be observed outside the laboratory as well as under experimental conditions. If you have an employee who makes you uneasy and seems not to respect you, watch him the next time you talk to him—perhaps he is failing to follow the customary low-status pattern.

| DIRECTNESS | Immediacy or directness is another good source of information about feelings. We use more distant forms of communication when the act of communicating is undesirable or uncomfortable. For example, some people would rather transmit discontent with an employee's work through a third party than do it themselves, and some find it easier to communicate negative feelings in writing than by telephone or face to face.

| DISTANCE | Distance can show a negative attitude toward the message itself, as well as toward the act of delivering it. Certain forms of speech are more distant than others, and they show fewer positive feelings for the subject referred to. A speaker might say "Those people need help," which is more distant than "These people need help," which is in turn even more distant than "These people need our help." Or he might say "Sam and I have been having dinner," which has less immediacy than "Sam and I are having dinner."

| GESTURES | Facial expression, touching, gestures, self-manipulation (such as scratching), changes in body position, and head movements—all these express a person's positive and negative attitudes, both at the moment and in general, and many reflect status relationships as well. Movements of the limbs and head, for example, not only indicate one's attitude toward a specific set of circumstances but relate to how dominant, and how anxious, one generally tends to be in social situations. Gross changes in body position, such as shifting in the chair, may show negative feelings toward the person one is talking to. They may also be cues: "It's your turn to talk," or "I'm about to get out of here, so finish what you're saying."

| POSTURE | Posture is used to indicate both liking and status. The more a person leans toward his addressee, the more positively he feels about him. Relaxation of posture is a good indicator of both attitude and status, and one that we have been able to measure quite pre-

cisely. Three categories have been established for relaxation in a seated position: least relaxation is indicated by muscular tension in the hands and rigidity of posture; moderate relaxation is indicated by a forward lean of about 20 degrees and a sideways lean of less than 10 degrees, a curved back, and, for women, an open arm position; and extreme relaxation is indicated by a reclining angle greater than 20 degrees and a sideways lean greater than 10 degrees.

Our findings suggest that a speaker relaxes either very little or a great deal when he dislikes the person he is talking to, and to a moderate degree when he likes his companion. It seems that extreme tension occurs with threatening addressees, and extreme relaxation with nonthreatening, disliked addressees. In particular, men tend to become tense when talking to other men whom they dislike; on the other hand, women talking to men *or* women and men talking to women show dislike through extreme relaxation. As for status, people relax most with a low-status addressee, next most with a peer, and least with someone of higher status than their own. Body orientation also shows status: in both sexes, it is least direct toward women with low status and most direct toward disliked men of high status. In part, body orientation seems to be determined by whether one regards one's partner as threatening.

| EYE CONTACT | The more you like a person, the more time you are likely to spend looking into his eyes as you talk to him. Standing close to your partner and facing him directly (which makes eye contact easier) also indicate positive feelings. And you are likely to stand or sit closer to your peers than you do to addressees whose status is either lower or higher than yours.

Applications to Education

What I have said so far has been based on research studies performed, for the most part, with college students from the middle and upper-middle classes. One interesting question about communication, however, concerns young children from lower socioeconomic levels. Are these children, as some have suggested, more responsive to implicit channels of communication than middle- and upper-class children are?

Morton Wiener and his colleagues at Clark University had a group of middle- and lower-class children play learning games in which the reward for learning was praise. The child's responsiveness to the verbal and vocal parts of the praise reward was measured by how much he learned. Praise came in two forms: the objective words "right" and "correct," and the more affective or evaluative words, "good" and "fine." All four words were spoken sometimes in a positive tone of voice and sometimes neutrally.

Positive intonation proved to have a dramatic effect on the learning rate of the lower-class group. They learned much faster when the vocal part of the message was positive than when it was neutral. Positive intonation affected the middle-class group as well, but not nearly as much.

If children of lower socioeconomic groups are more responsive to facial expression, posture, and touch as well as to vocal communication, that fact could have interesting applications to elementary education. For example, teachers could be explicitly trained to be aware of, and to use, the forms of praise (nonverbal or verbal) that would be likely to have the greatest effect on their particular students.

Applications to Treatment of Schizophrenia

Another application of experimental data on communication is to the interpretation and treatment of schizophrenia. The literature on schizophrenia has for some time emphasized that parents of schizophrenic children give off contradictory signals simultaneously. Perhaps the parent tells the child in words that he loves him, but his posture conveys a negative attitude. According to the "double-bind" theory of schizophrenia, the child who perceives simultaneous contradictory feelings in his parent does not know how to react: should he respond to the positive part of the message, or to the negative? If he is frequently placed in this paralyzing situation, he may learn to respond with contradictory communications of his own. The boy who sends a birthday card to his mother and signs it "Napoleon" says that he likes his mother and yet denies he is the one who likes her.

In an attempt to determine whether parents of disturbed children really do emit more inconsistent messages about their feelings than other parents do, my colleagues and I have compared what these parents communicate verbally and vocally with what they show through posture. We interviewed parents of moderately and quite severely disturbed children, in the presence of the child, about the child's problem. The interview was video-recorded without the parents' knowledge, so that we could analyze their behavior later on. Our measurements supplied both the amount of inconsistency be-

tween the parents' verbal-vocal and postural communications, and the total amount of liking that the parents communicated.

According to the double-bind theory, the parents of the more-disturbed children should have behaved more inconsistently than the parents of the less-disturbed children. This was not confirmed: there was no significant difference between the two groups. However, the *total amount* of positive feeling communicated by parents of the more disturbed children was less than that communicated by the other group.

This suggests that (1) negative communications toward disturbed children occur because the child is a problem and therefore elicits them, or (2) the negative attitude precedes the child's disturbance. It may also be that both factors operate together, in a vicious circle.

If so, one way to break the cycle is for the therapist to create situations in which the parent can have better feelings toward the child. A more positive attitude from the parent may make the child more responsive to his directives, and the spiral may begin to move up instead of down. In our own work with disturbed children, this kind of procedure has been used to good effect.

If one puts one's mind to it, one can think of a great many other applications for the findings I have described, though not all of them concern serious problems. Politicians, for example, are careful to maintain eye contact with the television camera when they speak, but they are not always careful about how they sit when they debate another candidate of, presumably, equal status.

Public relations men might find a use for some of the subtler signals of feeling. So might Don Juans. And so might ordinary people, who could try watching other people's signals and changing their own, for fun at a party or in a spirit of experimentation at home. I trust that does not strike you as a cold, manipulative suggestion, indicating dislike for the human race. I assure you that, if you had more than a transcription of words to judge from (7 percent of total message), it would not.

Experiment in Perception

Bela Julesz

In perceiving depth, both monocular and binocular cues can be used. Since it is extremely difficult to separate these two sets of cues, it has not been possible to evaluate completely their relative contributions to perception. Bela Julesz has brilliantly employed computer techniques to organize experiments in depth perception. With these techniques he produces complex dot patterns that provide only binocular cues. He is thus able to separate relevant stimuli, to pit monocular and binocular cues against each other, and to analyze central versus peripheral aspects of perception.

Most of us take it for granted that objects will look much the same whether we view them with one eye or with both eyes. Except for a certain loss of depth perception, the world we see when we shut one eye is almost identical to that we see with our normal two-eye, or binocular, vision. Shapes, textures, and contours of the objects about us do not change much when we view them with one eye shut.

But what would our perceptual experience be like if somehow we could create an environment that looked entirely different, depending on whether we looked at it with one eye or with both eyes? If we could separate monocular and binocular cues, what could we learn about the laws of perception?

And would the results differ from the established findings of classical psychology, with its centuries of studying images in which the monocular and binocular perceptual cues are not separated?

Intrigued by these ideas, I have been working since 1959 to devise techniques that would permit creation of images in which the monocular and binocular information are independent of each other. I have been able to "eclipse" the powerful monocular visual cues and thus reveal a previously hidden psychology of binocular vision.

It was particularly challenging to find a way to create complex stereographs with no apparent shapes or contours when viewed with one eye but that would yield predetermined shapes when seen with both eyes.

For more than a century we have known that binocular parallax—the relative difference in the horizontal location of corresponding points in the left eye and the right eye—is the principal binocular depth cue. Because the distance between the two eyes and the focal length of the eyes at a given fixation are constant for any individual, there is a simple trigonometric relationship between the parallax shift and the actual distance of the object. In traditional investigations, the aim has been to relate the amount of parallax shift to the amount of depth perceived.

It is commonly thought that the problem of depth perception is relatively simple because of the analogy between the eyes and a range finder. The most intriguing part of this problem is not the relationship between binocular parallax and depth, but rather how the brain *matches* corresponding points in the two monocular fields so that the disparity can be perceived.

In traditional investigations of stereoscopic vision, images with only a few dots or lines are ordinarily used. These present only a few visual targets, and so the question of which dot in the left eye's view belongs to which dot in the right eye's view does not arise. My previous interest in stereo radar systems (that use two or more search beams) taught me that the "false-target probability" increases as the number of targets increases. When there is one "blip" on the stereo radar screen, there is no problem in matching the blip to the target. But if many blips appear, the chances of assigning a blip to the wrong target increase tremendously.

This false-target-probability problem also occurs in perception. For example, when four targets cast their projections on the retinae, there are sixteen possible ways the brain can combine the information it receives. In this case, only four of the target localizations are correct, and twelve are false, yielding a false-target probability of 0.75. The probability of making a false-target localization approaches 100 percent as the number of targets increases (see Figure 1).

How does our perceptual process eliminate these ambiguities? In determining binocular parallax, do we first scan the monocular patterns in the right and left eyes individually, and then fuse them? Or are the two

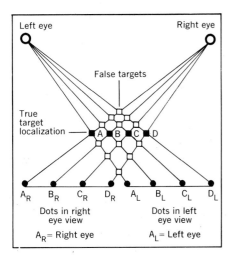

Figure 1. A view of 4 dots produces 16 possible localizations, of which 12 are false targets.

Figure 2. Hypothetical models of perception processes; the random-dot stereograph experiments indicate that Model II is the process that permits depth perception and pattern recognition.

Figure 3. (a) This computer-generated random-dot stereograph has identical left and right images except that the center square of dots in the left image has been slightly shifted on a horizontal plane. (b) Schematic plan of how center square in (a) is shifted. Note that the uncovered area (X, Y) is refilled with random dots.

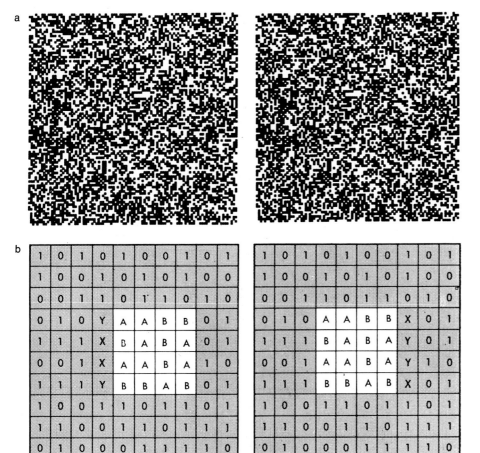

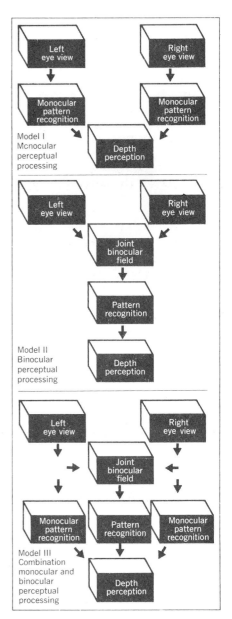

visual fields first combined in some manner, and all further processing conducted on the fused field? Or do we use a combination of both processes? (See Figure 2.)

One possible way we process visual information is by *form recognition*. It has been tacitly assumed that in the act of recognizing form, we combine thousands of dots in each eye's view into gestalts—or unified patterns. These gestalts are then identified in each eye's view as corresponding to each other.

For example, a person looking at a football crowd obtains a binocular picture presumably by matching corresponding faces that he recognizes and identifies separately in his left-eye and right-eye images.

To test this theory, I developed stereographs that contain no recognizable forms or shapes when viewed with one eye. A computer was programmed to print a square containing 10,000 randomly selected black and white dots. The dot patterns in the left and right images are identical, except for a center square in one image that has been shifted a few units to one side, as if it were a solid sheet. Because of this shift, an area is uncovered, and this area is filled with randomly selected dots (see Figure 3). The horizontal shift of the center square corresponds to binocular parallax.

The task of producing these stereographs is an ideal job for the computer—which can print out and manipulate patterns containing thousands or even millions of dots. Without the computer, these studies would have been extremely difficult, and probably impossible. With enough patience, of course, one could turn out a random-dot stereograph by hand. The pointillist painter Georges Seurat painstakingly placed tiny dot after tiny dot of color on a canvas until he created the overall effect he sought. The sheer magnitude of creating a single finished painting by this method explains why there are so few Seurats.

Our computer-generated dot patterns can be made to appear completely random when viewed with one eye. But if viewed binocularly, certain correlated areas are seen in depth. I have created a number of such stereographs, and my research with them at Bell Telephone Laboratories over the past nine years has borne out my earlier expectations that when monocular cues are *eclipsed*, a new aspect of the visual system emerges, which in some ways is richer than any known before.

We are now ready to begin our experiments with binocular fusion and depth perception.

First Computerized Anaglyphs

Examine the left and right images of the *stereo image pair* of Figure 3. When viewed with one eye, the dot distribution in each of the two images appears to be uniform. However, when these images are fused binocularly (a feat that some of the readers will be able to do without a stereoscope), the hidden center square emerges in vivid depth above the larger surrounding square.

To facilitate binocular fusion, a similar stereograph is reprinted as a red-and-green anaglyph in Figure 4.

Anaglyphs are composite pictures printed in two colors, usually red and green; they produce a three-dimensional effect when viewed through red-and-green spectacles. Anaglyphs are well known in the printing industry, but are difficult to produce because any areas in which the red and green overlap must be printed in yellow. With the aid of computer-controlled printouts, we are presenting here for the first time anaglyphs in which no red and green dots overlap.

The anaglyph illustrations in this article have been set up as experiments, which you, the reader, can perform. Each experiment is self-contained, with a full description of the procedure and explanation of the results.

Pause for a moment now and carry out the experiments in Figures 4 and 6.

Since the stereographs in Figures 4 and 6 appeared completely patternless when viewed with one eye, it appears that monocular gestalt organization is not nec-

essary for binocular fusion. These experiments also demonstrate that complex surfaces as well as simple depth planes can be binocularly portrayed by this technique. However, one still might argue that something simpler than gestalts, such as line segments and small clusters of dots, could be extracted from each monocular field and then compared during binocular fusion. Some sort of preprocessing of the images in each eye could occur before binocular fusion. This hypothesis has been tested in an experiment similar to the ones shown here.

The results show that even in the total absence of small clusters of dots, binocular fusion can still occur. Thus, for these examples at least, there is no preprocessing of the separate monocular images, either at the macro or micro levels before binocular fusion takes place. This shows that binocular depth perception results from the brain's processing of the combined images.

How, then, do we relate the dots in the left eye's view with the dots in the right eye's view when all the usual monocular cues have been removed? With two squares, each with 10,000 dots, there are theoretically billions of ways that binocular fusion could take place. One plausible hypothesis is that binocular fusion occurs where the black and the white dots in the two images happen to be in identical positions. In a random-dot stereograph, such as the stereo image pair (Figure 3), by chance 50 percent of the dots are in identical positions in the left and right images. These dots are said to have "zero disparity." The majority of the remaining dots can be matched at either +1 or −1 unit disparities, since nearly all of these remaining dots are located either one unit to the right or one unit to the left of a zero-disparity dot.

Therefore, in the fused binocular percept we might expect to see three planes staggered next to each other in depth: the zero-disparity plane, the +1-disparity plane, and the −1-disparity plane. Also, because only 50 percent of the dots in any of the three depth planes have the same disparity, the planes should appear semitransparent, or lacelike.

However, this is not what we actually perceive in this stereograph. What we do see is not three planes, but two—the plane of the center square and the plane of the surrounding square—at considerable depth. And these two planes are solid, not transparent.

This indicates that when visual images are fused binocularly, the fusion mechanism prefers to look for dense surfaces. Thus, the binocular process consists, in part at least, of matching clusters of adjacent dots in each eye's view. In other words, the fusion process consists of locating as many dots as possible with the same disparities. For example, in the anaglyph in Figure 4, while there are probably many tiny clusters of dots with the same disparity values, only two large areas have dots with the same disparities—the center square and the surrounding square.

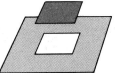

Figure 4. The floating square experiment.

OBJECT: To demonstrate that depth perception can occur even when no contours or shapes are visible to either eye alone.

METHOD: Using the anaglyphoscope, view the figure through the red *or* green filter with one eye shut. You will see no shapes in this 20,000-dot figure. Now, with both eyes (red filter/left eye; green/right) view it from arm's length or more. Within minutes, you will see a center shimmering square. Try to bring the center-square dots into sharp focus; concentrate on the dots that seem higher than the surrounding ones. Gradually, the center square will float toward you. Take your time. The depth effect does not occur quickly. Please be sure there is no glare on the page. Next, reverse filters (green filter/left eye; red/right). The square will appear as beneath a glass surface. Focus through the "glass" onto dots that seem lower than others. The square will move back.

RESULTS: The usual monocular contour or depth cues are unnecessary to perceive shape or depth. This implies that visual fields from each eye are first combined in the cortex, and binocular processing occurs on the combined field (see Model II, Figure 2).

Depth Fields

One simple model of binocular depth perception (see Figure 5) to explain these findings is: In the brain (cortex), the left and the right retinal images are *subtracted* point by point from each other. The "difference" is scanned for dot clusters of similar horizontal disparities. The cortex creates several difference fields by horizontally "shifting" the images prior to each subtraction. These difference fields are stacked in depth above each other. For example, take the stereograph with a displaced center square (Figure 4). Of the several difference fields created, only two contain dense clusters of dots. The zero-disparity field is perceived as the surrounding square, and the field displaced one unit is seen as the center square. There are no dense clusters of dots with similar disparities in the other difference fields, and so these fields play no part in forming the stereoscopic image. What we see, then, is the center square in depth either above or below the surrounding square.

This simple model based on difference fields has been tested in a practical application. A computer program based on this model, called AUTOMAP-1, has been developed for automatically compiling three-dimensional maps from two-dimensional aerial photographs. Each exposure is taken from a different aircraft position to produce the proper amount of parallax shift in the images. Previously, contour maps had to be made by clerks who plotted the contours point by point. The clerks fused two aerial photographs of the terrain with the aid of a stereoscope and then subjectively tried to align a floating point of light with the three-dimensional percept of a mountain top or valley bottom. The successful automation of this task frees people of a tedious and time-consuming chore. The fact that an object does not have to be recognized in order to locate it in space

makes conceivable the automation of many tasks that now require humans as operators or observers.

Competing Cues

In the first three experiments, we have learned that binocular fusion and depth perception are possible even when all monocular pattern cues are eliminated. But what happens when monocular cues, such as shapes or symmetry, are present in one or both of the stereograph images? Do monocular cues affect binocular fusion? In the next experiment, we will explore a new class of computer-generated images in which symmetrical patterns are visible when viewed with one eye.

The anaglyphs in Figure 7 demonstrate what happens when images of this type are fused binocularly. When viewed with one eye, the top half of stereograph (a) appears to be a mirror image of the bottom half. When stereograph (b) is viewed with one eye, a fourfold symmetry becomes visible. Viewed binocularly, the symmetry in each is scrambled in the fused binocular image. In a similar experiment that I conducted in my laboratory, a word or text is clearly visible when the stereograph is viewed with one eye but fragments into random dots and disappears when the stereograph is viewed binocularly.

This phenomenon should not be confused with binocular rivalry, which occurs when two dissimilar images, say a page of print and a picture, are presented simultaneously, one to each eye. The two images can be fused in a stereoscope, or the two objects can be placed side by side on a table, separated by a vertical sheet of paper and viewed so that the left eye sees only the left object and the right eye sees only the right object. We do not see the two images at the same time but rather we alternately see one object and then the other. This rivalry, or alternation, does not occur during the binocu-

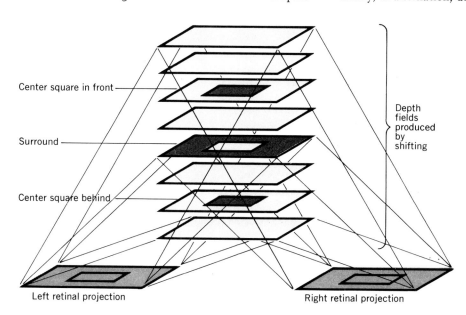

Depth fields produced by shifting

Center square in front

Surround

Center square behind

Left retinal projection   Right retinal projection

Figure 5. Hypothetical model of depth perception: the right and the left retinal images are compared and then "subtracted" on a point-by-point basis. The resulting "difference field" is scanned for dot clusters of similar disparities. A stack of difference fields is then created by mentally "shifting" the images prior to the subtraction.

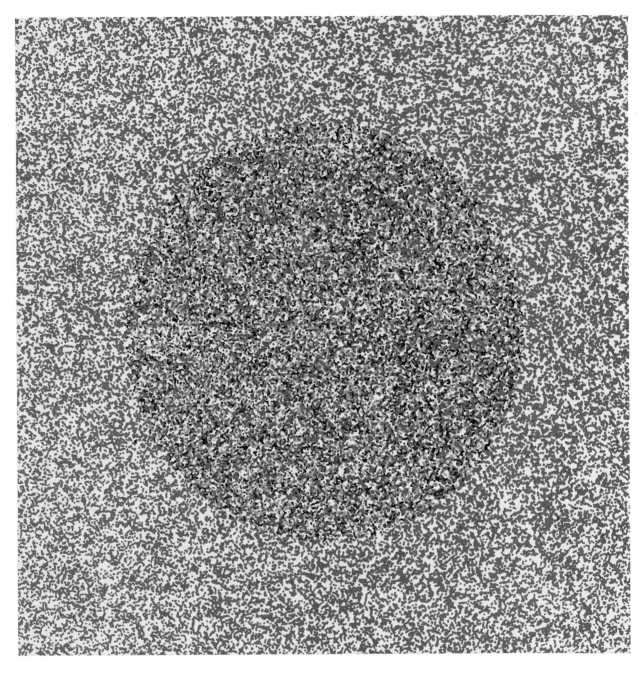

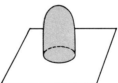

Figure 6. The expanding dome experiment.

OBJECT: To demonstrate the dramatic sensation of perceiving a paraboloid dome in great depth by viewing an array of one million random dots.

METHOD: View the figure at arm's length or more. When seen through the red filter only, the dots appear randomly distributed. When viewed with filters on both eyes (green filter/right eye; red/left), the center circle takes on a translucent quality of indeterminate depth. Locate the higher dots in the circle and bring them into sharp focus. The surface of the dome will take shape slowly. Initially, it looks like a transparent bubble with dots scattered on the surface. As you watch (take your time), the bubble will elongate until it has grown about 6 inches from the page. Move your head from side to side and watch the dome move with you. Keeping the dome in focus, move back slowly. The dome will follow you. If you have difficulty in raising the dome, hold a pencil tip a half-inch off the page and over the circle. Focus on the pencil tip and watch for dots that seem to rise to the pencil. As the dots rise, slowly lift the pencil as though pulling up the dots. Watch patiently; the dome will emerge. Next, reverse filters (red filter/right eye; green/left). The circle will seem to be covered by a glass. Look through the glass and try to find the dots below the surface. The dome will expand back into the page in great depth.

RESULTS: Continuous complex surfaces, as well as single planes, can be portrayed in depth with random-dot computer-generated stereographs.

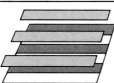

Figure 7. Lost symmetry experiment.
OBJECT: To demonstrate the effect of monocularly visible patterns on binocular fusion.
METHOD: View anaglyph (a) through red filter only. The top half is a mirror image of the bottom half. View through filters with both eyes (red filter/left eye; green/right). Gradually, horizontal stripes will emerge in depth and scramble the symmetry. Next, view anaglyph (b) through red filter only. A fourfold symmetry becomes visible. View through filters with both eyes (green filter/right eye; red/left). Gradually, a transparent plane floats up and obscures the symmetry.
RESULTS: The suppression of the monocular pattern by the binocular percept indicates that binocular fusion dominates monocular pattern recognition.

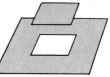

Figure 9. Broken connectivities experiment.
OBJECT: To demonstrate that binocular fusion can occur on a point-by-point basis without extracting features such as lines. The anaglyph (a) is derived from the stereo image pair in Figure 3, of which (b) and (c) are portions; (d) is derived from (b) by breaking the diagonal connectivity of the dots.

METHOD: View anaglyph (a) through red filter only. The images are strikingly different even though only 16% of the dots are different. Viewed through filters with both eyes (red filter/left eye; green/right), a center square is seen in depth.
RESULTS: Binocular fusion can occur on a point-by-point basis.

 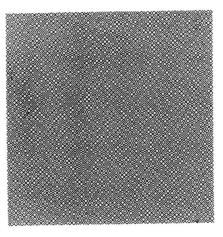

Figure 8. This diagonal-line stereograph is created by having the computer randomly select diagonal line segments instead of dots. When viewed through a stereoscope, a center square emerges above a background square, as seen in Figure 4.

lar suppression of monocular images. Once binocular fusion takes place, it remains stable. This indicates that if binocular fusion occurs, it precedes or dominates recognition of monocular patterns or gestalts.

These findings do not exclude the possibility of certain simple preprocessing of monocular cues prior to binocular combination. For example, research by physiologists David H. Hubel and Torsten N. Wiesel of Harvard has shown that receptor cells in the retina carry out considerable preprocessing of stimuli. They have discovered "line detectors" in the retina that are directly connected to certain cells in the cortex of the brain. These line detectors respond primarily to lines of light with specific orientations.

To find out if simple monocular preprocessing interferes with binocular fusion, we made a stereograph using short diagonal line segments (see Figure 8). Fusion can easily be obtained—the process can operate by extracting features such as lines or edges. Nevertheless, we must emphasize that binocular fusion can operate on a point-by-point basis without extracting monocular features. We have demonstrated this in the laboratory with stereographs in which the diagonal connectivity is one of the images that is deliberately destroyed. That is, wherever three diagonal dots in the left and right images were identical, the middle one was changed to its complement: black to white, or white to black. Only 16 percent of the dots in the two images are different when viewed monocularly, but the two images look strikingly different. (See Figure 9.) Binocular fusion is easily obtained, demonstrating that fusion can occur on a point-by-point basis.

Random-Dot Movies

Experiments with random-dot stereographs can be extended to motion pictures. For example, a film can be made of a stereograph with the raised center square. When viewed with one eye, the motion picture appears to be no more than the "snow" often seen on empty television channels, but when viewed binocularly, not one but two "snowstorms" appear. The center square appears in depth above the larger surrounding square.

By employing the proper sequence of random-dot images, a binocular illusion of movement can be created. The center square can be made to move up and down through the surrounding square. Watching the center square, a viewer experiences a unique sensation of movement, in which an object appears to move independently of its texture.

New perceptual phenomena different from those obtained with classical stimuli can be produced with this film technique. For instance, a classical stroboscopic experiment alternately presents pictures of two lines in different positions. If the rate of presentation is slow enough, each line is seen successively in its proper position. If the rate of presentation is increased, the viewer thinks he sees a single line jumping back and forth. At a still faster speed, the viewer sees the two lines simultaneously. This experiment performed with a random-dot stereograph containing two bars produces almost identical results—with a very interesting exception.

At the point where the viewer sees a single bar jumping back and forth above the background, as the speed of presentation is increased the movement of the bar appears to slow down. Eventually it appears to stand still while the surrounding margin jumps back and forth.

Seymour Papert of MIT, using the random-dot motion-picture technique, has determined the perceptual level at which the "waterfall illusion" occurs. If you stare long enough at a waterfall and then close your eyes, you will appear to see movement in the opposite direction to the waterfall. This effect is commonly explained as the result of fatiguing of the motion detectors in the retina or just beyond. The waterfall illusion can be created using movies of the random-dot stereographs. Since there are no moving patterns perceivable at the retinal level in these films, this strongly suggests that the illusion is caused by some process in the cortex that occurs after binocular fusion.

Panum's Fusional Area

Do these results with random-dot stereographs mean that the findings of classical depth-perception studies are wrong? The answer is no. In the classical investigations, the images used had only a few dots or lines, while the experiments described in this article use complex images containing thousands of dots. The relationship between classical research and the present studies can be likened to the relationship between atoms and molecules. And just as experimental findings about molecules do not disprove the findings on a single atom, neither do the findings with complex random-dot stereographs disprove those obtained with simpler images. The questions raised in studies using random-dot stereographs are at a different hierarchical level than the questions posed in classical studies.

In another experiment, Derek Fender, of the California Institute of Technology, and I have shown how much a perceptual phenomenon depends on the particular stimuli used. This experiment alters one of the basic physical findings of stereoscopic perception—Panum's fusional area, named after the nineteenth-century Austrian physiologist, P. L. Panum. He found that two images on the left and right retinae could be distinguished as separate images only if they were farther apart than 6 minutes of arc (one tenth of a degree). If the two images were registered within 6 minutes of arc—Panum's fusional area—then the two images seemed as one.

In our experiment, four graduate students submitted to the discomfort of contact lenses fitted tightly to their eyeballs. With mirrors attached to the contact lenses and with optical projectors, we stabilized the location of images on the students' retinae, despite ever-present eye motion. We began by projecting left and right stereograph images onto the left and right retinae. The students had no control over what they saw. When the images were brought within Panum's fusional area, the student experienced binocular fusion. Then we pulled the images apart slowly.

We found that the images remained fused binocularly until they were separated horizontally by 120 minutes of arc (2 degrees, or twenty times Panum's fusional limit). At this point they break apart suddenly. The images had to be brought back to within 6 minutes of arc alignment before they fused again.

Thus, the area of maintaining fusion for random-dot stereographs is much larger than Panum's fusional area.

Because of this experiment, the notion of the limits for corresponding points must be changed. Two dots that are 120 minutes of arc apart can be considered corresponding points if they are part of a dense structure that has been previously fused binocularly (but not if they are part of a simple structure). The binocular fusion mechanism has a sort of memory—once fusion has been obtained, it tends to be maintained.

In retrospect, it is not surprising that when we use thousands or millions of dots or lines, we can study a deeper structure of the visual system than we could by using only a few lines or dots.

Depth Blindness

This article serves merely as an introduction to the growing field of complex stereographs.

In random-dot stereographs, all of the monocular depth cues can be eliminated. These are so powerful that the illusion of depth persists even when we use only one eye. Monocular cues include: interposition (near objects blocking part of the background); motion parallax (near objects appear to move more rapidly than objects far away); perspective (parallel lines seem to meet in the distance); texture; and shadowing.

With the random-dot stereographs, for the first time it is possible to make an objective, quantitative test of stereoscopic vision based only on binocular disparity. Our tests of several thousand people indicate that there may be as many people who are "depth blind" as are color blind. Clinical tests for "depth blindness" in applicants might be useful for certain jobs—jet pilots, for instance, or heart surgeons. The random-dot stereograph can also be used to learn more about color perception, optical illusions, perceptual learning, and eye movements.

In my investigations, I have developed techniques to "paint" binocular shapes in which the monocular shape cues are eclipsed. Although I started out to explore the problem of binocular depth perception, these techniques now can be used by psychologists to explore any visual phenomena involving our perception of shape. Out of these investigations, using stimuli with a richer structure than can be obtained with simple line targets, we may hope to get a deeper understanding of our visual system.

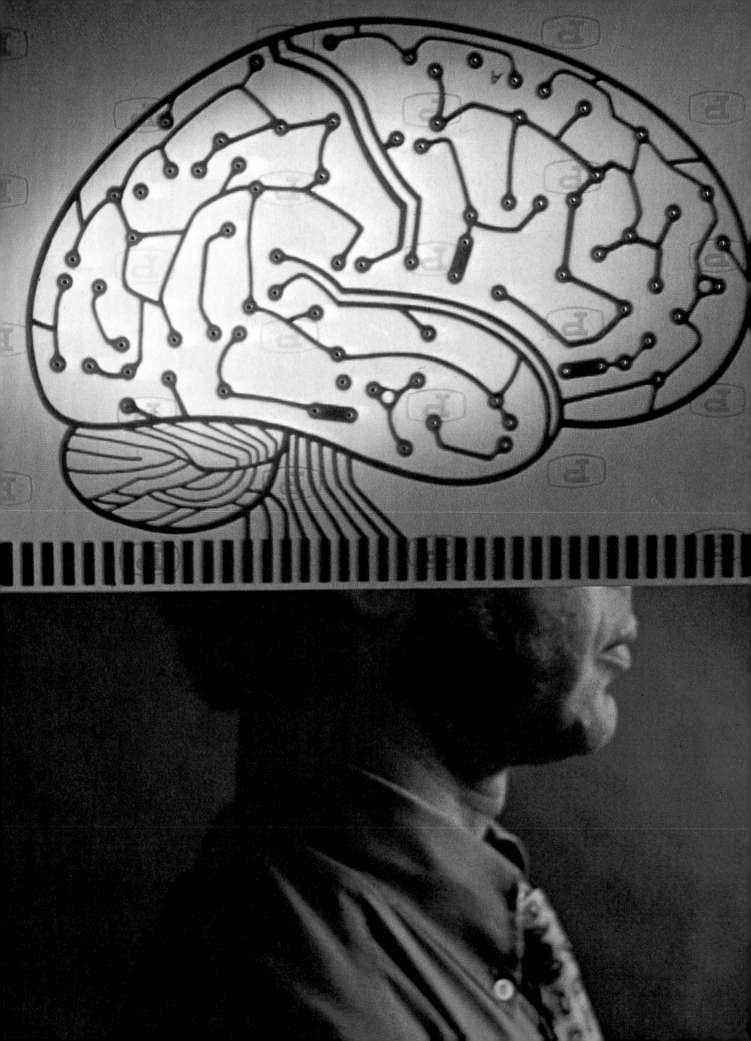

Conscious Control of Brain Waves

Joseph Kamiya

Kamiya, like Hebb in a previous article, attempts a synthesis of the mental and physical aspects of man's behavior. He shows how the occurrence and even the frequency of human brain waves can be manipulated by the individual. After presenting highly original experiments on conditioning the emission of alpha waves (one of the recognized patterns of electrical brain activity), Kamiya discusses the implication of these experiments for the control of conscious states. This work thus bridges the fields of cognition and the modification of behavior.

A young girl sits alone. Her eyes are closed and electrodes are pasted to her skull. By consciously producing a particular brain wave, she turns on a steady tone that fills the darkened room. When she ceases to produce the brain wave, the room falls silent.

This is not a scene from a science-fiction drama, but an experiment in operant conditioning. Just as rats can be taught to press a bar, so people can be taught conscious control of their brain activity in a relatively short time. My studies indicate that by combining methods adapted from experimental psychology, computer technology, and electrophysiology, we can increase our knowledge of the brain's function and of the elusive dimensions of consciousness, and can teach man to perceive and to control some of his brain functions.

The brain produces electrical activity from the moment of birth, and this activity can be recorded easily by means of the electroencephalograph. An electroencephalogram, or EEG, shows a continuously changing series of wave patterns, waxing and waning in both size and rapidity of fluctuations and produced in seemingly random sequence. A number of these wave patterns—the alpha, beta, theta, and delta rhythms—have been identified and named according to the number of cycles per second and the amplitude of the wave.

My experiments have been concerned with the alpha wave, a rhythm between eight and twelve cycles per second, with an amplitude up to about fifty microvolts.

The alpha wave is the most prominent rhythm in the whole realm of brain activity and tends to come in bursts of a few waves to many hundreds. When one opens his eyes and reads or stares at something, the alpha rhythm disappears and is replaced by a random, low-voltage, mixed-frequency rhythm. Alpha rhythm is recorded most prominently from silver disk electrodes pasted to the scalp at the back of the head. These electrodes are connected to equipment in another room by means of wires.

While conducting experiments in sleep in 1958 at the University of Chicago, I compared EEGs made during the sleeping and waking states. I became fascinated by the alpha rhythms that came and went in the waking EEGs and wondered if, through laboratory experiments with this easily traced rhythm, a subject could be taught awareness of an internal state.

We began with a single subject. He was placed in a darkened room, told to keep his eyes closed, and his EEGs were monitored continually with equipment in an adjacent room. He was told that a bell would ring from time to time, sometimes when he was in state A (alpha) and at other times when he was in state B (non-alpha). Whenever he heard the bell, he was to guess which of the two states he was in. He was then told whether he was right or wrong.

The first day, he was right only about 50 percent of the time, no better than chance. The second day, he was right 65 percent of the time; the third day, 85 percent. By the fourth day, he guessed right on every trial—400 times in a row. But the discrimination between the two states is subtle, so subtle that on the 401st trial, the subject deliberately guessed wrong to see if we had been tricking him. In order to be sure that he was differentiating between the two states from internal clues, we tried the experiments again without the bell. Perhaps, we speculated, since alpha and non-alpha are physiological states, they are connected with the threshold of hearing. But again he discriminated between the two states, saying A or B as he changed from one to the other.

We investigated the possibility that eye position might be related to alpha activity. We found that whenever our subject raised his eyes, there was a burst of alpha. Another test was run. This time he was required to look straight ahead, and his performance dropped from 100 percent accuracy to 80 percent. Yet within forty trials he was back up to 100 percent. Whatever relationship had existed between his eye position and his discernment of the alpha state was now destroyed.

These tests were repeated with eleven other subjects, and eight reached a significant proportion of correct guesses within seven sessions of about an hour each, although none reached the level of performance of our first subject. These results suggested that a conditioned, introspective response had been established. When asked to describe the difference between the two states, all those who had taken part in the experiment described various kinds of visual imagery or "seeing with the mind's eye" as occurring in the non-alpha state. The alpha state commonly was reported as "not thinking," "letting the mind wander," or "feeling the heart beat." The task demanded focused attention, for when trained subjects were asked to repeat the alphabet backward during the trials, their discrimination of alpha dropped dramatically.

Interestingly we found that when subjects had successfully learned to discern the two states, they were able to control their minds to the extent of entering and sustaining *either* state upon our command.

Experiments with Control of Alpha Waves

Our studies here at Langley Porter Neuropsychiatric Institute in San Francisco have been on a somewhat different basis. The goal of these experiments has been to see if subjects can learn to control their alpha waves without first going through discrimination training. With the aid of digital logic components, we devised a circuit to respond to the occurrence of alpha waves by sounding a tone. As long as the alpha waves persisted, the tone sounded. When the alpha waves stopped, so did the feedback (see Figure 1).

The volunteer was seated in a darkened, sound-deadened room and challenged to find a way to keep the

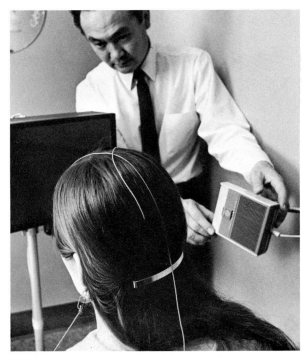

Figure 1. Electrodes record when subject consciously produces a particular brain wave.

tone sounding. It was explained only that certain mental states produced the tone. Overt muscular movements were not allowed. At the end of each minute-long trial, he was told the percent of time that he had been able to sustain the tone. After five such trials, his task was reversed. He was to suppress the tone for five additional one-minute trials. After forty such tests, eight of the ten subjects were able to control the tone, emitting or suppressing alpha waves in accordance with our instructions (see Figure 2). Again, visual imagery

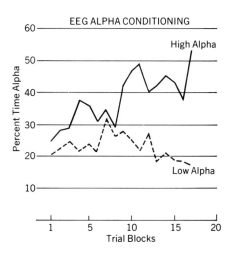

Figure 2. Results of one-minute trials in which subjects were asked to maintain the emission of alpha waves (unbroken line), then to suppress them (broken line).

was reported as effective in decreasing the tone—and the alpha—while an alert calmness, a singleness of attention, and a passive "following" of the tone sustained it. Alpha waves apparently result from an alert, nondrowsy state, devoid of concrete, visual imagery.

This experiment on trained self-control of alpha waves has been confirmed at several other laboratories. Dr. Barbara Brown of the Sepulveda Veterans' Administration Hospital has successfully used a light instead of a tone to help people turn on their alpha waves with their eyes *open*. Each time the alpha train was interrupted, the light dimmed and went out. Even though visual imagery has an initial suppressive effect on alpha activity, her subjects also learned to control their alpha waves.

People describe themselves as being tranquil, calm, and alert when they are in the alpha state, and about half of our subjects report the alpha state as very pleasant. Some of them asked us to repeat the tests so that they could experience once again the high alpha condition.

Alpha Rhythm, Zen, and Yoga

The reports, so closely resembling descriptions of Zen and Yoga meditation, were so provocative that we invited seven practiced Zen meditators to participate in our experiments. These men, who were experienced in Zen meditation, learned control of their alpha waves far more rapidly than did the average person. Meditation means long periods of sitting still, of turning the attention inward, and of learning to control the mind and body, and so the conditions required for the experiment were perhaps not strange to this special group.

The work of Tomio Hirai and of Akira Kasmatsu of Tokyo University is especially interesting in this context. They found a high correlation between EEG patterns and the number of years of Zen practice and the proficiency rating of Zen masters. These two researchers described progressive changes in the EEG of Zen masters during meditation: prominent alpha activity (with eyes open); increased alpha amplitude, particularly in the central as opposed to the posterior cortical regions; the slowing of alpha frequency; and—in mystics with twenty years or more of Zen practice—the appearance of trains of theta activity. (The theta wave is even slower than the alpha wave and has a rhythm of five to seven cycles per second.) In another study, B. K. Anand, G. S. Chhina, and Balden Singh of the All-India Institute of Medical Sciences in New Delhi, found that beginning Yoga students with pronounced alpha activity in their EEG patterns while they were at rest had an unusual aptitude for the practice of Yoga.

The great interest at present in comparing various subjective states with that state produced by psychedelic drugs—and the deliberate use of these drugs to alter states of consciousness—indicates a possible value in studies of alpha-wave control during the LSD experi-

ence. A study by Barbara Brown indicates that, by listening to the subject's report of his drug experience, one can predict the drug's effect on his alpha activity. If he reports only diffused states of feeling, his EEG will reveal little or no change; if he reports visual hallucinations, his EEG will show low alpha activity.

It must be stressed that there is no connection between alpha waves and extrasensory perception. People tend to associate the two because radio waves are involved in communication, but radio waves are generated at several thousand cycles per second, while brain waves range between a fraction of a cycle and about one hundred cycles per second, with most of the energy limited to about fifteen cycles per second. Also, the amount of energy involved is so infinitesimal that a powerful receiver placed half an inch from the skull could never detect it. There is thus no evidence of electromagnetic radiation to the outside world by brain activity.

Control of Alpha-Wave Emission

While the alpha rhythm covers the range from eight to twelve cycles per second, the dominant alpha frequency for each person is different and probably varies no more than half a cycle at any time. With this in mind, we tested the ability of ten volunteers to increase or decrease consciously the frequency of their alpha rhythm (see Figure 3). Each volunteer heard a series of clicks instead of a steady tone. With digital logic devices we compared single alpha-cycle durations with a standard duration preselected for the subject, so that about half of his cycle would be shorter than this standard. If the alpha rhythm took longer to complete its cycle than the individual's standard (fewer cycles per second), he heard a high-pitched click; when the rhythm was completed before his standard (more cycles per second), he heard a low-pitched click. The subject was told only

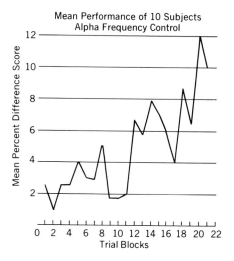

Figure 3. Mean performance of 10 subjects in test of frequency control.

skilled at controlling their own brain waves than are adults.

Implications

We have only scratched the surface of a challenging new field. These studies need to be expanded even further into what might be called a "psychophysiology of consciousness." Each of the different brain rhythms could be investigated as we have studied the alpha wave. The activity of the autonomic nervous system is now being explored in my laboratories. The heart rate, visceral contractions, palm sweating, and muscle tension can be brought under control by this method. Our preliminary studies already indicate that the systolic blood pressure of some hypertensive patients may be subject to learned control.

Dimensional analysis of the specific psychological states associated with the control of physiological processes seems to be a worthy goal. This would require a computer that can store information, compare the relation among several measures in a single subject, and produce an instantaneous feedback. The fact that for many centuries mystics have been doing something measurably real suggests that the meditative tradition is worth examination. Learning the essence of this obscure, dimly comprehended tradition might strip it of much of its mystical quality.

We have expended very little systematic effort in our culture on teaching people to discern and control the inner workings of their bodies. Once we are able to control these body functions, immense possibilities suddenly lie before us. We then will have the tools for an intensive exploration of the consciousness of man. Different subjective states—anxiety, misery, euphoria, or tranquility—might be mapped with the aid of trained subjects. Their reports of these various internal states could be related to their EEGs and to the various reactions of their autonomic nervous systems. Perhaps, through methods like factor analysis, we can discover that anxiety consists of a particular proportion of beta and a wave not yet identified, together with specific degrees of certain measurable autonomic responses. We suspect that tranquility and alpha activity somehow are connected.

Psychiatrists and psychologists, today's specialists on matters of the mind, disagree on most of the fundamental issues concerning consciousness. Through an intensive investigation such as we have proposed, the discontinuity between the subjective and the objective aspects of psychology and psychiatry might dissolve, and we would have a unified science. Someday it might be possible to examine a patient's physiological states and diagnose his neurosis just as the physician now detects tuberculosis by examining an x-ray. And if certain mental states can be defined, people can be trained to reproduce them. Instead of gulping a tranquilizer, one might merely reproduce the state of tranquility that he learned

that the clicks were generated by his brain waves and that his job was to increase the number of high clicks. Most people managed to control their average alpha frequency by this method, although they found it difficult to describe precisely what they did to gain control.

Since we first began experimenting at the University of Chicago, we have tested over one hundred people. A few produced no alpha waves at all. Of those who did produce alpha waves, 80 to 90 percent learned to control them to at least some degree. We found that people who were relaxed, comfortable, and cooperative tended to produce more alpha waves than those who felt tense, suspicious, and fearful, or who actively thought of what was going to happen next. We found that people peak and then level off in the extent to which they can control the emission of alpha waves. Most of the people with whom we worked have been young, college-educated adults, from eighteen to forty-five years old. The youngest person we tested was fifteen, the oldest, sixty.

More work needs to be done with other groups to determine what results can be obtained with uneducated people, people with low IQs, and with professional groups such as bankers or insurance salesmen. It would be revealing to do a study with young children, who do not have a differentiated, sophisticated vocabulary and who lack abstract concepts for these internal states. They might give us a fresh look at what goes on inside our bodies, and they might prove even more by the kind of training used in our studies. Perhaps our increasing concern over control of the individual by psychological persuasion could be diminished. People with full control of their internal states might be better prepared to resist external control. Studies of learning as a physiological process might disclose ways to increase the efficiency of learning in our schools and colleges. Trained control of bodily states might well be added to the curriculum, perhaps beginning as early as elementary school.

Suppose that we can measure the effect of a Beethoven concerto or a Shakespearean sonnet or a painting by Van Gogh. Would critics of the future be replaced by psychologists? They might at least be compelled to use a precise language. For the first time we might have a precise language for them to use because, to the extent that brain waves and other physiological states represent various states of mind, man would at last have an exact vocabulary for interpersonal communication.

Today we are little better informed about human consciousness than were Plato and Aristotle. By combining the methods of modern psychology and the advances in electronics and data-processing, perhaps one day we will make the same kind of stride physics has taken since the days of Democritus.

The Sonar Sight of Bats

James A. Simmons

One of the major problems in the study of behavior is how the organism senses the world. Much of man's advanced technology for gathering information, such as sonar, can be found in a highly evolved state in the animal kingdom. In this account of bat echolocation, Simmons describes experiments on the remarkable discriminative ability of bats. These animals, even when blinded, use their sonar systems to judge the area, shape, and distance of objects in their environments.

Living creatures have developed a remarkable variety of ways to obtain information about their environments. An animal's surroundings contain many different forms of energy and a variety of substances. As different animals go about their daily or nightly activities, they sense an impressive number of these energies and substances. Every aspect of behavior in any animal is under direct, immediate control by the information abstracted from the light, the heat, the vibrations, the chemical concentrations, the physical environment.

Nature has been particularly ingenious in providing ways for animals to detect objects without having to move up to them and bump them. Vision serves a wide range of different animals, from the invertebrates to the most elaborate mammal. Airborne and waterborne sound provides many organisms with information about things somewhere in their vicinity. Vibrations of the ground also act as stimuli for terrestrial animals. The sense of smell tells many animals that something is near, and the rattlesnake can even detect heat radiated from a source warmer than the rest of his surroundings.

In a few instances, nature gives animals portable sources of energy with which to explore the environment. Orientation by self-emitted energy is analogous to a man exploring a dark room with a flashlight. Whirligig beetles, insects that live on the surface of water, detect objects by rippling the water and picking up reflections of these ripples. Some species of fish generate electrical fields in the water around their bodies and detect objects by means of the disturbances the objects cause.

The most famous and best-studied type of emitted-energy orientation is found in bats. These little animals, already interesting to zoologists in their means of locomotion, reproductive processes, and choice of living quarters, find their way around with a full-fledged sonar system. For a number of years research on the hearing and perceptual capabilities of bats has been underway at the Auditory Research Laboratories of Princeton University.

Bats are creatures of the night. They sleep by day in caves, abandoned mines, culverts, attics, old barns, trees, and any of a hundred other quiet, sheltered places in which they can hang. In the evening they emerge to seek food and water. Their nocturnal habits have resulted in their inclusion with other beings of darkness in most of our folklore.

The bats owe their enormous biological success to the night and to their peculiar adaptations to life in darkness. With hardly any light to see by, they fly at daredevil speeds through trees, bushes, and jungle thickets, dart about in the air catching small flies and mosquitos, and fly in and out of deep caves, often through winding passages and in the company of hundreds and hundreds of other bats. Yet a bat rarely bumps a branch or misses a meal.

In geographic range, in numbers of individuals, and in the number and variety of different species bats are indeed flourishing. They have existed in basically the same form for over 50 or 60 million years. Although often regarded as rodents, "mouse-angels," bats are in fact a separate group of mammals, distinct from rats, mice, and squirrels. Zoologists classify bats in the order Chiroptera (wing-handed). The order is divided into two groups.

One of the suborders, Megachiroptera, is composed of bats less specialized for flight than the other. Megachiropterans have excellent vision and live on a diet of fruits. Perhaps the best-known of these is the "flying fox," a large fruit bat with a wingspread of five feet.

The other suborder, Microchiroptera, consists of bats that are well equipped for life in the air. They have powerful wings, and they also seem to have relatively poor vision and habits that usually keep them well away from light. Microchiropterans differ considerably in their diets. Some eat insects captured in the air or on the ground, some eat fruit or the nectar of flowers, and some capture and eat small birds and mammals, including other bats. The vampire bats are so specialized they eat only the blood of mammals or birds. To get by without being able to see, the various bats of the suborder Microchiroptera have evolved a remarkable way of getting information about objects in the environment.

The Bat Problem

The little, insectivorous bats of North America and Europe have long been zoological curiosities. Their proficiency in moving around at night attracted some attention. In the eighteenth century an Italian monk, Spallanzani, and several of his collaborators discovered that blinded bats could live and fly around without any apparent trouble. They found that impairment of hearing was the only way to disorient a bat. The science of the day reacted against the unconventional implication that bats "saw" with their ears, and most of Spallanzani's contemporaries assumed that the bat's skill in flying arose from touch sensitivity to nearby objects.

Little more became of the question of how bats found their way about until the twentieth century, when knowledge in acoustics provided a basis for renewed speculation. In 1912 the British inventor Hiram Maxim suggested that the bat detects obstacles by feeling echoes of the sounds of its wing beats as they reflect back from objects. Several years later, H. Hartridge, an English physiologist, proposed that bats navigate with a kind of sonar, emitting high-frequency sounds and detecting echoes of these sounds.

In 1938, Donald R. Griffin, a zoologist then working at Harvard University, found that bats do indeed emit high-frequency cries, often much higher in frequency than the upper limit of human hearing (or 20,000 cycles per second). Griffin and Robert Galambos worked together for several years on the discovery and established that the bat's ears can respond to such high-frequency sounds, and that the basis for obstacle avoidance in bats is the detection of echoes of its cries.

Bats navigate with a sophisticated biological sonar, called *echolocation*. They emit a series of short, sharp cries that contain frequencies from 25,000 cycles per second to well over 100,000 cycles per second. Some kinds of bats emit loud sounds, some emit soft sounds, some emit sounds of almost constant frequency, some emit frequency-modulated sounds, and some emit sounds rich in harmonic frequencies (see Figure 1). All

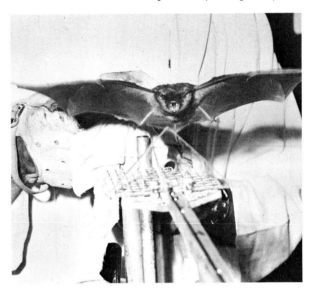

Figure 1. Bat with mouth open for emission of sonar cries in experiment for distance discrimination.

of the microchiropteran bats use echoes of their own characteristic cries for sensing objects in the environment.

Echolocation is an active process in which the bat generates a sound and identifies objects and obstacles with the reflected echoes. Although many animals can detect and locate nearby objects by picking up sounds that the objects themselves may emit or by sensing changes in the environmental noise level near the objects, relatively few animals use active sonar. The excitement stirred up by the discovery of the bat's echolocation led to the discovery of the use of sonar by porpoises and to the possibility that other animals, including some birds and terrestrial mammals, might also echolocate. Man himself can echolocate, as has been shown by several experiments on blind persons and on blindfolded subjects. To be sure, man can also echolocate with apparatus built for that purpose, as in the cases of ultrasonic scanning devices in medicine and underwater sonar systems.

We are accustomed to *seeing* objects in our surroundings. It is ordinarily with vision that we locate and identify objects, navigate from place to place, and find our way around obstacles. Qualities such as size, shape, distance, and texture have underlying visual cues like relative size, visual angle, perspective, parallax, and stereoscopic vision. These visual cues are in turn based on the physical properties of the light that stimulates our eyes.

Hearing is another important human sense, but not in entirely the same way as vision. We use hearing for communication; for detecting, locating, and identifying sound sources; and for music.

But bats use hearing in place of vision to gather information about distant objects. Banished for its own good to a life away from light, the bat perceives the important qualities of objects not with the intensity, wavelength, and distribution of light striking the retina, but rather with the intensity, frequency, and time of arrival of sounds at the ears. The bat "sees" nearby objects, in terms of the physical parameters of the echoes of its own cries as they return from the objects. The ears and brain of the bat have become highly specialized for rapidly processing the auditory cues in the echoes so that the essential details about obstacles or targets are detected in time to catch a moth or avoid a branch.

The bat's behavior is exquisitely controlled by the perceptions of the environment it derives from echolocation. We can inquire about the bat's mode of perception in much the same way as we traditionally have investigated vision. What kinds of judgments can a bat make about objects that it perceives with sonar? Animals that use vision easily can perceive object size, shape, location, and distance. Can the bat also detect such things? The bat's performance in flight and skill in hunting of course suggest immediately that it readily can perceive size, shape, movement, and so on, but can we demonstrate some of these perceptions experimentally?

In an attempt to learn more about the extent to which echolocation can substitute for vision, I have been working on the ability of several species of bats to make judgments of the size of objects, the shape of objects, and the distance to objects. I have found that when examined by the methods normally reserved for visual perception, the bat's sonar is very versatile, every bit as flexible as would be expected from the performance of bats in nature.

The species that I have used for the study of distance, size, and shape discrimination is the big brown bat, *Eptesicus fuscus*. This hardy insectivorous bat thrives in captivity, easily adapts to discrimination training, and can echolocate with great skill. It emits sounds that sweep in frequency from just under 50,000 cycles per second down to about 25,000 cycles per second, and its cries easily can be detected, even with crude, homemade condenser microphones (see Figure 2).

Since bats are among those mammals that occasion-

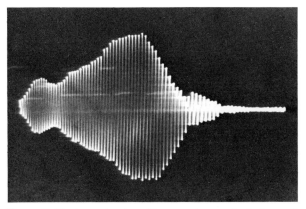

Figure 2. Photograph of oscilloscope trace of a bat cry; it lasts about 2 milliseconds and is frequency modulated.

ally carry rabies, all our staff members are vaccinated against the disease, and no one handles any bat without protective gloves.

When beginning discrimination studies with bats, there is one important experimental precaution to consider. The visual capabilities of echolocating bats are not well known. Available evidence suggests that bats are probably not very good at visual pattern perception, but no one is certain. To eliminate the possibility that vision may be used in discrimination-learning experiments, at least some of the bats must be deprived of sight. For most species, the best way to do this is actually to remove their eyes while they are anesthetized. The operation is safe, and the animals appear to recover completely. In discrimination experiments with dozens of bats of several species, no instance of the use of vision has come up. That is, blinded bats and normal bats do *not* perform differently on discrimination experiments.

Sonar Perception of Object Size

To find out whether an animal's vision is sufficiently acute to perceive the size of a stimulus, you can try to train the animal to distinguish between a large stimulus and a small stimulus. If it can learn to respond to one of the two stimuli, say the larger, but not to the other, then you have demonstrated that in some way the animal is able to perceive the relative size of each stimulus and to identify correctly the larger one. This technique is called *simultaneous-discrimination learning*, and it is a basic tool for the study of sensory and perceptual capabilities in animals.

Although size discrimination is a problem usually encountered in connection with visual perception, there is no reason why we cannot try to train echolocating bats to discriminate between objects differing in size. A simple experimental setup can be used for training bats to distinguish between a large stimulus and a small one (see Figure 3). The bat is taught to sit on the platform at the left and to examine the other two platforms and the triangular shapes mounted on them. The targets are

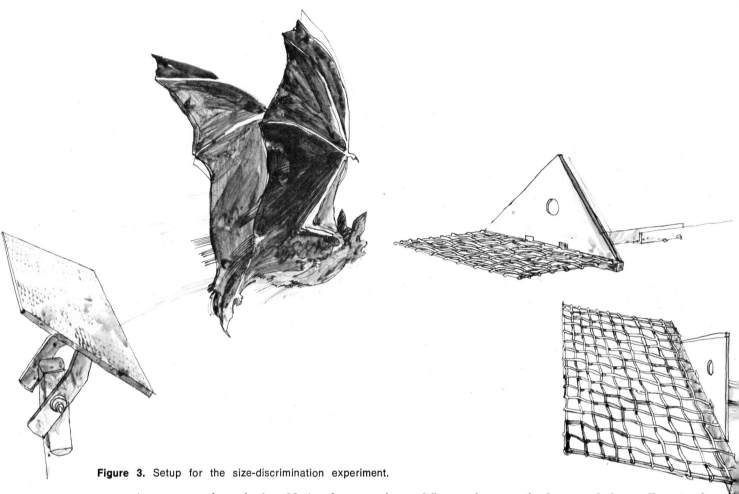

Figure 3. Setup for the size-discrimination experiment.

30 centimeters away from the bat. Notice that one of the triangles is larger than the other.

Each time the bat flies from the starting platform to the landing platform that has the large triangle, he is rewarded with a choice bit of food—a piece of an insect. The positions of the triangles are "randomly" interchanged from right to left and back again to ensure that the bat is responding to the size of each stimulus and not to its position. After a week or two of training the bat can choose the platform with the larger stimulus more than 90 percent of the time.

Acuity of Size Perception

We used a series of triangles to demonstrate that the big brown bat can distinguish between objects of different sizes with surprising accuracy (see Figure 4). We first showed the bat a pair of triangles that differed greatly in size. Each bat was trained to fly to the large triangle in this pair until it could do so with a minimum of errors for seventy-five trials. As expected, the bats learned to discriminate between the triangles easily. Then we transferred the bat to a pair slightly closer in size. We carried out fifty trials on this second pair, rewarding the bat with food for every correct response. Pair by pair, with fifty trials on each pair, the bat moved through a series of six additional pairs of triangles.

As each new pair was shown to the bat, the size

difference between the larger and the smaller triangle became a little bit smaller. Finally, the bat came to the seventh pair, in which the size difference was reduced to zero; the triangles were equal in size. As the size difference got progressively smaller, it became harder and harder for the bat to pick correctly the larger of the two triangles. Eventually, the size difference became too small for the bat to choose the larger triangle. The bat responded half of the time to one triangle, and half of the time to the other.

We charted the performance of three bats trained on the entire series of triangles (see Figure 5). Using an *arbitrary* level of 75 percent correct responses, we established the threshold of size discrimination for the bats. This threshold is an approximation of the smallest size difference that the bat can detect with any kind of consistency. The light level in the lab was very low for the sessions with sighted bats.

One of the three bats that had been trained was blinded and run on the series of triangles again. The blinded bat had a threshold of about 16 percent difference in stimulus surface area, which was almost the same as the average threshold for the three normal runs.

It is clear that visual cues did not play a decisive part in the discrimination performance of the bats. (Bats that were blinded from the start of training performed the same as these three bats, so it appears that *Eptesi-*

cus simply does not need to use vision at all for these size discriminations.)

The threshold difference for the blinded bat lies between the fifth and sixth pair of triangles shown to the bat (see Figure 4). By looking at the outlines and dimensions of the stimuli, you can see that the bat's sonar appears to be an adequate substitute for vision as far as size is concerned.

By bouncing artificial sounds off the triangular targets used in the experiment, you can learn something about the auditory cues the bats used to discriminate the triangles. The targets in the pairs turn out to differ in the intensity of the echoes they reflect. The triangles in the most easily discriminated pair differ by about eight decibels in the intensity of their echoes. As the size difference gets smaller, pair by pair, the echo intensity difference gets smaller, too.

Sonar Perception of Shape

As we have seen, an echolocating bat can determine the relative size of one of two stimuli with a good deal of acuity. If the stimuli were the same in size but different in shape, could the bat still learn to choose between them? To see if echolocation can be used to tell something about the shape of an object, I have used triangular stimuli of the same kind used in the size experiments.

One stimulus was an isosceles triangle 10 centimeters wide and 5 centimeters high, the same size as the largest triangle in the first experiment. The other triangle was 5 centimeters wide and 10 centimeters high. Both targets had the same surface area, but one was short and wide and the other was tall and thin. These triangles were mounted on landing platforms and used in the same way as before.

Both sighted and blinded bats learned to discriminate between the two different shapes. When the training was carried out exactly as in the size-discrimination experiment, the level of performance reached by the bats corresponded to an intermediately difficult size discrimination, something like the fourth pair of triangles in the size experiments.

What about the echoes that the bats use to distinguish the shapes? Over the frequency range used by the big brown bat, the echoes differ somewhat in intensity. The difference is from one to three decibels, depending on the frequency. These intensity differences are about the same as the difference between the members of the fourth pair of triangles in the first experiment. It seems quite possible that the shape difference was detected by means of the echo-intensity differences.

Depth Perception by Sonar

Humans find it rather easy to judge the distance to an object with vision, and there exists a large variety of visual depth cues. Can bats use their echolocation to determine how far away an object is? Considering the

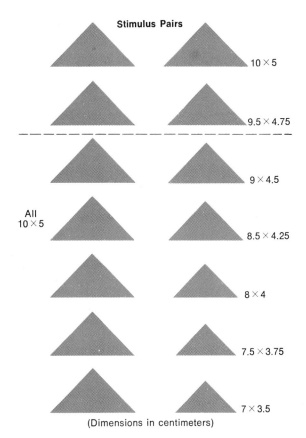

Figure 4. Target sizes in the size-discrimination experiment; the bat begins with targets having the greatest size difference (bottom pair) and is presented with targets successively closer in size until they are the same (top pair). The broken line indicates the bats' threshold of discrimination, set at 75% correct discriminations.

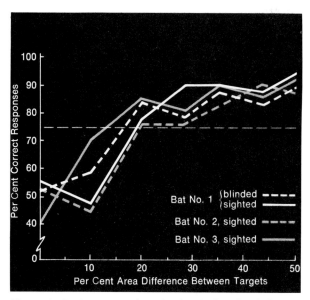

Figure 5. Performance chart for bats' size-discrimination ability (see Figure 4). Note that vision plays no part in these discriminations.

exceptional ability of many species of bats to accurately track flying insects, one expects them to be able to judge the range of a target. The discrimination procedure used for size and shape perception was adapted to the study of range determination by bats.

Just as before, the bat was placed on a starting platform and confronted with two landing platforms and targets. The triangles on the platforms were identical in size and shape, both were 10 centimeters wide and 5 centimeters high. The distance to the targets was previously fixed at 30 centimeters. Now it was the distance to the targets that the bat had to discriminate.

The bat was trained to fly to whichever platform was closer. At first, the near target was 20 centimeters away, and the far target was 30 centimeters away. The distances were alternated left and right in the same random fashion as the sizes and the shapes had been. After the bat learned to discriminate between targets that differed in distance by 10 centimeters, the difference was reduced by moving the nearer target back to 21 centimeters. A number of trials were completed, and then the distance difference was reduced by another centimeter, moving the nearer target back to 22 centimeters. In steps of about a centimeter, the difference in distance between the targets was further reduced to 7 centimeters, then 6 centimeters, and so forth until the two targets were finally presented to the bat at equal distances. This procedure allowed us to estimate the range-difference threshold for two stimuli presented at the same time.

We trained two blinded specimens of the big brown bat on a series of distances beginning with a difference of 10 centimeters and proceeding down to zero (see Figure 6). Large differences, between 10 and 3 centimeters, were easily discriminated; the bat flew to the closer platform on nearly every trial. When the range difference fell below 3 centimeters, however, the bats'

discrimination performance declined. The average threshold for a large number of specimens of *Eptesicus* is 1.2 centimeters. This threshold, a measure of the accuracy of the bat's determination of distance, is only 4 percent of the total distance of 30 centimeters.

The extreme accuracy of the bat's determination of the range of a target is not restricted to *Eptesicus*. In addition to the insect-eating *Eptesicus*, a European insectivorous bat, *Rhinolophus*, and a carnivorous, tropical bat, *Phyllostomus*, have also been studied. These other bats are about as accurate as *Eptesicus* in judging distance.

Besides the great accuracy of the bats' discriminations, there were several other surprises in the range experiment. Suffice it to say that the results of this experiment, together with more recent ones, show that the bat determines which target is closer by the difference in arrival time between echoes from the nearer and farther targets. The signal processing done by the bat on echoes from targets separated by a few centimeters is a complicated matter, and current experiments on sonar ranging by bats are just beginning to clarify what happens.

Echolocation: A Biological System

As we have seen, echolocation does a creditable job of providing a way for bats to appreciate objects in the environment without vision. Their sonar allows bats to do a lot more than merely to detect the presence or absence of objects "out there." They can make rather fine distinctions between the nature of the objects and also their location. There are other questions that arise. Can a bat localize an object horizontally and vertically as well as it can in distance? Does a bat get information about the texture of objects? Experiments now in progress are, hopefully, going to answer such questions.

In addition to the straightforward study of stimulus perception by sonar, there is the problem of the basis for echolocation in the bat's hearing. New techniques for electronically simulating targets by presenting faked echoes to the bat are proving very useful in analyzing the auditory cues used in the exploration of targets. These techniques are designed to study the mechanisms of echolocation, and perhaps they will even tell something of the brain processes of the bat's sonar.

The twentieth century has been a century of surprises for scientists. This is no less true for the student of animal behavior than for the particle physicist, molecular biologist, or neurophysiologist. The unearthing of the means of orientation in bats has been one of the more unexpected events for zoologists and comparative psychologists.

Interest in bat sonar is but an example of a general trend. Scientists have rediscovered biology with great enthusiasm in recent years. The ingenuity in design and

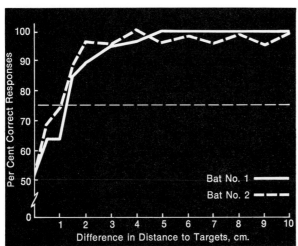

Figure 6. Performance chart for bats' distance-discrimination ability. Both bats used in this experiment were blinded.

function of biological systems has attracted many people to research on living systems. Discoveries in sensory physiology and psychology, in the molecular basis of genetics, and in many other areas of biological activity have highlighted the impression that really challenging problems are to be found in the study of organisms and their workings. The more that we find in the processes of living creatures, the more humble we may feel as fabricators of mechanism and machinery. What man can yet compress a multipurpose sonar system into the form of a lump of jelly about as big as your thumb, make that system seek out its own operating power, and even more, use such a system to produce others like it as a by-product of its own operation?

Chemical Perception in Newborn Snakes

Gordon M. Burghardt

In addition to asking how a sensory system works, psychologists can investigate how it came to work that way. Does the sensory process occur soon after birth, without specific learning, or does it require experience? In this article Burghardt examines the perceptual ability of young snakes. He shows that they respond to species-specific patterns of chemical stimuli, and he explains how this pattern correlates with the snake's nutritional requirements.

A face in a crowd, a familiar voice in a busy conversation, a delicate perfume in a summer evening's breeze, a hint of spice in a culinary masterpiece—each of these sensations leaps forward forcefully into our consciousness. We see the face, not the crowd; we hear that special voice, not any of the others; we smell the perfume, to the momentary exclusion of summer's other scents; we taste the spice, for a moment forgetting the impression of the dish as a whole. Out of what William James called the blooming, buzzing confusion of our raw sensory experience, we selectively admit into our consciousness only some of these myriad perceptions.

It is not simply a matter of our being especially sensitive to these salient perceptual events. Each face in the crowd, for example, is equally large and equally bright—perhaps even equally interesting on close examination. Rather, some events excite our interest and attention because they have particular meaning to us as individuals.

One source of this meaning is, of course, our past experience. The mother has come to recognize and respond to her baby's cry among all those in the nursery; the chef comes to detect the missing spice in the complex aroma rising from the stew; the wine taster comes to sense the particular essence that identifies the truly great vintage. All of us, highly trained or not, constantly select perceptual events from all the hundreds of stimuli imposed on us—and in so doing we project a perceptual structure onto the entire outside world.

The perceptual world of the normal human adult seems at first glance to be largely a matter of experience. Each of us finds a different face in the crowd to be particularly exciting and interesting. But perception is also tempered by natural, inherited limitations and saliences. It is true that a musician learns by experience to appreciate a great composition, but the range of tones that he can hear and the discriminations between tones that he can make are determined largely by the inherited structure of his ear. It is also true that each individual develops his own personal set of appreciated forms and colors. But commonly shared illusions and hallucinations suggest commonly inherited characteristics within our visual and nervous systems.

In fact, perhaps the most amazing and instructive cases of imposed perceptual structure are those that are not learned by a lifetime of experience but are dictated by nature through generations of evolutionary experience. The young child, for example, without any specific training or experience, will select a balanced diet from a multitude of offered foods, if left solely to his own devices. My research with snakes has shown that the infant snake is peculiarly fitted out by evolution to attack and eat specific nutritious organisms from among the many potential prey animals. More important yet is the finding that the snake seems prepared by nature to eat only those objects that it normally will encounter in its natural habitat. The wisdom of generations of evolutionary development has imposed on these small animals a perceptual structure that facilitates their survival from the moment of birth.

Sign Stimuli and Perception

We owe most of our knowledge of this form of natural perceptual selectivity to the ethologists who have elaborated the concept of the "sign stimulus" or "releaser." Basically, they have discovered that a given behavior often is critically dependent on just one aspect of the stimulus situation, while other equally perceivable qualities are without effect. For example, the red belly-feathers of the male British robin trigger an attack by another male robin if it is introduced into his territory. A dummy, accurate in all respects except that the belly is not red, elicits no attack, but a bundle of red feathers alone is sufficient to release the behavior.

There are many other examples of these critical relations. From them, such pioneers of ethology as Jacob von Uexküll and Konrad Lorenz arrived at a seminal concept known as the releasing mechanism. This mechanism is keyed to respond to perceptual cues from the relevant stimulus object, and these cues are known as releasers or sign stimuli. Another aspect of interest is that in many cases these releaser-response relations did not have to be learned in any normal sense during the individual organism's life. Eckhard Hess, at the University of Chicago, has shown that newly hatched, inexperienced chicks prefer to peck at some colors rather than at others. Why this should be is not known yet, but the point is that previous pecking experience was not necessary; releasing mechanisms are innate. It is almost as if there is an innate perceptual schema somewhere inside the organism, to which the environment must correlate in order for a response to occur. Thus nature imposes structure on the organism's perceptual world.

Whereas most work on releasers is and was concerned with vision, my research has been with chemical releasers, odors, which elicit behavior patterns.

The Sense of Smell

The chemical sense of smell is perhaps the most interesting and intriguing sense that we possess. We are certainly selective in our response to odors, many of which elicit profound emotional experiences. Why is there such a mystery surrounding perfumes, and why do only a small proportion of those developed win lasting favor? Why do some smells repel us, while others brighten our outlook throughout the entire day? Yet the mechanisms of smell, even the stimuli themselves, are little understood. There are even authorities who believe that, through generations of disuse and societal taboos,

Western man has become insensitive to his sense of smell.

When we try to study smell in man, methodological problems appear immediately. These include the inaccessibility of the sensory receptor itself, the difficulty of presenting an odor in a standardized manner, problems of adaptation and conditioning, and our inability to specify what in the physical stimulus correlates with the subjective impression. There have been some ingenious attempts to overcome these problems. For instance, John Amoore, with the U.S. Department of Agriculture, has had considerable success in correlating the smell of a substance with its molecular shape. But the fact remains that at present man is not a very good organism to use in the study of the chemical senses. Man's reliance on other sensory modalities confounds the precise assessment of the role and mechanism of smell.

Enter the Serpent

What would be a good experimental animal other than man? Many mammals below the primates rely on the chemical senses, but with them a behavior is rarely completely dependent upon olfaction. Most closely related to the mammals are the reptiles, the behavior of which is without question the least studied of all the vertebrate classes. Nevertheless, no one questions the great importance of the chemical senses to snakes. Snakes evolved from lizards and have reached a degree of specialization of the chemical sense unrivaled by any other group of terrestrial vertebrates.

Snakes possess numerous advantages as experimental animals, and many species do very well in captivity. Since some species such as garter snakes are viviparous and often give live birth to sixty or more babies at a time, they are especially useful in the study of early development. Nevertheless, snakes have been neglected as experimental subjects, probably because of society's antipathy toward them. The Biblical story of the Garden of Eden probably didn't help. But perhaps a different attitude is needed. As Robert G. Ingersoll put it, back in 1872:

If the account given in *Genesis* is really true, ought we not, after all, to thank this serpent? He was the first schoolmaster, the first advocate of learning, the first enemy of ignorance, the first to whisper in human ears the sacred word "Liberty," the creator of ambition, the author of modesty . . . of inquiry . . . of doubt . . . of investigation . . . of progress . . . and of civilization.

Snakes, besides having a well-developed sense of smell, have another modality derived from their olfactory nervous apparatus. The receptor for this modality is known as Jacobson's organ or the vomeronasal organ. It is present in some amphibians, reptiles, and mammals, but it reaches its highest degree of specialization in snakes. The organ consists of a pair of sacs that open into the anterior roof of the mouth. The epithelial lining of the sacs contains typical olfactory cells, and their cytoplasmic extensions form a branch of the olfactory cells that terminates on a specialized portion of the olfactory bulb.

The chemical senses in snakes and their behavioral importance were studied by a number of scientists who did their experiments some twenty-five to forty-five years ago. While the discussion of the individual contributions of such scientists as Baumann, Kahmann, Noble, Weidemann, Wilde, and Bogert is not possible here, we can list what seem to be the major results of often conflicting research. First, taste seems to be of rather minor importance and plays a role only when food objects are actually in the animal's mouth. Secondly, Jacobson's organ functions in conjunction with the tongue. The snake's frequent tongue flicking is a mechanical means of picking up and transferring chemical substances to the vicinity of Jacobson's organ within the mouth. (Of interest is the fact that snakes have an indentation in the upper lip that allows them to flick the tongue without opening the mouth at all.) The third point is that many behaviors in snakes—including prey trailing and courtship—seem to involve both Jacobson's organ and normal olfaction. However, Wilde in 1938 demonstrated that the attack on prey by the adult common garter snake is dependent almost totally upon Jacobson's organ. By severing various nerves, Wilde was able to show that only when Jacobson's organ was functioning did an attack take place. Olfaction alone was neither necessary nor sufficient. To prove that only a chemical stimulus was involved, he used a clear and colorless solution of earthworm mucus, which was presented to the snakes on cotton attached to glass rods. The snakes, which normally ate earthworms, attacked this cotton as they would a normal prey object. Wilde's research inspired ours. The behavior pattern and its elicitation were clearly commensurate with the ethological concept of the releasing mechanism. Perhaps feeding behavior in newborn snakes could tell us a great deal, not only about serpent behavior but also about the potentialities and functioning of chemical sensory mechanisms in general.

Analysis of Prey-Attack Behavior in Newborn Snakes

We started by asking questions: Would newborn garter snakes respond with prey-attack behavior to chemical stimuli from worms before they ever had experience with any type of food object or its odor? Would they respond to extracts from other normally eaten classes of prey? And if the above answers were affirmative, was this stimulus-response connection reasonably permanent? If the answers to these three questions were yes, then we would be dealing with a highly precise biological relationship that would offer limitless opportunities for studying, among other things, learned versus unlearned factors in chemical perception, the relations of selective chemical releasers to evolution and ecology,

and the development of a behavioral bioassay technique for chemical stimuli.

Using a litter of three-day-old previously unfed garter snakes (*Thamnophis s. sirtalis*), we found that the answer to all three questions was yes. The chemical stimuli were prepared by placing a standard weight of either redworms, minnows, mealworms (larvae of a beetle), or horsemeat into warm distilled water for one minute. The prey then were removed, and the resulting water solution filtered and refrigerated until use. Of the four items, the first two (redworms and minnows) are readily eaten in nature by this species of snake; the other two are rarely, if ever, eaten.

Naive newborn snakes dramatically attacked a cotton swab that had been dipped in either worm or fish extract. They did not attack swabs dipped in the insect extract, meat extract, or pure water. The attack response, given an effective stimulus, comprised the following: The snake increased its rate of tongue flicking and then lunged forward at the swab with its jaws wide open at about a 45-degree angle (see Figure 1). This response was identical with that seen toward live redworms and small fish. Moreover, although these young snakes normally refused to eat pieces of horsemeat, they readily attacked and ate horsemeat dipped in the worm extract. The inexperienced snake somehow can recognize, on the basis of chemical stimuli alone, what it "should" attack as a potential prey object.

The stability of the response to chemical stimuli first was tested in completely naive snakes from the same litter by presenting the worm extract at five-minute intervals for twenty trials. An attack was given every time and no progressive weakening of the response was apparent. In a later test for stability, forty trials were given to a snake with still no weakening of the response. (See Figure 2.) Naturally, the response cannot be elicited indefinitely at such short intervals. However, the stability shown is more than sufficient for the testing of the same individual repeatedly with the same or with a different extract.

After we obtained the above results, we were convinced that this phenomenon was worthy of intensive study. A series of experiments was designed to investigate various aspects of chemically released attacks by newborn snakes.

One of the first experiments concerned the role of vision in eliciting this behavior. With the same litter, we investigated the responses to visual aspects of prey animals from which the snakes could obtain no chemical information. A variety of small sealed glass vials was introduced into the home cage of each individual snake. Vials were either empty or contained a type of small organism, which was either dead or alive. The results were as follows: If there were moving organisms in the vials, the snakes would orient themselves, flick their tongues, and explore; however, they never opened their mouths or tried to attack the animals through the glass. Further, the amount of interest in the vial shown by the

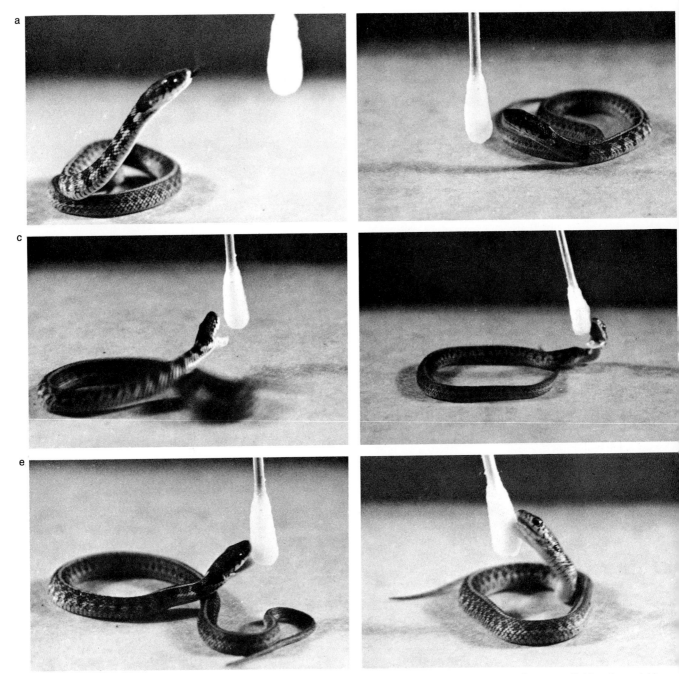

Figure 1. In a characteristic attack on a swab dipped in extract from a prey, the garter snake orients toward the swab and increases its rate of tongue flicking (a and b); lunges toward the swab (c and d); and bites the swab (e and f).

snakes was clearly proportional to the amount of movement going on in the vial at the time. For instance, quickly swimming guppies elicited the greatest response, while dead guppies of exactly the same size and coloration elicited no response. This response to movement in the vials disappeared rapidly when the vials were reintroduced a short while later, indicating that the novelty of the moving animals was involved. Indeed, at this point we can conclude that the role of vision is limited to the orientation toward and exploration of a potential food object, particularly if moving, but that the attack of prey can be elicited in naive subjects only by chemical stimuli.

Further experiments with inexperienced garter snakes whose eyes or nostrils (or both) had been artificially closed showed that neither olfaction nor vision is at all necessary for the prey-attack response to occur. Jacobson's organ is apparently responsible. Naturally, the

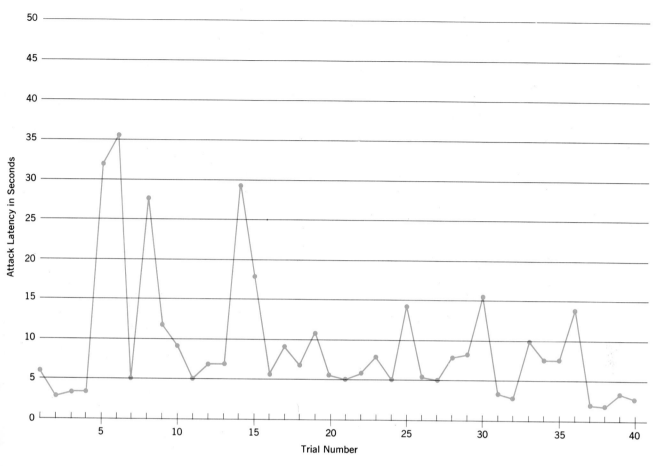

Figure 2. Newborn garter snakes reliably and repeatedly attack a swab dipped in extract made from worms normally eaten by adult garter snakes. An inexperienced snake attacked on 40 successive trials at 5-minute intervals; no habituation took place.

attacks of blind snakes were not well directed, but attacks they were.

Comparative Studies

One of our main interests has involved the study of species of snakes that have feeding habits in nature and captivity quite different from those of the garter snakes with which our work began. Would newborn young of these species respond to chemical stimuli from animals that the species normally ate? We began by looking at other species of snakes in the garter snake group (genus *Thamnophis*). In this large and widespread group of snakes are found forms with very different food habits. We tested seven species and subspecies with a series of extracts from prey representing most classes of animals known to be eaten by at least some species in the genus. The congruence between the responses of the inexperienced newborn young and the known feeding habits of the species was very close. For instance, the Chicagoland garter snake (*Thamnophis sirtalis semifasciata*) will eat fish, worms, amphibians, and leeches very readily and we obtained highly significant responses to those extracts, but not to extracts of slugs, mice, insects,

and crayfish, which in fact this species rarely, if ever, eats. (See Figure 3). As in many snakes tested, there was a big difference in the relative effectiveness of larval and adult salamanders. It appears that during metamorphosis changes occur in the chemicals from the skin that elicit prey-attack behavior.

Consider another species, the eastern plains garter snake, *Thamnophis r. radix*, which has similar habitat and feeding preferences. We tested a litter of twenty-two newborn young and obtained the profile of responses to various extracts (see Figure 4a). Again, all extracts but those of the baby mouse, slug, cricket, and metamorphosed salamander were significantly higher than the water control. Although no extensive ecological studies have been done on this species, it appears that earthworms, amphibians, fish, and leeches are eaten readily, with worms being probably most common in the natural diet. Extracts from three kinds of earthworms and three kinds of fish were tested. Again, it was found that the larval salamander had a higher releasing value than the adult form. This is a relationship that has frequently been found in species of newborn snakes that include amphibians in their normal diet.

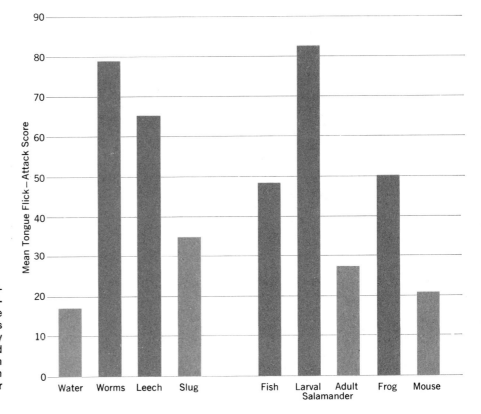

Figure 3. Results of attack experiments with newborn Chicagoland garter snakes. The prey normally eaten by adults of this species are indicated by the green; the prey indicated by the gray, though common snake prey, are rarely eaten by adult Chicagoland garter snakes.

In sharp contrast to the above were results obtained from the western smooth green snake (*Opheodrys vernalis blanchardi*). This species, unlike others we studied, is oviparous instead of bringing forth young alive. In one experiment, eggs were laid and hatched in captivity. The young were tested at the same ages as were the plains garter snakes, and with the same extracts. The same extracts were presented to the two species (see Figure 4b). The cricket extract was the most potent; indeed, it was the only extract to which actual attacks were made and the only one significantly higher than the water control on the basis of the tongue-flick-attack score. The result becomes more meaningful when it is realized that, out of all the extracts presented, the cricket extract is the only one that represents an organism eaten by the green snake. In fact, it appears that this species will eat nothing but insects, spiders, and soft-bodied arthropods.

The differences between the smooth green snake and the plains garter snake are striking. In contrast to green snakes, plains garter snakes never eat insects, and the cricket extract received the lowest score of all the extracts. It is obvious, therefore, that clear and biologically useful differences exist between the chemical perceptions of food objects by these two species of snakes.

The green snake and the plains garter snakes are rather widely removed from each other both taxonomically and ecologically. The common garter snake, dis-

cussed first, and the plains garter snake are much more closely related, live in similar habitats, and appear to eat the same food. With these two species, the extract-response profiles show no clear differences. Is it possible to find differences between closely related forms? Just how precise is the technique? A final answer to the last question cannot be given yet, but it is possible to generate some dramatic differences between species of the same or related genera. Let us look at a couple of examples:

Two species of garter snakes and one of the brown snakes (*Storeria*) were exposed to extracts from three earthworms, three fish, and one slug. We tested eight inexperienced newborn midland brown snakes (*Storeria dekayi wrightorum*), known to eat only worms and slugs. The second species of naive young tested was Butler's garter snake (*Thamnophis butleri*). We tested a litter of fifteen from a female caught in southern Michigan. In captivity, Butler's garter snake readily eats worms and fish but not slugs. The third species to be compared on these three classes of extracts was the western aquatic garter snake (*Thamnophis elegans aquaticus*), known to eat only fish. We tested a litter of nine from a female found in southern California. The results were clear. The responses of the different species of inexperienced snakes to skin extracts parallels the feeding habits manifested by specimens freshly caught in the field (see Figure 5). Scores for the brown snake

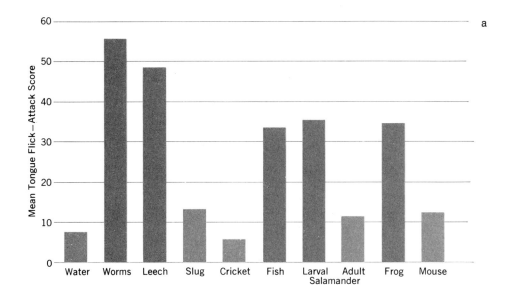

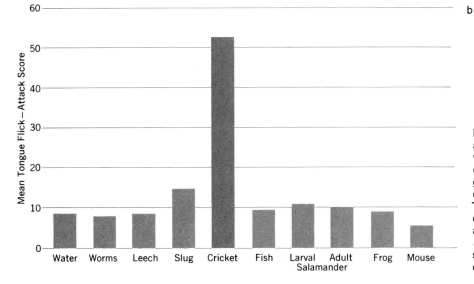

Figure 4. Strikingly different attack profiles were obtained with newborns from two different species: the eastern plains garter snake (a) and the western smooth green snake (b). The newborns attacked extracts of prey normally eaten by adults of the species (green) and ignored other common snake prey not eaten by adults of the species (gray).

were on a different scale from the garter snakes—about half as high, due to a lower frequency of tongue flicking. This reduction also was found in another species from the same genus.

Turning to the water snakes (*Natrix*), we found some more remarkable differences. Most water snakes (such as *Natrix s. sipedon*, the common banded water snake) eat fish and amphibians, but Graham's water snake (*Natrix grahami*) and the queen snake (*Natrix septemvitatta*) eat practically nothing but crayfish, and newly molted ones at that. Here the newborn young attacked only crayfish extracts and gave even greater response to extracts from newly molted crayfish (see Figure 6).

Taken together, these results dramatically indicate the species-characteristic nature of chemical perception in newborn snakes. That these are related to the natural feeding ecology of the different animals is equally clear. But what do these comparative results mean? First of all, they can best be understood in terms of evolutionary principles. By natural selection each kind of newborn snake comes to recognize, by chemical cues, the type of prey that it is best adapted to eat. Our present interpretation is that there is an innate perceptual schema, or releasing mechanism, based upon genetic information that enables the newborn snake to recognize, by chemical cues, the type of prey that it should eat. Differences between species then can easily be seen as ecological adaptations that have evolved through natural selection. As such, they can be as useful in the study of the

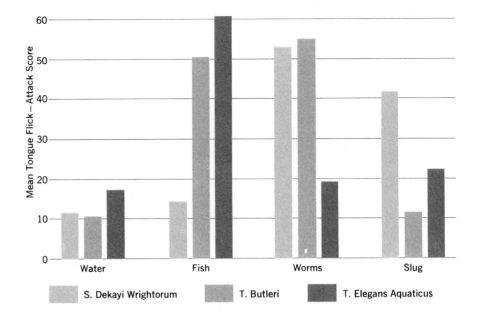

Figure 5. The attack profiles for newborn snakes of 3 species tested on 3 classes of extracts reflect the diets of the adult snakes of the species. (Scores for *S. dekayi wrightorum* are doubled.)

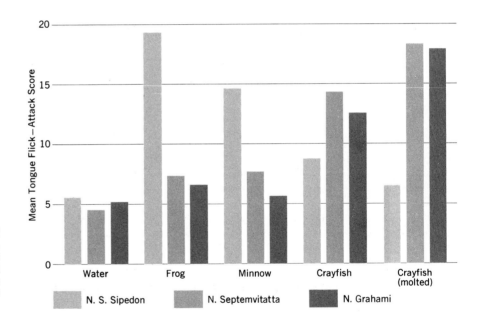

Figure 6. Three species of snakes from the same genus, *Natrix* (water snakes), have different natural diets, and these attack profiles of the newborns show the same differences.

relationships and differences among species as skeletal structure, scale patterning, or other morphological characteristics. For instance, the two species of water snakes responding to crayfish extract are closely related by the usual taxonomic criteria. But too facile an evolutionary interpretation does not do justice to the data. This technique shows that a naive snake will respond to chemical cues that cannot or do not figure in the normal feeding behavior of the species. For instance, where it is found, the aquatic garter snake would rarely, if ever, encounter the guppy, yet the newborn young

responded to the guppy extract readily. However, since the aquatic garter snake normally eats fish, it is probable that the guppy possesses chemical cues similar or identical to those found in fish that the snake normally eats.

In Butler's garter snake the situation is quite different. An extensive field study by C. C. Carpenter, now at the University of Oklahoma, showed that in nature the diet of this species comprises only worms and leeches. Yet captive specimens readily eat fish and amphibians, and newborn young respond to extracts from all four groups. Indeed, the complete profile of responses to extracts by Butler's garter snake is very similar to those of the plains garter snake or the common garter snake, which does eat all four types of prey in nature. It is apparent, therefore, that the normal feeding habits and ecology of a species are not sufficient to "explain" the response to chemical cues in newborn young. But we should remember that evolution is a process of time and that the past may exist in the present. A feasible hypothesis in this instance is that Butler's garter snake has retained the perceptual side of a releasing mechanism that appears to be of no selective advantage in its present mode of life. Of course, retention of the potential of naive snakes to respond to chemical cues from fish would be advantageous if a change in the environment occurred so that fish became a necessary or more easily obtainable food source. The same could be true for amphibians in this species. It is interesting to note, in this connection, that on the usual taxonomic criteria several authorities feel that Butler's garter snake has evolved from the plains garter snake.

We are beginning the construction of species profiles based upon the responses of newborn young to a series of extracts. So far we have investigated over fifteen forms from seven genera. It is by looking at very closely related forms, however, that the most valuable comparative conclusions may be gleaned, since here the traditional taxonomic canons of anatomical distinctions among species may be of only limited value.

Other Considerations

The problem of how these responses by naive snakes can be modified through subsequent experience is interesting, and work is underway in this area. However, the strength of these innate releaser-response ties is often more striking than is their lability. For instance, a large litter of garter snakes was divided into two groups. One group was tested on the standard series of extracts during the first week of life and then released. As with all our testing, it was possible to rank the stimuli in order of effectiveness. The rest of the litter was raised for either 64 or 191 days on an artificial, unnatural diet (strained liver). Since they would not eat this food, we periodically forced it down their throats. At the end of the predetermined number of days on the artificial food, the snakes were tested in an identical fashion on the same series of extracts as were the snakes in the litter tested at birth. Remember that for this period of time these snakes had never had the opportunity either to receive a chemical stimulus normally eliciting an attack response or to perform the attack response itself. In nature a similar amount of deprivation would have resulted in the early death of the snakes. Yet the snakes in both deprived groups attacked the same extracts in the same way as did their littermates tested earlier. No degeneration of the releaser-response system had taken place during the long periods of inaction. The artificial diet, by the way, was refused at the end of the experiment, as it had been at the beginning.

There is some evidence, however, that early feeding experience can influence subsequent behavior if the snake actually attacks and eats the prey object. Further experiments are in progress on this aspect of the problem.

Currently, studies also are being carried out, in collaboration with John Law of the biochemistry department at the University of Chicago, on the chemistry of the effective extracts. Once we know the nature of the chemical stimuli involved in this behavior, it should be possible to study stimulus structure and releasing value on a molecular level.

If the chemical perception of the newborn snake is so well adapted to the ecological and evolutionary aspects of its existence, it is reasonable to inquire into the possibility of similar situations elsewhere in the animal kingdom, including man. But many psychologists, while admitting the existence of complex inherited sources of stimulus information in birds, fish, and insects, feel that mammals, especially humans, are so perceptually and behaviorally plastic that evolutionary considerations of the type discussed here are unimportant or irrelevant, or perhaps even dangerous. Possibly a new approach is needed. Gene Sackett, at the University of Wisconsin, recently has shown that rhesus monkeys raised in visually restricted environments respond in species-characteristic fashion when confronted with pictures of monkeys having certain expressions such as threat. Robert Fantz has shown that the newborn infant brings into the world more complex visual abilities than previously thought and, on the physiological level, David Hubel and Torsten Wiesel have demonstrated the extensive visual abilities built into the newborn kitten. Daniel Freedman and Eibl Ebesfeldt are directing our attention to the implications of evolutionary, ethological thought for our understanding of human behavior.

But as concerns the chemical senses, we only can speculate. Probably no odor would elicit as specific an overt response in man as in the snake. But many of the responses of men to situations and stimuli are internalized. Feelings and affective states replace the motoric responses measured with animals. Perhaps many of the feelings aroused daily in the odoriferous world of man are influenced in part, at least, by evolutionary memories recorded in the genes many ages ago, fleeting emotional bonds with our ancestors. And this memory might be a little bit different for each of us, for we all have had a unique voyage from the past.

The highly precocial nature of young snakes and their dependence upon the chemical senses allow the phenomenon to be elucidated clearly. But the point is that we should not be concerned just with whether the newborn organism has or has not certain perceptual abilities of vision, olfaction, and the like. We would like to know if he can use these abilities innately to recognize stimuli having biological and evolutionary significance. In many cases we may never find out. Nevertheless, the search is both exciting and meaningful.

skimp·y

dv. 1. lacking in
a skimpy din
ousewife. [sk
i·ness, n.

up the
of chai

notors

one's kno
ething well.
mpetent ex-
xteri   : The
rade   wr job
ing   skill hich
What
d?   4. O   do
on;   uses
renc

cle

2.
ki
a

Skin (skin),
external cover
en soft and
the bod
skin
outer coatin
brane, the r
skin of thin
4. Jewelry.
outermost la
color and
aut. a.

Body English

Frank A. Geldard

Employing the measures of classical psychophysics (thresholds, and temporal and spatial discriminatory abilities), Geldard discusses the sensory characteristics of the skin. He compares the performance of this sensory modality with vision and hearing and shows how the skin can "understand" language. These experiments illustrate not only how basic information on sensory functions is gathered but also how such information can be applied. "Body English" can be taught to and used by the blind or by normal humans in situations where visual or auditory language cannot be used.

What kind of language can the skin understand? Well, most people would say, the skin can understand the "language" of texture—the rich, complex, unmistakable feels of silk, velvet or tweed. Or the language of hot and cold, the message of the insect's sting, the language of warning, the affectionate touch on the shoulder, or the small number of pokes and jabs which can mean anything from "Shhh—the boss is coming" to "Isn't that the most ridiculous thing you've ever heard?"

But what about language in a narrower sense—can skin receive and understand a complex impersonal system of symbols like Morse, semaphore, or even English?

And even if the skin can handle language in the communications sense, aren't the eyes and ears enough?

Eyes and ears were not enough during the early years of World War II, when fighter pilots were shot down too often because they could not hear their wing commanders, and they did not peel away fast enough when enemy planes closed in. Thus research was begun to find out if warning signals could be built into cushions so that pilots could "hear" by the seat of their pants.

Certainly it is painfully obvious that the eyes and ears are not enough if you are blind or deaf or both. Braille, for instance, is an arbitrary, very difficult language to learn, and most blind people do not read well in it. It is

also obvious that there are a myriad of conditions in which even the nondefective eye or ear may be absorbed, or baffled, or in some way at a grave disadvantage—you can't hear when the water's running or bombs are falling or crowds are screaming. You can't see in the dark or in the fog. The human voice is wildly distorted by helium under deep-sea pressure, and so on.

Assuming, then, the practical need to explore all possible channels of communication, we can and should ask: What can the skin do? What kinds of signals can it handle? What kinds of discriminations can it make? How can these discriminations be used as the building blocks of a sophisticated, easily intelligible vehicle for hard information?

The Compromising Skin

As a receiving instrument, the skin combines the best abilities of the eye and ear; it doesn't perform quite as well as the eye and ear do in their specialized fields, but it is the body's only receptor that can handle both fields fairly well.

By the ear's field, I don't mean sound—the blessed human voice, for instance, or the divine noise of the Prelude to *Parsifal*—I mean time. Within a continuous sound, the ear can detect a break or silence only two- to four-thousandths of a second long. The ear has a rather poor space-sensing ability, however; more often than not we speak of a sound coming from "somewhere." Space is the eye's province: the eye can be fooled, of course, but it can make extraordinarily fine discriminations—indeed the finest the human organism is capable of. On the other hand, the eye is a sluggish time organ; home-movie screens, which reflect only twenty-four discrete flashes of light per second, are seen as a continuous picture or blaze of light.

The skin handles time almost as well as the ear. Under proper conditions, the skin can detect a break of about ten-thousandths of a second in a steady mechanical pressure or tactile buzz. For the eye, comparable time discriminations are much slower; eye discriminations are about twenty-five to thirty-five thousandths of a second. (Ball-park time figures for the ear, for the eye, and for the skin are thus .003, .030, and .010 seconds, respectively.)

In terms of space, the skin can identify and distinguish between coded signals delivered from five to seven different locations within the chest area. The ear cannot identify the source of a sound (provided this sound is produced at some distance from the hearer) with anything like the same fineness, as anyone who has ever tried to "spot" a buzzing insect by ear can testify.

The Skin's Vocabulary

Given the skin's fairly accurate spatiotemporal perception, we can begin to talk about a language that uses discriminations in time and space as vocabulary items. The skin's time sense provides us with two vocabulary elements—duration and frequency.

When using duration in a system of signals, it is not worth considering vibratory pulses or buzzes shorter than 0.10 second (they are not felt as buzzes, and could easily be mistaken for an accidental poke or jab); at the other end, buzzes lasting more than two full seconds would slow any signaling system to a crawl. Between these limits, the skin can distinguish some twenty-five discrete, just-noticeable differences in length, at least four or five of which can be judged with absolute correctness. When presented in isolation, these four or five signals are felt to have a distinctive length—short, medium-short, medium, and long, for instance. These distinctive lengths can be coded and hence become meaningful elements in a language.

Frequency is a somewhat finer aspect of temporal discrimination, analogous to heard pitch. Such felt frequency depends primarily on the rate at which successive impacts are delivered to the skin. Usable or "hearable" frequency ranges for the skin are rates below 150 impacts per second, which is of course below the frequencies present in speech or the midmusical range. But within this limited range, the skin does almost as well as the ear; for example, a frequency or pitch of 40

impacts per second can be distinguished from one of 39.5 or 40.5 impacts per second! Sixty impacts per second provides a good general carrier frequency or note upon which pitch variations can be played conveniently.

Another valuable vocabulary item or codable discrimination is that of intensity or "loudness." Sensitivity to loudness or softness varies from one location to another on the skin, so that figures have to be specified for particular body sites. But, in general, from the threshold below which nothing is felt, to a safe distance under the discomfort level, the average subject can detect some fifteen just-noticeable differences in intensity. As with duration, some of these intensities can be recognized as having a unique value, like soft, medium, and loud, for instance, even when there is nothing to compare them with, and hence can be suitably coded to mean something.

The fourth useful dimension in cutaneous talk is location or space. There are a number of problems connected with the skin's space sense that are only now being investigated. (For example, when two chest vibrators are activated simultaneously, they are felt as one, but more about this later.) But so long as they are buzzed in sequence, with just a tiny time differential separating the signals, as many as seven vibrators may be placed on the chest and used as codable signal elements.

Vibratese—A Workable System

Vibratese was a language having forty-five separate signals: three intensities (weak, medium, strong) and three durations (short, medium, long) were delivered to five different spots on the chest. (All steps could be combined with all others, 3 × 3 × 5, giving forty-five steps or signals.) Letters of the alphabet were each assigned a signal representing a unique combination of duration, intensity, and location. The times were kept short—0.1, 0.3, 0.5 second for short, medium, and long, respectively. The most frequently occurring language elements were assigned shorter durations, enabling the system to "fly" at a rapid pace. The code proved quite efficient, since each of the all-important vowels was assigned its own vibrator, and since letters followed each other promptly, with none of the wasteful silences that are built into International Morse.

The vibratese alphabet could be mastered in only a few hours, and it was not long before two- and three-letter words could be introduced, and then short sentences. Trainees found that, as with radio or telegraphic codes, they could "follow behind" and combine letters and words into larger patterns. When the training sessions were finally discontinued—not because the learning limit had been reached, but because the sending equipment could go no faster—one subject was receiving at a rate about twice that of proficient Morse reception.

The vibratese experiment taught some valuable lessons but, more important, it raised questions about the possibility of making far better use of the space dimension. Could vibrators be scattered all over the body? Could they be activated simultaneously? These questions had to remain open, given the purely technological limitations imposed by the equipment then available—the vibrators were extremely cumbersome, and the chest area was the only place to put them.

By the time the Cutaneous Communication Laboratory at Princeton University was established in 1962 (hitherto most work in this field was done at the University of Virginia), a major technological breakthrough had taken place. A small, compact, yet powerful vibrator somewhat like a hearing aid was developed in 1959 by R. C. Bice at the University of Virginia. Later, a more rugged and reliable vibrator of the same general type was developed at Princeton by Carl Sherrick. Both these instruments can be attached quite simply and firmly at any desired body site and can be counted on to perform accurately over long periods.

It is possible that systems using only coded variations in spatial location can provide languages thoroughly adequate for many purposes—simple warning or tracking systems, for example.

In one experiment at Princeton we placed the vibrators on ten different body sites (see Figure 1). These sites weren't arbitrarily selected, and many others were tried. It was surprising how far from each other vibrators had to be in order to act in relative independence of one another. It was also surprising how many potential sites had to be abandoned because they provided ready paths to the ear; subjects complained of hearing, rather than feeling, the vibratory bursts. Though we really don't know as yet whether exactly corresponding points on the two sides of the body need to be avoided—as they are, intentionally, in the illustration—neurological principles seem to suggest this.

Subjects were exposed to patterns consisting of two vibratory bursts one-fifth of a second long, and separated by a half-second silence. Each of these two bursts activated from one to nine sites at the same time. In some of these patterns, both bursts were identical: exactly the same sites were involved. In other patterns, the two bursts were different in varying degree. The same number of sites was involved, but they weren't the same ones. Altogether, 1,000 patterns were presented (more than half a million are possible); 500 were "sames" pairs and 500 were "differents." The subject's task was merely to report which were which.

The really important error-causing factor turned out to be not the sheer number of sites involved, but rather the extent to which successive bursts had elements in common. That the number of sites alone was not primarily the culprit became evident when patterns utilizing no more than four vibrators were consistently misjudged to be the "same" because they had three sites in common (see Figure 2).

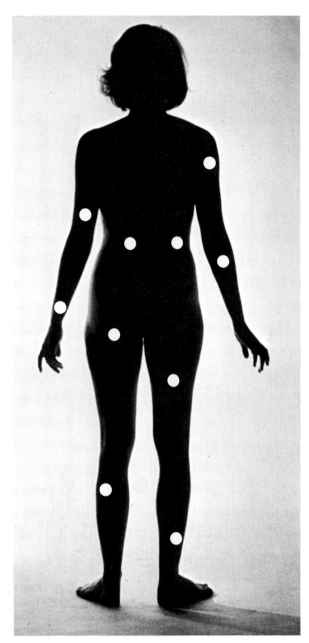

Figure 1. These vibrator sites, far enough apart and well separated from bone, form recognizable elements of language in spatial terms.

More elaborate patterns were discriminated perfectly, as long as they were different enough.

Space-Time Cooperation

It is clear now that tactile communication not only permits, but fairly demands, the coordination of both spatial and temporal variations. A peek into the future reveals at least one of the many possibilities to be explored.

At Princeton, we developed an instrument called the optohapt. The symbols supplied by a typewriter are

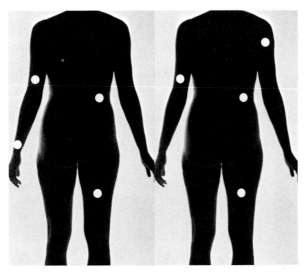

Figure 2. A common cause of error in subjects' being able to differentiate vibratory patterns was too many vibrator sites in common, as shown here, where 3 of the 4 sites are the same.

transmuted into sequences and combinations of vibratory bursts distributed over the body surface. Nine locations (see Figure 3) are used.

A glance at the circular inset in Figure 3 will reveal the essential mode of operation. In the case of an E

passing steadily from right to left, the vertical backbone of the letter first activates in a single burst the entire array of nine vibrators, then continues with only #1 (top), #5, and #9 (bottom). The middle one quits a little sooner than the top and bottom vibrators because of the shorter middle branch of the E. A distinctive spatiotemporal pattern is thus created, one that belongs exclusively to the E, though differing from an F only by the inclusion of a long burst on the #9 (bottom) vibrator. Some of these time-space patterns are extremely attention-getting, to say the least; the letter W, for instance, sweeps vividly across the body, shoulder to ankle, shoulder to ankle, like a sort of tactile neon sign.

Actually, letters do not provide the best material. Punctuation signs and a variety of literary and business symbols are more distinctive and more readily learned.

In the exploratory stage, we examined a group of 180 symbols, searching for the most easily understandable signals. The final survivors for alphabetic coding are shown in Figure 4. These, if presented at the optimal speed—optimal means having suitable "zip" and vivid movement—are easy to learn and retain. They are also easy to combine into word-forming sequences.

The optohapt represents only one limited set of possibilities for presenting spatiotemporal patterns; typefaces arbitrarily dictate the patterns flashed to the skin, and the typewriter carriage moves only one way, of

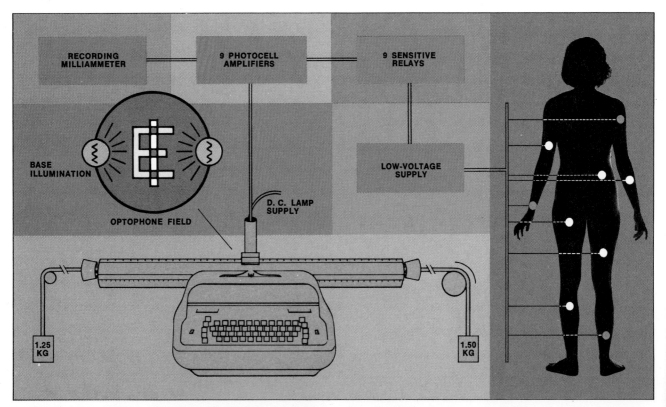

Figure 3. The optohapt transforms photoelectric impulses from typewriter symbols into sequences and combinations of vibratory bursts, which are played upon the skin as though upon a piano keyboard. The skin reads the bursts as a space-time "tune."

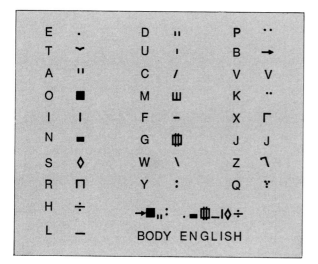

Figure 4. The optohapt alphabet. These symbols can be flashed to the skin rapidly and vividly; they are easy to learn and "read."

course. The Cutaneous Communication Laboratory is just now putting into operation a tape system that tells a different story. The new device—speedy, accurate, and reliable—will provide what appears to be the ultimate challenge to the skin, a set of patterns containing far more elements than even the most rabid dermophile would ever claim are within the skin's ability to conquer. Experiment will shortly decide if we shall ultimately arrive at a totally satisfactory "Body English."

A Friendly Look Backward

In terms of research history, we have made a good deal of progress since 1762, when Jean Jacques Rousseau proposed that the skin might serve as a channel of communication. In his revolutionary educational treatise, *Emile*, Rousseau drew attention to the common observation that the vibrations of the cello can be felt by the hand and fingers and that "one can distinguish without the use of eye or ear, merely by the way in which the wood vibrates and trembles, whether the sound given out is sharp or flat, whether it is drawn from the treble string or the bass." He asked whether "we might in time become so sensitive as to hear a whole tune by means of our fingers." Beyond that, he

estimated that "tone and measure" might ultimately become "the elements of speech" for communication with the deaf.

The idea that the skin ought to be trainable to receive complex vibratory patterns never really was lost sight of in the more than two centuries since *Emile*. People continued to suggest that speech and music might be impressed on the skin much as it is delivered to the eardrums. Indeed the argument was an evolutionary one: the eardrum is basically a derivative from skin, and the tactile sense should therefore be able to learn to do, at least crudely, what the tympanic membrane does so superbly.

During the first third of this century there were elaborate and painstaking experiments, both in America and in Germany, aimed at teaching the skin to recognize complex chains of vibrations delivered to the fingertips. In the most extensive of these, words and sentences were spoken into a microphone, which activated a small crystal speaker, an instrument known as the teletactor, which imparted its vibrations to the fingers. But the results were disappointing: only a series of poorly discriminated rhythmic accents could be learned, and not too effectively. In the mid-1930s the whole effort was abandoned, and it was many years before it was learned why these experiments had failed. Now we know that the frequencies important in speech are all but impossible for the skin to discriminate. The skin was being asked to do something at which it is quite inept.

The long course of research and speculation has led us to the knowledge that the skin can handle time and space discriminations fairly well. We have put this knowledge to the test and have shown that the skin can receive rapid and sophisticated messages. There is every likelihood that skin languages of great subtlety and speed can be devised and used.

But the point is that we have much more in the way of basic fact than anyone has yet put to work. This fairly solid ground floor of data is available for a host of applications, and I have touched obliquely on a few of them—warning signal systems, supplementary directional systems, a sophisticated language for the blind or deaf, and, of course, all sorts of secret military or commercial uses. But I confess to a certain sympathy with the classic remark attributed to Michael Faraday on the occasion of his being asked what good his induction motor was: "Maybe you can tax it some day."

Perceptual Adaptation

Irvin Rock

The perceived world differs from the physical world. In this article Rock analyzes aspects of the perceived world. He is concerned with which parts of our perceptual processes are fixed and which parts can be modified by learning. Investigating the learnable aspects of perception, Rock analyzes the means by which sensory adaptation is accomplished. This research leads into questions of sensory-motor coordination and plasticity of the nervous system.

Suppose you were forced to wear goggles with prisms inserted. Everything would be fringed with color; straight lines would seem curved, and all objects would appear to the side of their actual location. Would objects around you forever appear distorted or would you, in time, begin to see the world as it normally looks? Would you ever adapt to such a world?

To answer this question, let us consider first how we see the world without prisms. We all learned in school that the eye functions like a camera, with an image formed by the lens at the back of the eye and transmitted to the brain. There is much truth in this common explanation. And yet the camera theory cannot fully explain the way we see the world. Think about the problem of the perception of size. It is true that if we look at one cube that is twice as large as a cube beside it, the image of the larger cube on the retina will be twice as big as the image of the smaller, and we will perceive the large cube as twice as big.

But suppose the large cube is farther away? We know that the more distant an object is, the smaller its image is in the eye. But even if the larger cube is moved so far away that its image on the retina is the smaller, it still will seem larger. Psychologists call this size constancy.

The size of the image cast on the retina does vary with distance, but the perceived size does not change appreciably. And so the size of a retinal image is not the only basis for our perception of size. It would seem that the brain also takes into account the distance to an object before "deciding" on the size to perceive.

Constancy of size is not an exception, but rather a typical example of the way we see the world. When the sun goes behind a cloud, the light reaching our eyes from everything around us diminishes, but white objects continue to look white, gray continues to look gray (*achromatic color constancy*).

When we see a circle at a slant, the shape of its image becomes elliptical, but the perceived shape changes only slightly, if at all (*shape constancy*).

When we move, the image of everything in our field of vision shifts across the retina, but the objects do not seem to move (*position constancy*). Therefore, an explanation based purely on the photographic image cast on the retina does not explain adequately how we see.

You may argue that I have described not the act of seeing, but of knowing. You might well say that we *do* see the distant object as smaller, but judge it to be larger because we have learned about perspective and the effect of changing distance, or that we *do* see the world moving when we move, but *know* that we are moving, not the world.

But your argument is wrong. We do tend to *see* in terms of these constancies.

This point is illustrated by a photograph originally devised by Edwin G. Boring of Harvard University. In our illustration, the girl seated down the corridor looks much larger than we would predict from the small image she casts. This is borne out when the picture of the girl in the distance is cut out and placed alongside the other, at the same distance from the observer (see Figure 1). In the first picture, you take distance into account in reaching an impression of the girl's size.

Is the fact that the distant girl in the first picture *looks* larger than the same girl in the second merely a matter of knowing? Such a claim constitutes a forced and false description derived from what we think we ought to see based on our implicit acceptance of the camera model of vision. This model maintains that vision is directly determined by the retinal image and must be constant when the image is the same and change whenever the image changes. Years ago, psychologists such as Edward Titchener were caught up in

Figure 1. The small figures in both pictures are exactly the same size.

precisely this tendency of altering the facts to fit their theories of perception.

Recently, T. G. R. Bower of Harvard has shown that two-month-old infants perceive on the basis of constancy, namely that they take distance and slant into account in perceiving size and shape. The behavior of chickens, fish, and many other species suggests that they also see in terms of constancies rather than in terms of the physical properties of their retinal images. It is difficult to believe that lower organisms and infants *see* in terms of the changing image, but behave otherwise because they *know* better.

Research like this has led psychologists to claim that there is a separate discipline of perception. They believe that there are laws of perception that must be discovered and that these laws cannot come from the ele-

mentary facts of vision, or be understood as factual knowledge gained about the world.

One further argument may be mentioned. Optical illusions cannot be explained on the basis of the retinal image, since the image accurately mirrors the objective state of affairs. Nor can the illusions be based on knowledge; they defy knowledge. For example, we *know* the two line segments in the familiar Müller-Lyer illusion are of equal length, but even after we have confirmed our knowledge with a ruler, one segment still looks longer than the other (see Figure 2). Therefore, all optical illusions attest to the impotence of knowledge about a situation to affect its appearance.

Does this mean that perception is not based on past experience? Not necessarily. I have argued that we cannot reduce perception to knowing; we see the world on the basis of certain complex central processes that take into account information about things like distance, slant, illumination, or our own movement. We cannot rule out the brain's use of past experience in achieving these perceptual experiences.

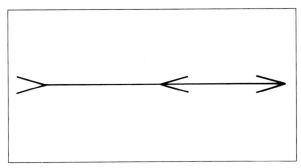

Figure 2. The Müller-Lyer illusion.

The two tablets shown in Figure 3 suggest that past experience plays a role in what we see. One tablet contains cuneiform writing in bas-relief; the other contains the same writing in intaglio. Yet the figure on the right is the one on the left turned upside down. The point I wish to emphasize is that we see the writing in this way: it looks as if it protrudes in one case and is indented in the other. The knowledge I have just given you—that these are pictures of the same object—has essentially no effect on the way they look. This illusion is based on the position of the shadows (shadow underneath—object protrudes; shadow above—object is indented).

There is reason for believing that this perceptual effect *is* based on past experience. Both sunlight and indoor artificial light typically come from above. Logically, then, a bump on a flat surface usually will be shadowed on the bottom and highlighted on the top. So we could learn—though quite unconsciously—that shadows are associated with protrusion and indentation.

One rather bold experiment supports this theory. E. H. Hess of the University of Chicago reared chickens from the time of hatching in cages where the only light came from below. These chickens, unlike normally

Figure 3. The tablet (a) appears to be in bas-relief; (b), in intaglio. Yet, (b) is the same photograph as (a) turned upside down.

reared chickens, pecked more at photographs of grain with the shadow at the top, suggesting that these photographs looked to them like protruding objects—and, therefore, like grain.

But this experiment is the exception. Even after a century of work dominated by psychologists—and before them, philosophers—who believed we learn to see the world the way we do, there is little solid evidence to support this belief.

In fact, there now is rather good evidence that form and depth perception are innate, that form and depth are perceptible at birth or soon thereafter. Bower's work shows that even perception in terms of constancy of size and shape is either not learned in humans or learned quickly—soon after birth—in some completely unknown way.

But what about the prismatic spectacles and the like that distort the world by refracting light? It has been known since the days of Herman von Helmholtz and Wilhelm Wundt in the last century that, if you continue to look through the prism, you will adapt to the distortions. Soon things no longer appear either as displaced or as curved as when you first looked through the prism.

This would appear to be a clear case of learning to perceive. If so, if we can demonstrate the effects of such experience on seeing in the adult, then perhaps we can conclude that perception in the young infant develops similarly. Study of adaptation to prismatic distortion now takes on real importance. In the laboratory we can produce, in a relatively short time, the effect of experience on perception. The next step would be to investigate the conditions necessary to induce these effects.

Many laboratory attempts have been made to study adaptation to visual distortion. As early as 1896, George Stratton at Berkeley undertook to view the world through an inverting lens system. His retinal image was reinverted—since the normal retinal image is an inverted one—and the world appeared upside down. He hoped to discover whether, in time, the world would appear normal—or right side up—again. Stratton wore the device continuously for eight days, never permitting himself to see the world except through the lenses. To

judge from his day-to-day description of his experiences, the outcome was not altogether clear.

This difficult and trying experiment has been repeated about once very decade since and—in my opinion—the results still are not clear. Stratton claimed he adapted or was well on the way to a complete righting of the scene. Others after him seemed to get no such effect, though T. Erismann and Ivo Kohler of Innsbruck recently claimed their observers did adapt.

There are several difficulties with Stratton's experiment. No objective methods were used to supplement and to clarify the observer's often unclear introspections. The choice of optical distortion—*complete* reinversion of the retinal image—compounds the difficulty. A less drastic change would have been advisable, because it is difficult to imagine partial adaptation with complete reinversion. The world will look upside down or right side up, but not tilted by some lesser magnitude. A further difficulty is the confusion between changes in behavior and changes in perception.

In addition to the altered appearance of things, lenses or prisms also lead to incorrect movements at the outset. Stratton reached upward for things that were actually below the head, and vice versa. Or he reached leftward for things that were actually to the right, and vice versa. One may learn to correct these errors and nevertheless continue to see the world upside down.

Indeed, everyone who has undertaken this experiment has adapted behaviorally. Incorrect movement tendencies have disappeared and some observers have learned to bicycle and to ski while wearing the inverting lenses. Whether they adapted to the distorted appearance of things is another matter. This is not to deny that these two aspects of adaptation are related.

Except for these sporadic experiments on reinversion, no systematic work on adaptation to distortion was done until recently. This delay in systematic investigation can probably be traced to the work of J. J. Gibson of Cornell University, who set out in 1933 to study the ability of observers to reestablish sensory-motor coordination when they viewed the world through prisms. However, his observers reported that straight lines that were curved by the prisms later tended to appear less curved. Gibson therefore shifted his focus of interest to this problem. Reasoning that a prism creates a curved retinal image and that this curved image later appears to straighten, he felt that the crucial thing was the curved image. His next—and plausible—move, one that I believe had an important historical impact, was to abandon the prism technique in favor of looking at a truly curved line. Surprisingly enough, he found that if you stare at a curved line for a few minutes, it will look less curved. If a straight line is then introduced, it will look curved in the opposite direction. This is the now well-known Gibson normalization effect. (He made a similar discovery about a tilted line.)

Gibson reasoned that objects tended to approach the norm from which they are departures. Since lines can curve symmetrically in either direction, a straight line is the norm or neutral point. If a curved image tends to lead eventually to an impression of straightness, then we may suppose that the entire coordinate system has shifted to a new neutral point. If this shift occurs, a straight image will no longer appear straight.

Prismatic distortion was no longer the focus of study. The prism seemed irrelevant to Gibson's work; it was only one method of creating a curved image. The normalization effect could not be adaptation to a distorted world based on learning to see the world more accurately. In this effect the observer came to see *less* accurately, for after a while the truly curved line looked less curved. Therefore, it was not learning in the usual meaning. Interest shifted from prism adaptation to adaptation effects based on fixating curved and tilted lines.

The field of prism adaptation had to be rediscovered. Investigators had to realize that there is a class of effects such as Stratton first studied: perceptual change based on learning to see a distorted world more correctly. The work of Erismann and Kohler played a major role, for when their observers wore the distorting devices over weeks or even months, they encountered dramatic changes and equally impressive aftereffects when at last the prisms were removed. Richard Held of MIT gave this work impetus by developing objective techniques for studying change and by showing experimentally that normalization effects of the kind Gibson discovered could not account for the changes that take place in wearing prisms.

A typical modern adaptation study is divided into three parts: pretest, exposure period, and posttest. In the pretest, the experimenter establishes just how each observer judges the perceptual property under investigation.

For example, the observer is asked to indicate when a flexible, luminous rod appears straight. Because he is shown the rod in a darkened room, he must respond in terms of the absolute appearance of the rod. He cannot compare it with other contours in his field of vision. Several measures are taken and the average computed.

Then the observer puts on the prisms, set in goggles, and his exposure period begins. He performs relevant activities, more often than not merely walking through the laboratory corridors. For the posttest, he is brought back to the darkened room, his goggles are removed, and once more he views the flexible rod. The difference between pretest and posttest is the measure of adaptation. Any adaptation will be revealed by an aftereffect. In this experiment, a curved rod will appear straight, since a curved image has—during exposure to the prisms—come to yield an impression of straightness.

It is also possible to conduct all three stages with the observer wearing prisms. Adaptation in this procedure is revealed by the selection of a curved rod in the pretest and a straight rod in the posttest. It can be argued that, if the observer wears prisms during the testing, he will try to discount the known distortion in order to give the "right" answer. Without prisms, he has no reason to compensate and adaptation will be revealed by an "error." Thus, the aftereffect obtained without prisms gives impressive evidence that a change in the nervous system does take place.

The findings of various adaptation studies indicate that adaptation to displacement occurs readily. If the observer is given enough exposure, this adaptation will be more or less complete. When an object straight ahead is prismatically displaced, the observer must turn his eyes to look at it. Many investigators agree that this kind of adaptation is based on the observer's interpretation of the turned position of his eyes as *not* turned. Hence, after exposure, an object fixated with eyes turned appears straight ahead.

There is now fairly good evidence that observers will adapt to a tilted image, a superior procedure to Stratton's 180-degree transformation. In the pre- and posttest, the observer sets a luminous line until it appears vertical. Exposures of a half hour to an hour induce changes of from 3 to 10 degrees, providing objective data that an image need not be in its usual position for the observer to see it as upright. Stratton's belief thus appears to be confirmed.

Adaptation to altered curvature exists, but is relatively small. In one study, adaptation was only 30 percent of the total distortion after observers wore prisms for forty-two days. Nevertheless, the adaptation—and this is also true for tilt—is greater than the Gibson normalization effect can explain. Within a very short time, there is also appreciable adaptation to distortions of size.

The curve of adaptation levels off after the first day or two of exposure. After that, adaptation increases very little. The reason for this is unknown, nor do we know whether adaptation other than that to displacement will be complete if the exposure is continued indefinitely.

Erismann and Kohler reported certain dramatic effects such as simultaneous adaptation to blue filters on the left side of both goggles and to yellow filters on the right; simultaneous adaptation to compression of images on one side and expansion on the other. However, it has not been possible to reproduce the color effect, and we still lack adequate confirming evidence about the compression-expansion effect and other effects of this kind.

We must now consider the theoretical problem of adaptation to distortion. Are we to suppose that perception is so malleable that no matter how we distort the retinal image, the observer ultimately will adapt and see the world as we do? If this is true, how can we reconcile it with the findings that many perceptual attributes are present at birth and do not depend on learning? What mechanism underlies such changes in appearance?

I believe the answer is that perception is not completely malleable. We can adapt only to certain kinds of distortion. The information within the retinal image does supply us with the necessary core of what we see.

Suppose we hypothesize that the retinal image provides crucial information about relationships between objects. Consider the following example. Imagine you are looking at two straight lines, A and B, with line A being vertical and line B tilted, and A being longer than B (see Figure 4a). Assume that line A is straight ahead of you. In terms of the relationship of the image of A to that of B, we can say that A is longer than B and that A and B diverge, being closer at one end than the other. That is all.

Now if you look at this same configuration through a wedge prism, holding the position of your eyes still, the image will be distorted (see Figure 4b). The entire pattern will be displaced sideways on the retina, and A and B will be curved. But the basic relationships are preserved: A remains longer than B, and A and B diverge from one another. If you look at the pattern through a lens that magnifies or minifies the lines, then, while the absolute size of the two images will be altered, the relationship of their sizes to one another will not be affected. If you look at the same pattern through an optical device that tilts the entire retinal image, the relationship of tilt of the lines *with respect to one another* will not be altered (see Figure 4c).

Therefore, if the crucial information given by the image is relational, the kinds of distortions that are being studied are not distortions at all! On the other hand, if a more drastic kind of distortion were introduced, such as a random scattering of points on the image, I think you will agree it is unlikely that an observer will ever adapt. He would never come to see A and B as we do.

But, if perception depends only on the relationships within the image, why does the world look distorted when first we look through prisms? This point has been completely overlooked by investigators, who have assumed that it is intuitively self-evident that the world looks distorted because the image is distorted.

Let us consider this previously ignored problem of the initial distortion. Perhaps the absolute aspects—not the

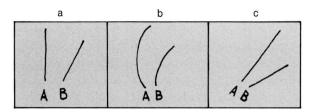

Figure 4. The lines in (a) when viewed through a wedge prism (b) or through an optical device that tilts the entire retinal image (c) will nonetheless retain the same relationship *with respect to each other.*

relationships of the two lines—will explain the distortion. Lines A and B produce images of specific size at any specific distance; A's image on the retina is vertical, B's is tilted; the images of both A and B are straight. Perhaps the visual experience of a lifetime associates these absolute aspects with their corresponding perceptual properties: the size of the image with the perceived size; the orientation of the image with the perceived orientation; the curvature of the image with the perceived degree of curvature. Such associations are preserved in the form of enduring memory traces, and these traces are faithful representations of the absolute features of the retinal image and the associated perceptual properties.

If this is true, A appears tilted when first viewed through a tilting prism, not for any innate reason, but because a vertical orientation of the retina has become a sign of the perceptual vertical in the neural organization underlying perception. (Orientation here is with respect to the observer. The prism does not change the orientation of A with respect to B.) A appears smaller when viewed through a reducing lens, not because a smaller image innately demands a smaller percept, but because the specific size of the image has become a sign of a specific perceptual size. A and B appear curved when first viewed through a wedge prism, not because a curved image innately suggests a curved line, but because only a straight image has become a sign of a perceptually straight line.

Given this explanation, it is obvious how we adapt to prisms. It is only when the perceptual properties of absolute tilt, size, curvature, and the like are not linked innately to absolute features of the retinal image that a theory of adaptation makes sense. For it would be hard to understand why, if image curvature innately determines perceived curvature, the perception of curvature is subject to change. But if the relationship of image curvature to perceived curvature is a learned one in the first place, then the formation of a new association while wearing prisms becomes plausible. Through learning, a curved image is associated with a straight line.

We have not yet explained how the observer forms these new associations. It is not enough to say he does so by looking through prisms. To illustrate this point, imagine a stationary observer who looks at A and B through a tilting prism. Suppose that he can see only

Figure 5.

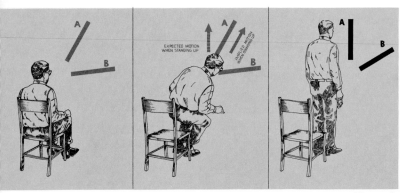

Figure 6.

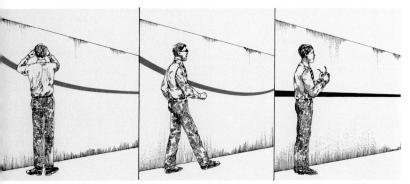

Figure 7.

this pattern; everything else being invisible. A will look tilted and B almost horizontal, and they will continue to do so. Unless information is provided that tilted A is vertical and horizontal B is tilted, no new associations can be formed. The observer would not adapt.

Suppose, however, the observer now can see his own body. The image of his body, seen through the prisms, will undergo the same tilting transformation. It, too, will appear tilted (see Figure 5). Consequently, he now can learn that the tilted image of A is actually "vertical," for it is parallel to his body.

Other information than direct sight of the body can lead to adaptation. Movement by the observer could be an important clue. The seated observer who can see

only A and B through the prisms has no reason to see the lines as they really are. But suppose he stands up (see Figure 6). Since A appears tilted with respect to himself, he would expect his movement in standing up to take him obliquely away from A. Instead, he sees that the direction of his movement is in alignment with A. He *knows* that his movement was vertical, so he *must* assume that A is actually vertical.

The same informative value of movement applies to curvature distortions. Imagine an observer who looks through curving prisms at a horizontal straight line on a wall. If he sits or stands still and sees only the line, there is no reason for its curved appearance to change. But if he walks parallel to the wall, peculiar changes of the line's image will occur (see Figure 7). That part of the line that had been in front of him will appear to move upward, and the part he is approaching will move downward. In other words, the lowermost bulge of the line will always remain directly in front of him. This is because the line is straight. Wherever he is, the tendency of the prism will be to displace that part of the line to his side upward to a greater degree than the part straight ahead. These changes in the image of the line inform him that its curvature is parallel to the direction in which he is moving. Because he moves in a straight path, the line must be straight.

We have not yet considered an obvious source of information—what we can find out from our other senses, particularly from touch. Suppose the observer who looks at A through tilting prisms then runs his hand along the line. You would expect that it would be easy for him to tell that the line is actually vertical.

In fact, in both philosophy and psychology there is a long tradition that can be traced to Bishop Berkeley of belief in the educating role of touch in the development of adequate visual perception. We see correctly in spite of the logical limitations of the retinal image as a source of information—for example, the image is two-dimensional, but vision is three-dimensional—so that it has seemed plausible to believe we learn to see by touching things and moving around in the environment.

But running the hand along the tilted line does not lead to visual change. Quite the contrary. The line will feel tilted. So dominant is vision that the impression yielded by our sense of touch is distorted to conform with our visual impression, even when it is wrong.

In our laboratory we have presented an observer with a conflict between vision and touch. In a simple experiment, the observer views a square through a lens that reduces the image to half its actual size. A one-inch square appears as a half-inch square. The observer is allowed to grasp the square, but a cloth below the square prevents him from seeing his hand. And he is not told that he is looking through a reducing lens (see Figure 8).

In this conflict between two senses, the observer

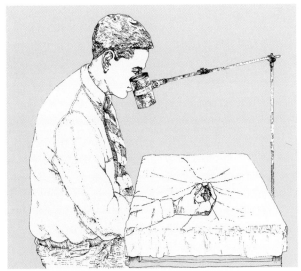

Figure 8. Experimental setup to test the conflict between vision and touch. The subject's hand is under the cloth, so it cannot be seen when he views the square object through the reducing lens.

Figure 9. Experimental setup in which the subject sees, by means of a convex mirror, much of his own body plus an array of familiar objects. Tests of size perception are conducted before and after the experiment.

experiences only what he sees, and the feel of the square conforms to the look of it. The "feel" is captured by vision. As for adaptation, if the observer is given a prolonged exposure to this contradictory experience, vision does not change at all. Touch changes! The impression of size by touch alone—with the eyes closed—has changed following exposure to the conflict. The one-inch square now feels smaller than it did before the experiment began. It is therefore hard to believe that adaptation to prismatic distortion can be based on touch.

Contrast this failure to adapt visually to a reduced image with a different experiment. The observer is exposed to a reduced image, but he is given visual information. He does not have to rely on his sense of touch. In this experiment, the observer looks through a convex mirror that makes everything appear diminutive. Through this, he sees a good portion of his own body and an array of familiar objects, such as playing cards or checkers and checkerboard (see Figure 9). Tests of size perception are conducted before and after exposure to this optically reduced scene. During the exposure period, which can be as brief as ten minutes, the observer either remains stationary or plays solitaire or checkers. The reduced images of objects lead increasingly to an impression of normal size. In the test following exposure, the observer judges a luminous line of about 10 inches in length seen in the dark to be about 12 inches long, suggesting that considerable adaptation to the reduced image has taken place.

I believe that the crucial information here consists of sight of the body and the array of familiar objects. If the observer saw only a rectangle through the convex mirror, it no doubt would continue to look about half its actual size. But when he sees a playing card maintain

its normal size in relation to other objects, particularly to his own minified hand, he receives information that the reduced image is of a much larger object than first it seemed to be.

If perceptual adaptation is a fact, and if my suggested hypothesis concerning memory traces is plausible, a difficult question remains. How can memories affect the way things look? I cannot answer this question, but it is interesting to consider other cases where memories probably have such effects.

Consider the familiarity and meaningfulness of objects. Logically, it must be the case that a figure "4" looks familiar and meaningful because of memories associated with it. If so, these memories must enter into the neural organization underlying such perceptual experience. Even more to the point, because it involves space perception, is the drawn figure of a cube. The memories of three-dimensional cubes apparently are aroused by the sight of the drawn figure, and these memories then must enter the neural organization that leads to the visual impression that a two-dimensional drawing is three-dimensional. Recall the photographs of the cuneiform carvings. The memories of how shadows fall on three-dimensional objects must play a determining role in the way these photographs appear to us.

These are examples of past experience contributing to present perceptual experience. It is in this way, I would speculate, that adaptation effects can be understood. In our laboratory experiments, memories of how a tilted or curved line "behaves" somehow affect the way these lines look to our observers after prolonged exposure. On the other hand, our perception of the *relationships* between objects in the environment is in all probability innately determined. Not learned, but there all the time.

III
Learning, Memory, and the Modification of Behavior

The Inspector General Is a Bird

Thom Verhave

Continuing in the tradition of radical behaviorism, B. F. Skinner and his co-workers developed the field of operant conditioning into a precise science. Using these operant techniques, Verhave has broken down an industrially important task into its component parts. In using the "prediction and control" that Skinner postulates as the criterion for all good science, Verhave has taught pigeons to perform complicated discriminations and to teach these discriminations to other pigeons.

It is common knowledge that two heads are better than one, and just as true when the heads belong to pigeons.

Properly conditioned, this ordinary bird can be taught the visual operations of commercial manufacturing. He can be, in fact, a quality-control inspector. But more surprising than the thought of pigeons as inspectors are the implications for certain aspects of socialization that come from two pigeons working together on an assembly line. Pigeons at work can give us new insights into the way man cooperates and transmits his culture from generation to generation.

My interest in pigeons began many years ago, but it was not until, as a psychopharmacologist, I toured the research and manufacturing facilities of a large drug company that I learned about the gigantic problem of quality control.

The company's facilities produced as many as 20 million gelatin capsules daily. All of these had to be inspected visually for possible defects—at great cost in time, money, and human patience.

A group of seventy women was required to inspect the capsules before they were filled. The capsules in a particular batch—all of the same shape, size, and color —dropped at a fixed rate onto an endless moving belt. The inspector scanned the capsules as they moved be-fore her and discarded all those that were off-color, bumpy, capped twice, or dented. After a batch of capsules was inspected, a supervisor scooped a ladleful of them out of the barrel and checked them for defects. If there were more than the allowed number of defective capsules (called skags) in a sample, the entire lot had to be reinspected.

Training Pigeon Inspectors

It occurred to me that this was work pigeons could do, and so I devised a method of training the pigeons to inspect capsules. In the procedure I developed, the pigeon was placed in the caged portion of an inspection apparatus. Before him were two pigeon keys (rounded disks that the pigeon could peck). One key was actually a small transparent window, the other was opaque. The capsules, on a moving belt, came into view behind the transparent key.

The training procedure consisted of a series of circumstances initiated and continued by the birds' behavior and discrimination. A single peck on the illuminated opaque key turned off the light behind it and, at the same time, weakly illuminated the window key, so that the pigeon could see that there was a capsule behind it. Next, the pigeon pecked a single time on the weakly lit window key to produce a bright, narrow beam of light clearly illuminating the capsule. Three more pecks on the window key sounded a tone briefly. The tone indicated the moment of decision.

If the capsule exposed to view was seen by the bird as a skag, it was supposed to make two more pecks on the window key. This turned off the beam of light, moved up the next capsule, and produced food through an automatic hopper. If the capsule was seen by the bird as acceptable, it indicated this by pecking on the opaque key, which also turned off the beam of light and moved up the next capsule. It did not produce the reward of food.

The pigeon determined its own inspection rate, and reinforcement, in the form of food, came only after the pigeon made the appropriate number of pecks on the window key and correctly identified a true skag. Skags made up 10 percent of the capsules on the belt. Incorrect judgments, either false alarms or misses, were not rewarded. Instead there was a thirty-second blackout. In a week's time, birds learned to inspect with 99 percent accuracy.

There is nothing earthshaking about a pigeon—or any animal with one intact eyeball—learning a simple visual discrimination, such as to distinguish between capsules that are disfigured and others that are not. But for anyone who wanted to put birds on an inspection line, there was an intriguing problem: making sure the pigeons *continued* to distinguish good capsules from bad.

From Concept to Action

To understand why the continued recognition of difference presents a problem, it is helpful to look both at discrimination and at concept formation, the way pigeons learn discrimination.

Whenever an animal discriminates, it is able to tell the difference between at least two different events, objects, or stimuli. A pigeon that has successfully been taught to inspect drug capsules can, for example, distinguish between a capsule with a dent in its surface and one without such a defect. The bird pecks on the glass observation window when a skag appears behind it, and on another key whenever a good capsule is shown.

This is an example of simple discrimination, which has been much investigated in such animals as rats and pigeons. It is of the so-called go/no-go variety, familiar to all who have cursed the red light at an intersection: The observer must respond to the presence of a particular cue and not respond in its absence (or to another cue). What is common to all discriminative behavior, from the simplest behavior on the part of an animal to the most complex on the part of a human adult, is the learned ability to act differently in the presence of at least two conditions.

This broad definition of discrimination is closely related to what traditionally has been called abstraction and concept formation. Consider the concept of a bear.

Bears come in many places, shapes, forms, colors, and sizes; they may be large or small, black, brown, or even white. In the forest or in the zoo, they sit, climb, curl up in a furry ball, beg for food, or snarl and threaten. Yet with all these variations, children learn the common elements of "bearness."

When a child identifies a bear, showing conceptual behavior, he ignores certain features of a situation and responds only to the essential aspect. His conceptual behavior is a more complex version of the simple discriminative behavior mentioned earlier. The distinction between the two is a matter of degree. Even the simpleminded pigeon is behaving conceptually when it responds one way whenever it observes a dented capsule, be it large or small, blue or green, and another way when it spots an undented one.

Learning Through Reward

One way to teach an animal or a child to discriminate is to reward the pupil when he reacts correctly to the essential aspect of a situation, and not otherwise.

In teaching a piegon to discriminate between skags and perfect capsules, the bird is rewarded if it pecks at the observation window when a skag appears. But if it pecks at the window when a good capsule is shown, there is no reward. Constant reward, or reward only for correct answers, is unnecessary. What *is* important is that the frequency of reward for correct responses be effectively larger than that for wrong ones.

In the laboratory, the experimenter knows whether the capsule before the bird is a skag or a perfect pill. Without this knowledge, the animal cannot be rewarded at the appropriate time, and learning does not take place.

The problem of using an animal in quality-control inspection is that one no longer knows whether or when to reward. Except by actual inspection, there is no way of knowing when a skag will turn up.

And that is exactly what we want our pigeon to do for us. We want an effective inspector. We want to be able to take a pigeon's word that when it reports a skag, a skag is a skag indeed.

The problem, of course, is that if the bird's discrimination is not rewarded, accuracy deteriorates, and we suddenly have an unemployable bird.

There are two possible solutions to this problem. The experimenter could plant a certain number of known objects—skags as well as perfect capsules—in any batch to be inspected. These could be coded so that they are detectable by special equipment, such as a magnetic sensing device. A certain minimum percentage of such informants could keep the bird's behavior at the required level and serve as a checkup on the bird's inspection.

A more interesting solution to the problem relies upon agreement between two inspector-general pigeons, which inspect each item more or less simultaneously. Each animal is trained separately, and once the desired discriminative behavior is well established, all outside checks on the birds' performance are discontinued. Instead, the birds are rewarded whenever they both agree whether or not a capsule is a skag.

The possibility arises, of course, that both inspectors occasionally may err. The frequency with which that happens is the product of the separate error frequencies of each bird if he were on his own. If each animal, working alone, makes one error for every hundred inspection trials, the likelihood that both birds will be wrong on the same trial is only one out of 10,000! If more than two animals are used as inspectors, the probability of reinforcement for incorrect responses is reduced even further.

Matching to Sample

My recent research has explored the maintenance of discriminations by pigeons whose only check is agreement with another bird. A basic but relatively complex form of discrimination behavior known as *matching to sample* is used in the experiments.

Matching to sample consists of teaching an animal to indicate whether colors or items such as cubes, pyramids, and cylinders are different or similar.

The ability to match lies at the core of much of the complex conceptual behavior so proudly exhibited by man. When a child learns to count, he matches the four apples and the four oranges on the table and learns that each set is *four*. The concept of equivalence, of course, is basic in mathematics.

A relatively simple form of matching behavior has been studied with pigeons. Much of this work has required color matching. These experiments use a modified version of an apparatus designed by B. F. Skinner, a chamber with three small opaque plastic disks and an electromagnetically operated grain-feeder mounted on one wall. A pigeon is trained to peck at these keys, which can be illuminated from behind with lights of various colors. Pecking the appropriate keys in a certain sequence is rewarded: The feeder makes grain available to the pigeon briefly, usually for about three to five seconds.

Each experimental session is broken up into distinct trials. First, the bird, which already has been trained to match colors, must indicate the two of three lighted keys that are the same color. The center key is illuminated with a white light as a trial starts. If the bird pecks the center key three times, the color changes to red or green. The side keys stay dark.

Next, the bird has to peck the colored center key several more times. The two side keys then light up, one red and one green. Which side key lights up with which color on any particular trial is a chance affair, except that red appears always on one side and green on the other.

Thus the pigeon sees three illuminated keys, two of the same color, and this is the crucial moment. If the pigeon pecks three times on the side key whose color

matches the center key, the trial ends and the pigeon gets his reward.

A *single* response to the other side key also terminates the trial, but without reward. In other words, the animal's task is to respond to the correct side key. After a short rest, the next trial begins (see Figure 1). In two

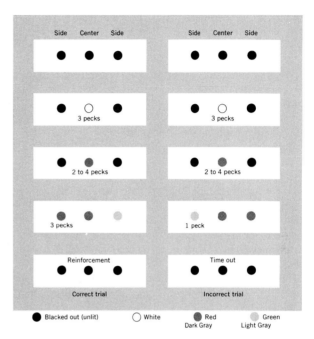

Figure 1. Two successive trials in which a trained pigeon attempts to match red or green lights; only the correct trial ends with the reward of grain.

or three preliminary half-hour training sessions, the bird learns to eat from the feeder and to peck the keys. In only a few more sessions, the bird learns to match two colors almost perfectly. Some pigeons learn so well that they make no mistakes in one hundred trials.

I indicated earlier that discrimination can be maintained even though correct responses are not always rewarded. The more difficult matching-to-sample behavior is no exception. There is even experimental evidence to show that the frequency of errors or mismatches is *less* when correct matches are rewarded intermittently, rather than constantly. Therefore, in my experiments only 50 percent of all correct matches are reinforced. Which ones pay off is determined by the flip of an electronic coin.

Feathered Teachers and Pupils

If two animals, taught discrimination individually and then put to work together, maintain their performance indefinitely at about the same level of accuracy, what will happen if one pairs a *trained* and an *untrained* animal? According to simple rules of chance, the untrained partner in time should learn the discrimination almost as well as his expert companion. If that were indeed the result, one would have a situation in which one animal automatically teaches another, even though pupil and teacher have no direct contact.

Suppose that one begins with two pigeons. The teacher-bird already has been trained in the matching task. Its performance can be assumed to have reached fairly high accuracy, say 90 percent. The pupil has had a certain amount of preliminary training but is unaware of red-green color discrimination, the essential of the matching-to-sample task.

To understand the outcome of an alliance between feathered teacher and pupil, we should remember that the probability of reinforcement of both partners is always equal. If they are rewarded, it is always on the same trial. The only prerequisite for reward is their agreement. The probability of both birds responding the same way on any particular trial is 50 percent.

Rules of Chance

Agreement, which brings the reinforcing reward, occurs when both birds respond correctly *or* when both birds make an error. The chance of agreement on any trial is the sum of the odds of both birds making an error and the odds of both birds matching correctly. And the odds that both birds will make a mistake on the same trial is the product of the two independent probabilities: the possibility that each pigeon will make an error separately.

The trained bird mismatches, on the average, in 10 percent of all trials; the untrained bird, responding at random, in 50 percent of all trials. Thus, the combined odds that both birds will err and receive a reward is $1/10 \times 5/10 = 5/100$ or 5 percent. By the same rule, the chance that both birds will respond correctly on the same trial and be reinforced is $9/10 \times 5/10 = 45$ percent.

Note that in the case of the trained bird—as well as the untrained one—the probability of being rewarded for a correct match is 45 percent, compared to a previous probability of 50 percent before the reward-for-agreement arrangement went into effect. This represents a decrease of only 5 percent, hardly enough to make a difference.

It is true that the birds also will be rewarded whenever both mismatch colors. But the rise in expected payoff frequency from zero to 5 percent for incorrect responses is unlikely to lead to a deterioration in the performance of the trained bird. Moreover, the reward probability of 45 percent for correct matches, in combination with a reward probability of 5 percent for incorrect ones, will lead to the formation of color discriminations in the untrained bird.

An attempt to explain or support these assertions would take us up to our necks in technicalities about intermittent reinforcement and discrimination. It may be granted, however, as quite plausible that 45 percent to 5 percent, or a 9 to 1 ratio in favor of correct responses for both birds, is very likely to lead to a better-than-chance performance by the untrained bird.

The picture is even brighter than the figures above indicate, because the ratios do not take *learning* into consideration. As the untrained bird begins to match at a better-than-chance level, the possibility of both birds agreeing on a mismatch decreases, further enhancing the prediction that the pupil will learn from the teacher (see Table 1).

TABLE 1

Matching Performance of an Untrained Pigeon Pair

	Trained Bird	Untrained Bird	Agreement	Ratio
Errors	10%	50%	5%	9/1
Matches	90%	50%	45%	
Errors	20%	40%	8%	6/1
Matches	80%	60%	48%	
Errors	30%	30%	9%	5.4/1
Matches	70%	70%	49%	
Errors	30%	40%	12%	3.5/1
Matches	70%	60%	42%	
Errors	20%	30%	6%	9.2/1
Matches	80%	70%	56%	
Errors	20%	25%	5%	12/1
Matches	80%	75%	60%	

Increasing the Odds

It appears that the chance that an untrained bird will learn to match depends very much on the error frequencies of the partners when they are first teamed. There are two ways by which one can greatly increase the odds in favor of learning to match.

First, the trainer should have a very low error frequency. He should be a competent bird. An error score of 1 percent, combined with the 50–50 score of an untrained bird, produces a probability of only 0.5 percent that both birds will mismatch on the same trial.

Second, there is no reason at all why other trained animals cannot be added to the fray. A combination of two trained birds, each with an error frequency of 10 percent, and an untrained bird that responds at chance level, leads also to the probability of 0.5 percent that all three birds will err on the same trial ($10/100 \times 10/100 \times 50/100$).

Perhaps we can assume that any animal inspector in a factory would be well trained. If so, then the odds of two inspectors agreeing are very high indeed, and this implies a high payoff frequency. It is desirable to cut such a high probability of reinforcement by 50 percent, and that can be done by never rewarding the animal who responds first. This may not seem fair, but at least it cannot produce jealousy, since pigeon participants do not know the rules of the game. (Strong believers in fair-employment practices may be assuaged by the fact that the chance of being first to respond can be made the same for all of the members of a team.)

If I have gone to great lengths to show that it is

possible to use pigeons as quality-control inspectors, it is not because I expect anyone to hire a pigeon. I want only to defend the honor of a loyal subject that has cooperated patiently during endless sessions of experiments in many a university laboratory.

Pigeons and People

Is it possible to apply to human behavior these observations about pigeons who peck on glass windows? How does the loyal and patient pigeon compare with a child in a similar task? The most important and obvious difference is language. The ability to communicate verbally makes it possible to skip many of the steps that must be taken in teaching a task to a nonverbal pupil.

From this, one might conclude that the proverbial superiority of men over animals lies not in man's ability to handle abstractions or to form concepts, but in his capacity to engage in symbolic behavior, particularly to use language. The Aristotelian question about whether, by means of special techniques, animals could be taught to speak (to behave symbolically) in my opinion is still open.

It is the unique aspect of an arrangement in which one pigeon teaches another and in which any reward is based upon agreement that leads me to speculate about socialization and cultural transmission. Would it be fair to say that, in an experiment where an untrained bird learned to match colors by agreeing with a trained bird, the trained pigeon functions as the socializing agent of the other? Perhaps socialization as a basic process of social interaction can be studied artificially in the laboratory with pigeons. Surely this is going too far! Aside from purely emotional objections to the idea, there must be many rational ones. Human socialization obvi-

ously differs in many ways from what goes on between pigeon teams.

For example, in the case of the pigeons, neither pupil nor teacher is in any way aware of what he is doing or what is being done to him. But then, many of us are not much more knowledgeable than pigeons when it comes to acute awareness of social forces. People function quite adequately, first as victims and later as agents of socialization.

A more important difference is that the pigeons are never in face-to-face contact. Ever since Charles H. Cooley made the distinction between primary and secondary groups nearly sixty years ago, socialization usually has been considered something peculiar to the former. Cooley defined primary groups as those characterized by intimate face-to-face associations and cooperation.

If one concedes that the matching-to-sample skill acquired by the untrained pigeon in the reinforcement-through-agreement arrangement is at least a rudimentary form of socialization, then it seems that face-to-face contact is not necessary. An arrangement where neither party sees the other, but where agreement is a prerequisite to reward, appears both sufficient and necessary.

Within the human family, our best example of a primary group member with a socializing function is the parent who rewards or punishes, depending on whether the behavior of his children is similar to his own repertoire. At the same time, he is only an intermediary, acting on orders and according to rules or norms set up by others outside the immediate family, or by cultural tradition he has been trained to accept. I have a feeling that the relationship of the trained pigeon to the experimenter is painfully similar.

Of Mice and Misers
Edmund Fantino

One of the justifications for the study of animal behavior is that it will ultimately verify the dynamics of human behavior. The acquisition of wealth and the phenomenon of the miser have fascinated not only writers such as Molière but also behavioral scientists. Gordon Allport has postulated that certain traits, like the acquisition of money, originally satisfy basic needs but that eventually the behavior continues unmotivated by obvious rewards—in psychological terminology, it becomes functionally autonomous. Edmund Fantino examines Allport's theory of functional autonomy and finds, through experimentation, that the concept is unnecessary to account for persistent behavior patterns in mice, rats, pigeons, and chimps.

As long as there has been money there have been misers. And almost as long as there have been misers there have been people—even kings—scrutinizing them. "Misers are very kind people: they amass wealth for those who wish their death," said Stanislaus I, eighteenth-century king of Poland. Hidden behind the elegant Polish irony of his aphorism is a psychological mystery.

The miser poses two questions for psychology. The first, and easier, question is, "How did he get that way?" Why and when did the miser begin the money-hoarding behavior that we find so reprehensible, unless, of course, we will benefit from his "kindness"? In some cases, the answer may be that he learned his thrifty habit in hard financial times; in other cases, the cause may be considerably more obscure. However, in this Freudian age we can surely accept the tenet that some experience or set of events in the individual's history has predisposed him toward this abnormal behavior.

Some experiments with rats make the point rather nicely: young rats frustrated by food deprivation will become hoarders. Later on, these rats continue to hoard food significantly more often than rats without a history of frustration. The persistence of the behavior indicates

a long-term effect. Similarly with the miser. He acquires his characteristic behavior in the same manner as the rest of us, by lawful interaction with his environment.

The second and knottier question is, why does the miser's behavior persist, even when the environmental conditions that gave rise to it are no longer present? There are two possibilities. One is that, contrary to appearances, the environment is indeed providing rewards and punishments that are maintaining the behavior. The second is that behavior can persist even when it is not maintained by rewards or punishments. If that is true—if there is evidence that behavior is independent of rewards in even a small way—then we have a principle of fundamental importance to an understanding of man and to the science of psychology.

Before accepting such a principle, however, we must examine very carefully the empirical evidence on which it rests.

Means into Ends?

One principle that might account for the miser is that of *functional autonomy*. "Activities and objects that earlier in the game were means to an end," said Gordon Allport when he formulated the concept, "now become ends in themselves." Or, in a later exposition, "What was once extrinsic and instrumental becomes intrinsic and impelling." In other words, behavior that has often led to reward may become rewarding *in itself*, even though it is no longer a mechanism for achieving the old reward. Robert S. Woodworth of Columbia University expressed the same idea in 1918, when he suggested that "the mechanism becomes the drive."

But before we conclude that an activity has become autonomous in relation to the conditions that gave rise to it, we must rule out any more parsimonious explanations. To illustrate, let us abandon the miser for a moment and consider the hunter. We might assume that the hunter hunts in order to gain the biological reward of food. Next, assume that the hunter becomes affluent and begins to discard his prey, but continues to hunt. Has hunting behavior acquired functional autonomy? Can we conclude that it is no longer a way of satisfying a biological need and, in Woodworth's terminology, that the mechanism (hunting) for obtaining a biological reward (food) has now become a self-sustaining "drive"?

Not necessarily. It might be, for example, that the hunter would hunt before hunting produced food—that the behavior began in response to some other biological or primitive need, such as a need to be aggressive, and that need is what maintains the behavior.

Before applying Allport's doctrine to the hunter, I suggest that we would have to demonstrate the following:

1. Hunting behavior does not originate when it does not produce food.
2. When food is available as a reward, hunting behavior originates and persists.
3. When the biological reward of food is no longer available, hunting behavior continues indefinitely, though not necessarily with the same frequency as before.
4. No apparent need (such as a need to be aggressive) has emerged since hunting began that is strong enough to explain the persistence of hunting behavior.

Points 1 and 2 would allow us to conclude that hunting behavior was established in response to the need for food; points 3 and 4 would show that the behavior had become autonomous of reward.

Demonstrating these things is necessarily difficult, particularly when considering that human behavior is influenced by a complex set of controlling variables. In order to approach the problem of functional autonomy, therefore, studies have been performed using subhuman organisms in apparently straightforward experimental designs. Of course, evidence based exclusively on lower animals should not be uncritically extrapolated to human behavior. (Allport himself distinguished among varieties of autonomous behavior and insisted that some

were exclusively human.) But experimental evidence should offer some insight into how the analysis of "autonomous" human behavior might proceed and should establish guidelines for an appraisal of the miser.

Sand-digging Mice

Two experiments in the animal literature have been used often and authoritatively as support for the concept of functional autonomy. One involves sand digging in mice; the other, ear scratching in rats. The study on sand digging in mice was done by Robert Earl at Stanford University in 1957. Earl discovered that mice that had learned to dig *nine pounds* of sand in order to reach a reward box containing food continued to dig nine pounds of sand even when food was no longer rewarding—that is, when the mice were not hungry. Earl remarked that the sand had developed an "invitational character"; others suggested that here was a perfect example of functional autonomy.

Michael Cole and I, then colleagues at Yale, decided to look into this phenomenon a bit further. We were interested in the implications of Earl's results for the doctrine of functional autonomy, but we were even more intrigued by the Herculean behavior the mice had displayed. We put thirteen mice, eighty days old at the start of the experiment, through their paces, using apparatus similar to Earl's (see Figure 1).

A mouse was placed in the digging compartment or start box. A rubber tube containing sand led from the start box to the reward box. As the mouse dug the sand out of the tube, it fell through the wire-mesh floor of the apparatus into a bucket, and more sand dropped into the tube from a jug located over a hole in the top of the tube. When the mouse had removed all the sand, it could walk through the tube to the reward box. As the mouse entered the box, a photocell beam stopped a time meter, giving us an automatic measure of how long the mouse took to dig through the sand. (Although watching mice dig is fun at first, it turns out to have little "invitational character.") The amount of sand dug was weighed after each session, and the digging rate recorded in grams per minute.

We gave our mice preliminary training by depriving them of food for twenty hours and by allowing them to explore the empty sand tube. For seven mice (Group 1), we placed food in the reward box, as Earl had. For the other six mice (Group 2), the reward box did not contain food. The amount of sand in the sand jug was gradually increased over a twenty-five-day period from 0 to 4,300 grams, or about nine pounds. Each mouse was put in the sand tube every day and left there until it had dug through all the sand and entered the reward box, where it was permitted to remain for fifteen minutes. On those few occasions when the mouse did *not* dig all the sand, it was removed from the digging compartment after two hours.

After these preliminary sessions, we conducted the

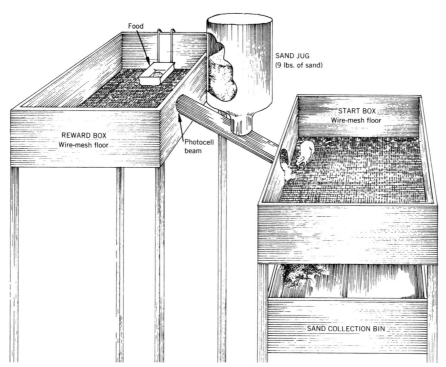

Figure 1. The sand-digging experimental setup.

experiment proper. It included three stages: fourteen sessions under strong (twenty-hour) food deprivation; eleven sessions during which food was always available in the home cages, so that the mice were not hungry; and twenty-seven sessions again under strong (twenty-hour) food deprivation. During the first and second stages, food was available in the reward box for Group 1 but not for Group 2; during the third stage, it was available in the reward box for Group 2 but not for Group 1.

There was a large range of digging rates. One mouse that was not receiving a food reward dug at an average rate of twelve grams per minute; two mice that were receiving food rewards dug at about one hundred grams per minute. But *every mouse did dig*, whether there was food in the reward box or not.

Our second finding was that hunger and the availability of food in the reward box both influenced the digging rate. Mice dig faster when there is a food reward available, and they also dig faster when they are hungry. One mouse dug at an average rate of fifty-four grams per minute when hungry, even though no reward was offered. In the next stage of the experiment, when this mouse was not hungry, its digging rate slipped to twenty-five grams per minute. In the third stage, when the mouse was hungry and food reward was available, its digging rate leapt to 109 grams per minute. It took this mouse less than forty minutes to dig nine pounds of sand—more than 200 times its own weight!

Three additional mice were also studied, using a different procedure. For these mice, food was always available in the home cage. In addition, food and water were placed in the start box, and there was no reward at all in the reward box. Nonetheless, when these mice were offered the opportunity to dig sand and gain access to the empty reward box, all three of them eventually dug nine pounds. Two dug at the rates of thirty-eight and seventy grams per minute, well within the range established by the other mice. Stable measurements for the third mouse were not obtained. Soon after it first dug nine pounds, this mouse was found buried in the sand; apparently it had dug itself to death.

Thus mice dig sand whether or not digging produces food. There is no need to invoke the concept of functional autonomy to explain Earl's results or our own. The "invitational character" that Earl referred to appears not to have "developed" with rewarded digging, but to have been present from the start.

Ear-scratching Rats

In discussing the hunter, I stressed the need to ascertain whether hunting behavior would begin and continue before hunting produced food. The studies with mice show why this is important. It is unlikely, though, that a miser would hoard money before its reward value had been established. Our next study, therefore, concerns a habit clearly acquired in response to environmental change.

In 1929, Willard Olson reported an experiment in which he placed the irritant collodion on rats' ears. The rats, he discovered, scratched their ears for several weeks after the collodion application, even though the evidence of tissue irritation had vanished. William Datel and John Seward of UCLA did a more elaborate version of Olson's study in 1952 and reported similar results. These studies have been widely cited as examples of functional autonomy by several authorities, including Allport himself in 1961.

J. J. Braun and I, together with two Yale seniors, William Vollero and Bruce Bradley, decided to investigate this persistent behavior a bit further, with greater attention to the possibility that tissue damage might explain the persistent ear scratching. We also continued the experiment for a longer period of time than either Olson or Datel and Seward had, in order to see whether ear scratching would return eventually to pre-collodion levels.

We used four groups of eight rats each. One group was never treated with collodion; the other three groups were administered three different concentrations of the chemical, so that the degree of irritation—and, we hoped, the amount and persistence of ear scratching—would vary.

Ear scratching did increase dramatically on the four days when collodion was applied, and the stronger the concentration was, the more scratching the rats did (see Figure 2). More than two weeks after the last application, the two groups of rats that had received the strongest concentrations were still scratching at a higher rate than they had before collodion was applied.

Up to the twenty-fifth day of the experiment, our results were similar to those obtained by previous workers, except that we used more than one collodion

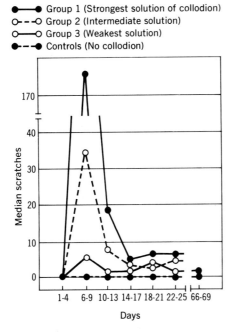

● ● Group 1 (Strongest solution of collodion)
○ - - ○ Group 2 (Intermediate solution)
○ ● Group 3 (Weakest solution)
● - - ● Controls (No collodion)

Figure 2. Observations of ear scratching in mice treated with collodion over a period of 69 days.

application. Previous workers, however, did not continue their experiments. When we observed our rats later on, at days 66–69, the scratching had virtually disappeared in all groups. (The very slight scratching by the first group was not statistically significant.) Thus the "persistent" habit eventually ends.

In addition to recording the ear-scratching rates each day, an observer (Bradley or Vollero) examined the rats' ears daily for signs of tissue irritation. The observer was not told whether an ear had been treated with collodion or not. He was asked simply to judge whether either ear showed signs of irritation (redness, wrinkled skin, scabs, or residual collodion) and if so, which one.

Our most important finding concerned these blind judgments of tissue irritation. The groups that persisted in ear scratching (Groups 1 and 2) were also reliably judged as having irritated ears. The four rats in each group were judged every day for sixteen days (days 10–25)—a total of 128 judgments per group. For Group 1, the treated ear was judged as irritated all 128 times; for Group 2, 126 times; in neither group was an untreated ear ever judged as treated. In Group 3, which had received the mildest concentration of collodion and did relatively little scratching, the ears were occasionally judged to have visible tissue irritation. The untreated rats in Group 4 were never judged as treated. In other words, persistent ear scratching was always accompanied by visible irritation.

So ear scratching does persist for a substantially longer time than the collodion application that gave rise to the behavior, but an interpretation based on functional autonomy is unnecessary. The behavior may be "autonomous" in relation to the stimulus narrowly defined as collodion application, but it is not autonomous in relation to the stimulus defined, broadly and properly, as collodion application and the irritation that follows. The persistence of ear scratching is a simple function of the persistence of stimulation, a finding that points up the need to define stimulus conditions with care.

Grain-gobbling Pigeons

We have reviewed two studies used to support the doctrine of functional autonomy and two similar studies from our laboratory that indicate the support is unwarranted. Are we to conclude that autonomous behavior never occurs? A third series of experiments, done in collaboration with Kurt Fischer of Harvard (at the time, a student of mine at Yale) sheds some light on this question.

In the first stage of these experiments, Fischer observed two pigeons for two or three hours each on over fifty occasions. The procedure was to place the hungry pigeon in a box and allow it to peck at a key that occasionally yielded a food reward. The rewards were substantial, and the pigeon rapidly became satiated. As its hunger diminished, so did its pecking rate. It pecked about once a second at the start of the session but only about once a minute at the end. This orderly decline occurred in every session. (Other procedures demonstrated that it was indeed the level of hunger and not the length of the session that brought about the decline.)

The question was, what would happen if the pigeon were fed to its satiated weight before it was placed in the box? If the pecking rate depended only on how hungry the pigeon was, a full pigeon would not peck at a high rate to obtain food; it would peck at the very low rate characteristic of the end of a session. Therefore, in the next stage of the experiment, we gave the pigeon enough food one hour before each session to bring its weight to the level that was usual *after* a session.

But both our pigeons pecked diligently and ate heartily nonetheless. Their pecking rates in the first test session were comparable to their rates when hungry, and in the course of the session, one pigeon ate half its usual amount and the other slightly more than its usual amount. The first bird, apparently aware of Victorian and ancient Roman dining customs, actually regurgitated during the third session, the only time we have seen a pigeon do so!

The pigeons' behavior did, then, become autonomous of their needs, and the same type of phenomenon might well occur in human behavior. Suppose a man is used to eating at home every evening at seven. Then one night he eats with a business colleague at six. If he returns home at seven, just as his family is sitting down to dinner, he may have a "second supper"—behavior that is autonomous of the state of his stomach.

However, the autonomy of our pigeons' behavior was short-lived. By the fourth or fifth session, the pre-fed pigeons pecked at a rate more characteristic of the end of the earlier sessions. It appears that the pigeons developed a response pattern appropriate to a certain level of hunger, and this pattern persisted for some time after the hunger level had changed. Their behavior seemed to become at least partly autonomous of hunger, but the autonomy was transitory.

If we now return to the world of humans and ask for experimental laboratory demonstrations of functional autonomy in human beings that satisfy the four criteria mentioned earlier, to my knowledge none emerge. Consider, for example, the many experiments with children and with chimpanzees that have been based on token rewards. Tokens, when they can be exchanged for such things as candy (children) and grapes (chimps), do become rewarding, and chimps will work to obtain tokens that they can use later to get food from a "chimp-o-mat" vending machine. But the reward value of the token is eventually extinguished when the child or chimp can no longer use it to obtain a reward. As with our pigeons, whatever autonomy the tokens acquire is temporary.

The Miser's Chimp-O-Mat

Is there a concept other than functional autonomy that will account for the miser? In my opinion, the miser's behavior persists because it continues to be, from time to time, rewarded; that is, the miser's situation is similar to that of a chimp who has access to a chimp-o-mat.

Food, just one of the many rewards for which money can be exchanged, makes a good example. A person sometimes exchanges money for food at a restaurant, when he is hungry. Or he may shop for a week's food supply at some time when he is not hungry. This variation in food-buying habits is important because it is a well-documented finding that behavior becomes more persistent and durable when it is coupled with reward under a variety of circumstances. Since money can be exchanged for a great many different rewards under a great many different circumstances, money itself should become a quite powerful and robust reward, and its reward value should be extremely *resistant to extinction*. Even if the miser were continually thwarted (say, when his money had been rendered worthless by inflation or revolution), we would expect his behavior to persist for a long time.

But, of course, the miser is not thwarted in his efforts to exchange money. He does buy essentials; he occasionally obtains rewards that give the reward value of money a boost. So it is not surprising that hoarding behavior persists throughout the miser's lifetime. The question of its eventual extinction is unanswerable, because the subject dies before the experiment is over.

There may be many different types of miser, and perhaps not all may be accounted for in the same way. But an analysis like the one sketched out above has an important advantage over explanations based on such principles as functional autonomy: it is consistent with empirical evidence about behavior. Indeed, the experimental work summarized here strongly suggests that functional autonomy is a concept that does not survive experimental scrutiny.

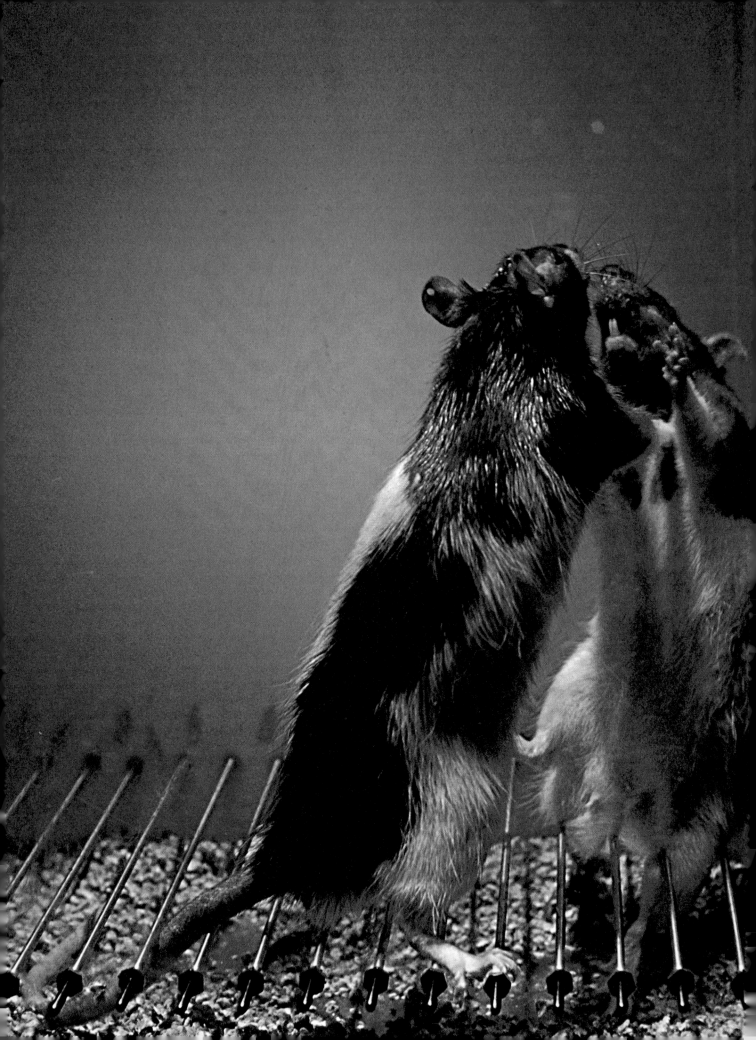

Pain and Aggression

Nathan Azrin

The scientific community's interest in the basis of aggression is evidenced by the recent publication of such books as Konrad Lorenz's On Aggression, *Robert Ardrey's* Territorial Imperative, *and Desmond Morris'* The Naked Ape. *Azrin, a psychologist, conducts experiments that differ from those of the three zoologically oriented authors. Employing operant conditioning techniques, Azrin presents a series of studies on the production and control of aggressive behavior in animals. He examines the role of pain in initiating aggression and the means of preventing aggression.*

With the advent of nuclear weapons and man's power to annihilate himself along with much of the planet's "thin film of life," the behavior we call "aggression" is of more than academic interest. Sooner or later any debate on the possibility of a warless world turns into a debate on whether aggression in man is based on nature or nurture. Recent books, such as *On Aggression* by Konrad Lorenz, that generalize animal behavior to man arouse unusually heated controversy in which one may detect overtones of "Tain't so," or "I told you so," depending on whether the debater views man as but little lower than the angels, or but little higher than the apes.

In fact, however, we know very little about aggression. What do we mean when we speak of "aggressive behavior"? Warning? Threat? Attack? Predation? What kinds of stimuli produce an "aggressive" response? Can we scientifically measure the amount or intensity of aggression?

For many years experimental psychologists have used the operant conditioning procedures developed by Skinner and extended by others to study various animal behaviors—particularly learning—under carefully controlled laboratory conditions. These conditioning techniques are based on the principle that behavior can best be studied when it is analyzed in terms of the following question: Under what conditions will there be a change in the frequency of an observable, measurable bit of behavior? The "bit of behavior" is called a "response," the occurrence of which is largely controlled by *reinforcement*. In *positive reinforcement*, a given response increases in frequency if it is followed by a reward, such as food for a hungry animal. In *negative reinforcement*, a given response increases in frequency if it is followed by the termination of an aversive event, such as electric shock applied to an animal's feet. By using only measurable units of behavior, the occurrence of which can be controlled through various procedures and schedules of reinforcement, the experimentalist need not depend on intellectual constructs such as "instinct" or "intention" as explanations for behavioral processes.

Serendipity

More than thirty years ago Lawrence O'Kelly and Lynde Steckle studied the "escape" behavior of rats by delivering an electric shock to their feet through an electrified floor-grid in the cage. They found that a single rat, alone in the cage, would attempt to escape or would "freeze" into immobility. But if a group of rats were shocked, they immediately began attacking one another, lunging, striking, and biting. However, since attempts by others to reproduce these results were only partly successful, there were no further tests of the puzzling report that foot-shock made rats "emotional."

About five years ago, at the Anna Behavior Research Laboratory, we were trying to see if negative reinforcement (escape from shock) could be used instead of positive reinforcement (food) in teaching two rats to interact with each other. Our plan was to increase the intensity of shock to their feet slowly until the rats happened to move toward each other, at which moment the shock would be abruptly stopped. By gradually changing the degree of proximity required to terminate the shock, we thought that the rats would learn to approach each other as a means of escaping the unpleasant shocks. Instead, much to our surprise, the rats violently attacked each other as soon as the shock became painful and before the experimenter had time to terminate it. This behavior did not occur all the time or with all rats, but so disruptive were these scrambling, attacklike episodes when they did occur, that we had to abandon our original objective.

Our interest was now aroused in this seeming relation between pain (foot-shock) and attack. Was the attack merely the result of random, agitated movements causing accidental collisions between the rats, or could we produce this shock-attack behavior whenever we wished? Was it produced only by foot-shock, or would other types of shock or aversive events produce it also? Was it an all-or-none reaction? Was it learned or innate? How was it affected by hunger? Did it occur only with male rats? Would it have occurred if the rats had lived peaceably together since infancy? Would it eventually die out as the rats became accustomed to the shock? Was such shock-attack behavior peculiar to rats alone—was it "species-specific," as is their well-known tendency to crawl into a hole? My colleagues, Roger Ulrich, Don Hake, Ronald Hutchinson, and I embarked on a series of studies to explore this seeming relation between pain and aggression or, more precisely, between shock and attack.

Measuring the Attack

Our first task involved "identification" and "quantification" of what we wished to study, so that our investigation would be orderly and disciplined, and so that other researchers could test our results by repeating our experiments exactly. We had, therefore, to define what we meant by "pain" and "aggression," and find ways of measuring them. To define and measure pain was easy: we knew that it was produced by electric shock, and that we could measure its intensity by the intensity of the shock. Our major problem was that of defining "aggression" and measuring its intensity or amount. The phenomenon we had observed was that of attack—but to identify it seemed impossible in the beginning, as we observed the rapid and seemingly random actions of the rats. But closer observation and slow-motion pictures showed that there were elements of consistency. Immediately upon receiving the shock, a rat would stand erect on its hind legs, face another rat, open its jaws so that the front teeth were clearly visible, and make physical contact with the other by striking with its forepaws.

This posture and these movements were observed only when another rat was present; otherwise a shocked rat held its jaws sufficiently closed so that the teeth were not visible, and usually kept all four feet on the floor. The posture and movements of a shocked rat in the presence of another rat were distinctive enough so that observers could be reasonably definite in judging that a particular episode constituted an attack. Each of these attack episodes lasted for about one second; the best method for quantifying the attack seemed to be a simple counting of the number of attack episodes.

Getting Down to Cases

Our first objective was to see if there was a relation between the intensity of the shock (pain) and the degree of aggression (number of attacks). Was it, we wondered, an all-or-none reaction, occurring in full intensity whenever some pain threshold was reached, and not at all below that threshold; or would the number of attacks increase as the shock-produced pain intensified? It turned out that there was a direct relation between the intensity, duration, and frequency of the shock and the amount of aggression—and this was limited only by the physical incapacity of the rat at high shock-intensities. As experimentalists, we were especially surprised and gratified to find that at optional shock-intensities, an attack accompanied almost every shock; having identified the appropriate stimulus conditions, we could produce this complex attack-response in almost "push-button" fashion.

We found, too, that the rats did not adapt to the shock; its effect did not wear off, and the rats continued to attack—sometimes to the extent of several thousand a day—as long as we delivered the shocks. This demonstrated that the attack was not a startle-response to a novel stimulus, but was a strong and enduring reaction.

But was it innate or learned? That is, had our rats learned, through association with other rats, to respond with attack to painful events or threatening situations? If so, then rats that had been isolated from other animals from infancy on would not display the shock-attack response. Not so. Social isolation did reduce the number of attacks somewhat but did not eliminate them. We found, too, that rats that lived together attacked one another just as often as rats that had been caged separately. Sexual competition or attraction was not involved in the reaction either; for males and females attacked members of the opposite sex or members of the same sex. Nor was this a predatory reaction, for hunger did not appreciably affect the number of attacks. We concluded at this point, therefore, that the shock-attack response is a reflexlike reaction in which a specific stimulus (pain) produces a fairly stereotyped response (aggression), which is relatively independent of normal learning experiences.

Rats Are Not the Only Ones

Now we wanted to find out if this shock-attack response is confined to rats or whether it is widespread in the animal kingdom. In other words, how far could we generalize our findings with regard to this particular psychological process?

First, we found that this response occurred in many different strains of rats. Then we found that shock produced attack when pairs of the following species were caged together: some kinds of mice, hamsters, opossums, raccoons, marmosets, foxes, nutrias, cats, snapping turtles, squirrel monkeys, ferrets, red squirrels, bantam roosters, alligators, crayfish, amphiumas (an amphibian), and several species of snakes including the boa constrictor, rattlesnake, brown rat snake, cottonmouth, copperhead, and black snake. The shock-attack reaction was clearly present in many very different kinds of creatures. In all the species in which shock produced attack it was fast and consistent, in the same push-button manner as with the rats. In testing other species, however, we found that the shock-attack reaction is not as easily generalizable as the above results might lead one to suppose. First, it does not reflect the general tendency to aggressiveness of a particular species; rather, it appears to be a special process. For example, many species that normally attack in their natural state frequently did not attack when shocked; fighting cocks and Siamese fighting fish are well known for their proclivity to attack members of the same species, yet shock not only failed to produce attack in either of these species but tended to suppress it.

Nor did shock produce attack in many other species known to attack under normal conditions: iguanas, skunks, rhesus monkeys, tarantulas, chickens, hawks (and several other species of birds), and fish, including the flesh-eating piranha. Further study may show that these animals failed to attack only because the experimenter failed to discover the condition that produces pain in these animals—a difficult task at best because different species vary greatly in sensory endowment. All we can say at this time is that the shock-attack reaction is present in a great variety of species, but we cannot as yet say that it is synonymous with aggressiveness in general.

Where shock did produce attack, we found that the reaction was not a stereotyped reflex—that is, each species attacked in its own distinctive way. The monkeys used their hands; several species slashed with their forepaws; the opossums hissed; and the snakes often hissed and sometimes encircled the target of their attack. But biting was common to all the attacks, and it appears that the aim of the attack is not merely to ward off or defend, but to injure or destroy, by whatever means the animal possesses.

Shocked Animals Are Not Choosy

Ethological studies of animals in their natural environment have demonstrated that many innate behavior patterns are "triggered" by specific physical characteristics of another animal. For example, the red, swollen belly of the female stickleback triggers courting behavior in the male. We wanted to find out, therefore, whether the shock-attack reaction is similarly related to specific physical attributes of the "target" or whether it is the expression of a general tendency to destroy. If the attack response to pain is triggered, then slight changes in the appearance of the target should change or eliminate the reaction. To test this, we conducted a long series of studies in which various animals were paired with target animals of a different species. For example, we shocked a rat caged with a target guinea pig, a raccoon with a rat, a monkey with a mouse, a monkey

with a rat, a rat with a rooster, and an opossum with a rat. In every instance, the shocked animal attacked the target, showing that the characteristics of the target animals are not relevant.

And this raised the question of whether, indeed, a live animal was needed; might not a model do as well? Stuffed dolls produced the same shock-attack reaction. Did the model have to be similar to an animal? We used the simplest geometric form, a sphere with no animal-like features—in actuality, a tennis ball. The animals attacked the tennis ball. It seems, therefore, that under the stimulus of pain, animals will attack and try to destroy almost any "attackable" object in the environment—animate or inanimate—regardless of its attributes.

Problems, Problems . . .

Though our studies had provided us with much information, they had also raised some serious methodological problems. First of all, the attack episodes had been identified and counted by a human observer; thus our results depended entirely on gross observation and subjective interpretation. And in the second place, the behavior of the target animal influenced the attacks. Attacked, the target animal often fought back, and in some cases the results were even more disconcerting. For example, often at the very first shock, the rat attacked the snake with which it was paired. But there was no second try, for the snake would fatally injure the rat. The selection of rats as our initial subjects was fortunate, since they usually do not inflict serious injury, but if we were to study more destructive animals, we would have to eliminate both counteraggression and the likelihood that one animal would destroy another.

The "Bitometer"

The discovery that pain would produce aggression against an inanimate object enabled us to solve both our problems, for it provided us with a means to record attack behavior objectively, and it allowed us to test the attack responses of very destructive animals. We suspended a tennis ball or other object from a cord that was attached to a switch. Whenever an animal struck or bit the ball, the switch closed and provided an output signal to a recording device. An even more direct and useful method of automatically recording attack was the "Bitometer"—a pneumatic tube that could be bitten by the shocked animal, giving us a direct measure of the number of bites as well as a measure of their duration and forcefulness. These and similar devices made it possible for us to study the shock-attack reaction of a single animal during many months, encompassing thousands of attack episodes, without injury to the subject or to the target, and eliminated the problems of counteraggression and reliance on human observers.

We developed a specialized apparatus for monkeys, and modified it for several other species. Restrained in a chair, yet permitted considerable freedom of movement, the monkey is positioned so that it faces the target—the Bitometer—and is maintained at a fairly close but fixed distance from it (see Figure 1). The Bitometer yields an output signal only if the monkey bites it; pulling, striking, or pushing it displaces too little of the enclosed air to produce an output. Since we had found that there is a direct relation between the intensity of the shock and the amount of aggression, we precisely controlled the intensity of the shock by fastening surface electrodes on the monkey's tail.

As Long As It Hurts . . .

Because electric shock is a novel experience for an animal, seldom if ever encountered in its natural state, we wondered whether the novelty of the stimulus, or perhaps the postural imbalance caused by foot-shock, might account for the attack reaction. Would attack be provoked by other painful stimuli? Shock delivered to rats and monkeys by means of surface or subdermal electrodes produced attack as before, eliminating postural imbalance as a cause; intense heat produced attack in rats; and a physical blow provoked it in monkeys. Clearly, it seems, attack is a reaction to many types of painful experience, and is not distinctively related to electric shock.

But is attack provoked only by events that produce physical pain, or might "psychologically" painful experiences have the same effect? For example, hungry pigeons have been trained to peck at a disk by reinforcing them with a few pieces of grain. Several observers have noted that when the reward for this response is abruptly stopped, the pigeon appears to become agitated. Might this abrupt shift from expected reward to no reward be psychologically painful enough to produce attack? We tested this possibility by exposing a hungry pigeon to this "frustrating" situation—with a target pigeon in a restraining box close by. The box was pivoted on a switch in such a way that if the target were attacked, the impact closed the switch and provided an

automatic measure of the attack. When the experimenters failed to reward the pigeon with the expected grain, the bird first made a flurry of vigorous attacks on the wall disk, and then turned around and with beak and wings attempted vigorously to attack the target bird. The same thing happened when a stuffed pigeon served as target. Because the recording procedure was completely automatic, we could study how the degree of hunger and the number of preceding rewards affected the amount of aggression.

This discovery that abruptly terminating a rewarding situation produces aggression greatly modified our view of the pain-attack reaction, for it provided experimental evidence to suggest that withdrawing reward is equivalent to physical pain. Thus attack will be precipitated by the psychological pain resulting from simple changes in the frequency of reward, as well as by physically painful events.

Since this sort of psychological pain seems to be more common in human experiences than are extremes of physical pain, these findings may help us understand some of the mechanisms that produce aggression in man. Being scolded, being fired from a job or expelled from school, losing a sexual partner, running out of gas, having one's allowance cut down or stopped, losing money to a vending machine, being thwarted by a stuck door—who has not experienced these noxious events and felt like kicking the door, taking a hammer to the vending machine, or just smashing the nearest thing?

Fight Versus Flight

"He who fights and runs away may turn and fight another day." How is the pain-attack reaction related to other effects of noxious stimuli, such as escape or avoidance? More simply, when does pain produce fight and when flight? To answer this question, rats and monkeys were exposed to a variety of procedures that provided them with a target for attack, as before, but that also made available a response that would allow them to escape or avoid the electric shock. The results

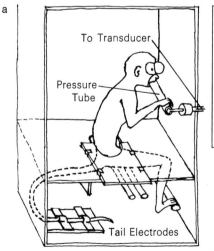

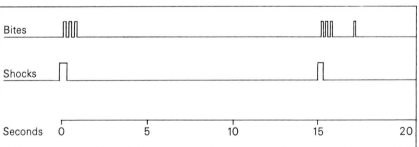

A Typical Bitometer Record

Figure 1. (a) Laboratory equipment designed to measure aggression automatically; the test box is equipped with a restraining chair and a Bitometer, which, when bitten, activates a recorder. Electrodes attached to the monkey's tail deliver electric shocks. (b) A typical Bitometer record.

all pointed in the same direction: the shocks produced attack only when the animals could not avoid them, because (1) no avoidance response was possible, (2) it was possible but not yet learned, or (3) the avoidance response was excessive. Once the rat or monkey learned that by pressing a lever he could avoid the shocks, the avoidance behavior (flight) was predominant, and the attacks (fight) took place only on those few occasions when a shock was delivered. Thus it appears that the attack reaction to pain can be eliminated by establishing effective avoidance behavior. Or, in everyday terms, it seems that pain-evoked aggression can be controlled or eliminated by establishing effective, peaceful means for avoiding the pain.

Aggression and Counteraggression

Attack need not be opposed to escape, however, as a reaction to pain; this is illustrated by the situation in which the aggressor inflicts injury on the target. For the injury causes pain to its victim, and this should lead to counteraggression—and the counteraggression will be rewarded if it eliminates the source of the initial pain. Counteraggression is thus analogous to pressing the lever that stops the shock. According to this analysis, then, counteraggression should be a very strong and quickly acquired reaction to aggression. We investigated this possibility by using the Bitometer as the target for monkeys to whom we delivered an electric shock; however, in these studies, the biting attack postponed the next shock. These monkeys learned almost immediately that biting was a way of avoiding shock, and their biting attacks did not decrease even when the shocks could no longer be avoided that way. When the pain-attack reaction is rewarded by escape from pain or avoidance of further pain, the two together produce strong and lasting counteraggression that continues even when the counteraggression no longer serves its original purpose. A vicious circle is formed that can be broken only by interpolating a nonaggressive means of escaping or avoiding pain.

The Urge to Kill

How flexible is this pain-attack reaction? Can it provide a means for teaching new behaviors? If not, we would have to consider it to be stereotyped and reflexlike, but if it could serve as the basis for acquiring new behaviors, this might explain the variations in the mode of attack. We explored this possibility in monkeys by using the appearance of an attack target as a reward. We put each monkey in a compartment without any target, and

then shocked him. Hanging nearby was a chain; if the monkey pulled the chain immediately after being shocked, a target appeared—the tennis ball. Did the monkey learn to pull the chain every time he was shocked, thus providing himself with a target for his aggression? Yes. This study confirmed our earlier findings that the pain-attack reaction is not stereotyped behavior. Rather, pain seems to create a changed state in the animal during which it is rewarding for him to injure or destroy.

What Does It All Mean?

What began as an accidental observation that some rats scrambled and attack one another upon receiving a painful electric shock has led to the discovery of a psychological relationship that has much greater generality than we could have anticipated. To sum up, these studies indicate that pain tends to provoke attack behavior (aggression) in many different species, and possibly in man as well. It is provoked both by physical and by psychological pain; it is directed at animate and inanimate parts of the environment; it can serve as the basis for learning new behaviors; and it can be eliminated by providing the animal with a nonaggressive means of escaping or avoiding pain. From the standpoint of evolution, pain-provoked aggression seems to have survival value, since it causes the animal to react instantly and vigorously to noxious events—and in a way that is likely to terminate them.

Aggression, like much other social interaction, is difficult to study with any exactitude. Because many individuals are usually involved, because the attacks are usually violent, brief, and quickly delivered, and because they can be manifested in a variety of ways, it has been difficult for human observers to agree as to what constitutes an act of aggression. Thus an important outcome of this study is the development of procedures for measuring and identifying aggression; valid automatic recording techniques can be used to quantify this important but complex social behavior, and to subject it to controlled laboratory analyses.

The discovery that pain provokes aggression and that the pain-attack reaction is not stereotyped or reflexive behavior is of major importance. Though it is but one of the many factors to be considered in analyzing aggression, it appears to be among the most amenable to laboratory study. If we can understand the many causes of aggression we may hope, eventually, to learn how to use it constructively for the further advance of our own species, rather than for our destruction.

Neural Basis of Memory
J. Anthony Deutsch

The psychological behaviorists, particularly the practitioners of operant conditioning, are essentially concerned with the external environmental control of behavior. They and the physiological psychologists frequently labor in isolated vineyards. With this extremely clever model of synaptic changes in memory, J. Anthony Deutsch furnishes a unique bridge between the behavioral studies of memory, especially the classic studies on massed and spaced memory practice, and neural function in learning.

At present the physiological basis of learning is unknown. We know that time alters the stability of memory, and this alteration presumably reflects in some way the underlying physical process. Many theories have been advanced to explain these changes, but only recently have discoveries been made that permit us to test the validity of the theories.

An old but still influential theory, put forward by an Italian physiologist, E. Tanzi, in 1893, postulates that the passage of nerve impulses causes some kind of physical change in the connections between nerve cells. The connections between the nerve cells, or neurons, are called synapses. While it is possible to show in the laboratory that the *functioning* of synapses can be affected by excessive use or disuse, these experiments do not show that changes occur in actual *learning*. A different kind of evidence is needed to show this, and I shall describe how such evidence has been obtained in some of my recent research.

We know that whatever changes produce the physical basis of memory, at least some of them must occur relatively slowly. Remarkable evidence for this comes from everyday accidents. For example, a person who has struck his head violently in an automobile accident may suffer from retrograde amnesia. He may be unable to remember what happened during the week before the accident, but he is able to remember what happened two weeks, two months, or two years before. The gap in memory covers a continuous stretch of time, with one end anchored to the time of the accident. As memories return, those most distant in time always return first.

This indicates that as a memory gets older it becomes more difficult to dislodge. So the physical change that underlies memory must alter slowly with time. If this change is an alteration in the *sensitivity* of a synapse, then it should be possible to show this by the use of drugs.

To understand how this can be done, we must briefly sketch what happens at a synapse when a message is transmitted from one nerve cell to another. The synapse is a microscopic gap (a few hundred angstroms, or less than a millionth of an inch) between adjacent neurons.

Inside the neuron itself a message is transmitted as an electrical impulse or disturbance. When this traveling electrical impulse reaches the synaptic region, it triggers the release of a chemical substance from vesicles at the end of the nerve cell. This chemical transmitter then travels across the narrow synaptic cleft to the receiving nerve cell. The chemical transmitter fits into certain sites on the second nerve cell as a key fits into a lock, mainly because the transmitter molecules have a specific size and shape.

The transmitter, it is believed, depolarizes the membrane of the receptor cell and initiates a new electrical impulse in the second neuron. The electrical impulse then travels along the neuron to the next synapse, triggering the release of a chemical transmitter, and so on (see Figure 1).

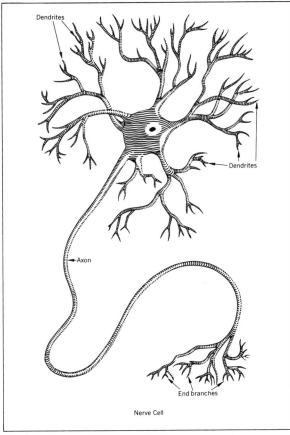

Figure 1. Neural pathway; a message travels along a nerve cell as an electrical impulse until it reaches the junction between the end branches of one neuron and the dendrites of another. At the synapse an electrical impulse triggers the release of a chemical transmitter.

There are many different types of synapses in the brain, and they may use different kinds of transmitters, such as acetylcholine or norepinephrine (a chemical related to adrenaline). One of the best understood synapses uses acetylcholine (ACh) as the transmitter. ACh is present in relatively high concentration throughout the central nervous system. One of the strange things about this transmitter is that when too much of it accumulates on the synaptic part of the receptor cell, the transfer of messages across that synapse is blocked. To prevent a breakdown in transmission across the synapse, ACh must be inactivated as soon as it has performed its function. This is accomplished by an enzyme called acetylcholinesterase (AChE), which rapidly destroys ACh after it has been ejected.

Interfering Drugs

There are two classes of drugs that interfere with synaptic activity, each in a distinctive way. One kind acts directly on the receptor nerve cells, while the other interferes with the destruction of the transmitter. The first kind is called the anticholinergic drugs, or blocking agents. These drugs fit into the same sites on the receptor nerve cells as does ACh. However, although these blocking agents fit into the same sites, they do not initiate an electrical impulse in the second neuron. In addition, these blocking agents are not rapidly destroyed by the enzyme AChE. This means that the drugs can put parts of receptor cells out of action. The larger the dose of a blocking agent, the more sites are inactivated. The effect of the blocking agent, then, is to subtract from the effectiveness of the transmitter ACh.

A number of blocking agents are found in plants. Scopolamine is found in henbane, whose effects were known to the ancient Greeks. In high doses, scopolamine is a nerve poison: it completely stops transmission across synapses. In lower doses it simply reduces the amount of transmission and can be used medicinally to relieve such disorders as stomach cramps. Atropine, another blocking agent, is found in the deadly nightshade or belladonna plant. In low doses, it is used to relieve muscular spasms and to dilate the pupil.

Drugs of the second kind that affect transmission across the synapse are the anticholinesterases, or inhibitors of the enzyme AChE. Since the function of AChE is to destroy the transmitter chemical ACh, inactivation of AChE will lead to an accumulation of ACh at the receiving sites of the synapse. As indicated previously, accumulation of too much transmitter at the receptor will block the synapse.

Another interesting effect of inhibitor drugs occurs when a neuron ejects too little transmitter to trigger an electrical impulse in the receptor cell. With the addition of the enzyme inhibitor, the transmitter is destroyed less rapidly and the amount of transmitter at the receptor cell builds up until it triggers an electrical impulse in that nerve cell.

This boosting effect is used in the medical treatment of myasthenia gravis, a disorder marked by progressive weakening of the muscles. A patient with this disorder may be unable to move, even though there is nothing physically wrong with his nerves or his muscles. The muscular weakness is caused by the release of too little ACh at the junction between nerve endings and muscles. By inactivating the enzyme that destroys the transmitter, enough of the transmitter can build up at the receptor sites to initiate muscle contraction, and paralysis disappears. However, the dose of the inhibitor drug is critical. If the dose is too large, too much of the transmitter will pile up at the receptor sites, causing a block, and paralysis will return.

Efficiency of Transmission

We therefore have drugs that enable us to track changes in the efficiency of transmission across a synapse. Blocking agents, or anticholinergics, can completely stop transmission when relatively small amounts of transmitter are released. Yet this same dose of a blocking agent should not interfere with transmission when the amount of transmitter is high. On the other hand, addition of drugs that inhibit the action of the enzyme AChE, which destroys the transmitter, should not hinder transmission when levels of the transmitter are low. In fact, enzyme inhibitors may even improve transmission in this situation. But when the level of transmitter is high, the same dose of inhibitor should block transmission because of the excessive build-up of transmitter at the receptor sites.

Another way of looking at this is to suppose that learning causes changes in the *sensitivity* of the receptor cell rather than changes in the amount of transmitter released. In some respects this is a more attractive explanation, but we will follow both interpretations in our guided tour of some of my laboratory experiments to discover the physical basis of learning.

In one set of experiments I studied the effect of drugs on learning in rats. A rat is placed in a maze on a mildly electrified grid. To escape from the electrical shock, the rat must choose whether to run into a lit alley or into a dark alley. If it runs into the lit alley it escapes the shock. If it runs into the dark alley the shock continues. It takes about thirty trials for a rat to learn to choose the lit alley. In these studies learning is defined as the ability to make ten correct decisions in a row.

After a number of rats have passed the learning test, they are put back into their cages. The rats are divided into several groups. Some are injected with a drug half an hour after the learning trials, others after one day, three days, seven days, or fourteen days. A control group does not receive any drugs. Although the rats receive their drug treatment at various times after learning, they all are tested at the same time interval after the drug injection.

It should be noted that the drug doses used in the experiments cause no apparent change in the rats' ability to learn. Groups of rats injected with the drug will later perform as well as untreated rats in learning tests.

When rats are injected with an inhibitor drug, such as diisopropyl fluorophosphate (DFP) or physostig-

mine, which inactivates the AChE enzyme that destroys the ACh transmitter in synapses, some interesting changes in memory occur.

Rats injected with the drug half an hour after the learning trials forget only a little. They take more trials to relearn the maze than rats from the control group, but require far fewer trials to learn than rats that have never been trained.

When rats are injected with the inhibitor drug one and three days after training, they show perfect retention of learning. But rats treated with the drug seven and fourteen days after training lose their memory of the training almost completely. A control group of rats not drug injected still remembers to choose the lit alley after seven or fourteen days (see Figure 2).

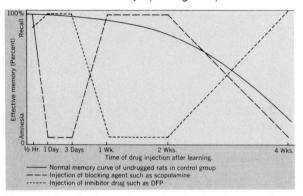

Figure 2. Results from rat experiments show how two types of drugs can each produce amnesia or recall, depending upon the time of injection after learning.

We might conclude that the inhibitor drug causes premature forgetting. However, this is too hasty a conclusion. If we retest undrugged rats four weeks after they have learned to run the maze, we find that they have forgotten which path to take. But if we then inject them with an inhibitor drug in the same dose as previously caused forgetting, the rats regain their memory almost perfectly. In this case, the injected drug could be called a "memory improver."

Experimental Conclusions

We know that the injected drug prevents the enzyme AChE in the synapse from destroying the chemical transmitter after it has been ejected. From these experiments we can draw the following conclusions. After one day, the amount of transmitter released in the synapse is relatively small (or we could say that the sensitivity of the receptor cell is low). At three days, the amount is still low, since injection of an enzyme inhibitor does not cause a pile-up of enough transmitter at the receptor sites to block the synapse. But at seven days, the amount of transmitter (or sensitivity of the receptor) rises and remains high even at fourteen days. Injection of the drug causes a pileup of transmitter at the receptor and blocks the synapse. After four weeks, the level of transmitter (or sensitivity of the receptor) has dropped to such a low point that the rat has forgotten the learned task. Injection of the drug, however, enables the small amount of transmitter still present to become effective and the rat regains its memory.

These conclusions can be cross-checked by repeating the experiments, this time with blocking agents—drugs that fit into the same sites on the receptor cell as the ACh transmitter. A blocking agent such as scopolamine should abolish memory where we have concluded that synaptic transmission is weak, and leave recall unaffected in cases where we suppose that transmission is high.

In repeating the experiment with scopolamine, we found that memory is unaffected by a drug injection half an hour after learning. But a drug injection one or three days later completely knocks out memory of what was learned. This is what we would predict on the basis of our previous conclusion that the synaptic transmission level is low at one or three days after learning. At seven and fourteen days, injection of scopolamine does not affect memory. This also confirms our interpretation that transmission is strong at seven and fourteen days.

We can check our conclusion that synaptic transmission gradually improves during the week after learning without the use of drugs. Rats are given only a small number of learning trials in a maze so that correct choices are only partially learned. The rats are divided into several groups. Each group is given a different waiting period—one day, three days, five days, and so on—before it is brought back to the maze. In this session, the rats are allowed to learn the task completely, and we count the number of trials they need to do so. We find, interestingly enough, that the rats who wait seven days before the second session learn with a much smaller number of trials than rats who are tested after one day or three days. This suggests that there is spontaneous strengthening of memory in rats a week after learning.

Temporary Memory Loss

If our theory is right, one of the things we can expect is that drug-induced disappearance of memory will be temporary. The action of the drug on the synapse should last only as long as the drug is present. And a number of experiments do show that memory returns when the effect of the drug wears off. There is also evidence that the inhibitor drugs, or anticholinesterases, do not completely inactivate the enzyme AChE in the dose strengths used in our experiments. It is likely that only a portion of the enzyme is inactivated and that the destruction of ACh transmitter is not halted but simply slowed down. If this is so, then the spacing of trials after the injection of the inhibitor should affect the degree of amnesia. If the trials are spaced farther apart, more transmitter should be destroyed between trials. Since too much transmitter at the receptor causes the block in the synapse, increased spacing of a well-learned

task should improve recall. And, indeed, it turns out that this is what happens. (See Figure 3.) In tests of drug-injected rats seven days after the learning session,

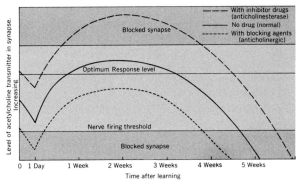

Figure 3. Synaptic transmission model. The middle curve shows changes in synapse after learning. The inhibitor drug (top curve) or blocking agent (bottom curve) can block transmission at certain times.

when the trials are spaced twenty-five seconds apart, the rats exhibit almost total amnesia. When the trials are set fifty seconds apart, the rats remember their learned task.

From the results of our experiments, it looks as if learning changes a synapse's ability to transmit messages. Our experiments consisted of a large number of trials, and each learning trial could have affected a different set of synapses. On the other hand, each trial could have affected the same set of synapses over and over again. We cannot observe changes in the synapses directly, even with an electron microscope. A typical synapse may measure as little as one millionth of an inch in size. There are millions of neurons in the nervous system and each neuron may have thousands of synapses on it. In the synaptic region the neurons are intricately intertwined, much like a mass of spaghetti. Detecting changes made by a single learning task is almost impossible. A major difficulty is finding a way to observe the same set of synapses before and after learning—a task similar to finding a needle in a haystack, except that in this case we are trying to find a specific piece of hay.

What Synapses Are Involved

Fortunately, we can again use drugs to determine whether learning affects the same set of synapses or a different set of synapses on each learning trial. If each trial increases the transmission across the same set of synapses, then the larger the number of learning trials (the more learned the habit), the greater the susceptibility of that learning to inhibitor blocking. Also, if the same set of synapses is affected by learning, then a small number of learning trials should produce weak transmissions and therefore memory will improve with injection of the inhibitor drugs.

On the other hand, if each learning trial simply

changes another set of synapses until enough synapses are altered to ensure correct performance, then the number of trials should not alter the susceptibility of the learned habit to blocking by an inhibitor drug. Each synapse will be altered in an all-or-nothing fashion, and each should be equally susceptible to the drug.

To test these two ideas, we trained three groups of rats. One group received 30 training trials, the second 70 trials, and the third 110 trials. The rats with only thirty trials could be considered undertrained. In their last ten trials, they chose the correct path only two out of three times. Five days later, half of the rats in each group were given a dose of diisopropyl fluorophosphate, a drug that inhibits the AChE enzyme. The undertrained group injected with the drug performed much better than their undertrained counterparts who were not given the drug. In their first ten trials, the drug-treated rats performed almost perfectly. Drugged and undrugged rats from the group with seventy trials performed identically. Overtrained rats (110 trials) injected with the drug, however, performed much worse than their undrugged counterparts, and even worse than the undertrained rats that had been drugged.

In other words a well-learned habit is blocked by injection of this drug, whereas recall of a poorly learned habit is improved. This indicates that the same set of synapses is stimulated more and more with each learning trial.

To show that the results had nothing to do with the number of trials but rather were concerned with the degree of learning, we performed another experiment in which the number of learning trials was the same for all rats. This was done by taking advantage of the rat's propensity to learn more quickly when the light in the safe alley of the maze is very bright. Groups of rats were given the same number of trials, but variations in the brightness of the light in the safe alley led to very different rates of learning. The group with a dim light had learned very little at the end of thirty trials, while a group with a very bright light had learned to make the right choice almost every time. Injection of the inhibitor drug produced the same results: the group with the well-learned habit forgot, the group with the poorly learned habit performed better.

This seems to confirm that the same set of synapses is affected as learning of the same task progresses. The same synapses are stimulated more and more with each trial. As a result of this stimulation, the synapse becomes gradually more efficient at passing messages. This increase in efficiency occurs without any apparent need for practice or repetition of the learned responses.

Transmission Efficiency

Our evidence supports the theory that the physical change underlying learning is the increase of transmission efficiency in a synapse. But our experiments do not provide enough information to decide whether the increased efficiency is caused by increased sensitivity in the receptor or increased amounts of transmitter in the synapse.

We can, however, set up an experiment that will identify the correct explanation. There is a class of drugs that mimics the transmitter action of acetylcholine. One of these drugs is carbachol (carbaminoylcholine), a very close chemical relative of ACh. Carbachol is strongly resistant to destruction by the AChE enzyme. When injected in low doses, carbachol acts together with ACh to excite the receptor nerve. Higher doses of carbachol will block memory. Results of research to date indicate that injections of carbachol will improve new memories but block older ones. When the amount of transmitter is small, the injected carbachol teams up with it to improve memory. When the memory is one week old, if we assume that the amount of transmitter increases, then it is hard to explain why the same dose of carbachol results in a blocked synapse. It is unlikely that the increased amount of transmitter would cause the block, because the transmitter would be destroyed at the normal rate by the AChE enzyme. A more likely explanation is that the receptor becomes more sensitive (requires less transmitter to become activated) and that the carbachol blocks synaptic transmission because it alone can now keep the sensitized receptor nerve cell depolarized, which prevents initiation of new electrical impulses in that neuron.

So, although we have good evidence that learning improves transmission across synapses that use ACh as a transmitter, the evidence that this improvement is caused by an increase in the sensitivity of the receptor is much more tentative.

These findings suggest that some human memory disorders may be due to a lowered efficiency in transmission across synapses, particularly those using ACh as the transmitter. If this proves to be the case, some memory disorders may be improved with relatively simple drugs. But in spite of the effect of our drugs on the memory of rats, we have discovered no memory pill. While one day such a drug might be developed, it is not likely to be one of those used in our research. All these drugs are potent poisons; their effects are mixed—they improve some memories while blocking others—and their effects are transitory. Seekers for a pill to end practice and study forever will have to look elsewhere.

IV
Motivation and
Biological Psychology

Chromosomes and Crime

Ashley Montagu

Scientists following the ethological tradition of Konrad Lorenz have concentrated their studies on genetically determined, stereotype behavior. American behavior geneticists have concentrated on the genetic control of more complicated, "higher" functions. In the tradition of both these schools, Ashley Montagu reports on investigations into the possible hereditary basis for criminal behavior. While this research is extremely controversial, it may ultimately offer biological insights into the dynamics of human society.

Are some men "born criminals"? Is there a genetic basis for criminal behavior? The idea that criminals are degenerates because of "bad genes" has had wide appeal.

Johann Kaspar Spurzheim and Franz Joseph Gall, the inventors of phrenology early in the nineteenth century, associated crime with various bumps on the head, reflecting the alleged structure of the particular region of the brain within. Later in the last century, Cesare Lombroso, an Italian criminologist, listed physical stigmata by which criminals might be recognized. Lombroso's marks of degeneration included lobeless and small ears, receding chins, low foreheads and crooked noses. These traits supposedly foretold a biological predisposition to commit crimes.

In more recent years, Earnest A. Hooton of Harvard and William H. Sheldon of New York claimed to have found an association between body type and delinquent behavior. These claims, however, were shown to be quite unsound.

Of all the tales of "bad blood" and "bad genes," perhaps the two most famous are those of the Jukes and the Kallikaks. The tale of the Jukes was first published in 1875 by Richard L. Dugdale, a New York prison inspector. In his report, "The Jukes: A Study in Crime, Pauperism, Disease, and Heredity," Dugdale covers seven generations, 540 blood relatives and 169 related by marriage or cohabitation. Although Dugdale did not invent the Jukes, he often fell back upon his imagination to bolster his theory of the hereditary causes of crime when the facts failed. When information about individuals was hard to come by, Dugdale resorted to characterizations as "supposed to have attempted rape,"

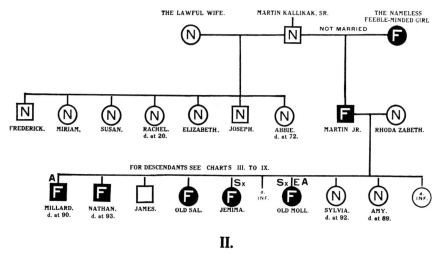

II.

Chart II.

N = Normal   F = Feeble-minded.   Sx = Sexually immoral   A = Alcoholic.   I = Insane.   Sy = Syphilitic.   C = Criminalistic.   D = Deaf.
d. inf. = died in infancy.   T = Tuberculous.

The good and the bad Kallikaks, from *The Kallikak Family* by Henry H. Goddard,
© Macmillan, 1912 (copyright renewed 1940 by Henry H. Goddard)

"reputed sheep-stealer, but never caught," "hardened character" and the like.

The Kallikaks were studied by Henry H. Goddard, director of a school for the mentally retarded in New Jersey. In his report, published in 1912, he followed the fortunes and misfortunes of two clans of Kallikaks. Both were descended from the same Revolutionary War soldier. The bad Kallikaks sprang from this soldier's union with a feeble-minded girl, who spawned a male so bad that he became known as "Old Horror."

"Old Horror" fathered ten other horrors, and they in turn became responsible for the hundreds of other horrible Kallikaks traced by Dr. Goddard. All of the good Kallikaks were descendants, of course, from the Revolutionary War soldier's marriage with a Quaker woman of good blood. Since none of the good Kallikaks seems to have inherited any "bad genes," something rather strange must have occurred in the lineage, for we know that a certain number of the good offspring should have shown some "degenerate" traits.

The Jukes and the Kallikaks are sometimes quoted as examples of what "good" and "bad" genes can do to human beings. While it is possible that a genetic defect may have been involved in some of these pedigrees, the disregard by the investigators of environmental effects renders their work valueless except for their quaint, anecdotal style of reporting.

Recently, the question of whether a man's genetic makeup may be responsible for his committing acts of violence has again come forward in the courts.

In France in 1968, Daniel Hugon was charged with the murder of a prostitute. Following his attempted suicide, he was found to be of XYY chromosomal constitution. Filled with remorse, Hugon had voluntarily surrendered to the police. His lawyers contended that

he was unfit to stand trial because of his abnormality.

The possible link between an XYY chromosomal constitution and criminals first came to light some years ago in a study of prison hospital inmates. In December 1965, Patricia A. Jacobs and her colleagues at Western General Hospital in Edinburgh published their findings on 197 mentally abnormal inmates undergoing treatment in a special security institution in Scotland. All had dangerous, violent, or criminal propensities.

Seven of these males were found to be of XYY chromosomal constitution, one was an XXYY, and another an XY/XXY mosaic. Since on theoretical grounds the occurrence of XYY males in the general population should be less frequent than the XXY type (the latter type occurs in some 1.3 out of 1,000 live births), the 3.5 percent incidence of XYY males in a prison population constituted a significant finding.

There is still too little information available concerning the frequency of XYY males among the newly born or adults, but there is little doubt that the frequency found by Jacobs and her colleagues is substantially higher than that in the general population. Few laboratories yet are able to do chromosome studies on a large scale, so information available is based on limited population samples from small areas. Current estimates of the frequency of XYY males at birth range from 0.5 to 3.5 per 1,000.

Jacobs also found that the XYY inmates were unusually tall, with a mean height of 6 feet 1.1 inches. Males in the institution with normal XY chromosomal constitution had a mean height of 5 feet 7 inches.

Since publication of the paper by Jacobs and her coworkers, about a dozen other reports have been published on XYY individuals, and all the reports confirm and enlarge upon the original findings (see Table 1).

TABLE 1

Summary of Published Reports on XYY Anomaly

No.	Population	Status	Height Inches	Intelligence	Traits	XYY	XXYY	XY/XXY	XXY	XYY/XYYY	XYYY	Investigator
10,725	Maternity	Newborn				—	1	5	12	—	—	Maclean, N. et al. *Lancet*, i: 286–290, 1964.
2,607	Ordinary			Subnormal		—	2	—	—	—	—	Maclean, N. et al. *Lancet*, i: 293, 1962.
197	Security	Criminal	73.1	Subnormal		7	1	1	—	—	—	Jacobs, P. et al. *Nature*, Vol. 208: 1351, 1352, 1965.
942	Institutional	Criminal		Subnormal		12	7	2	—	—	—	Casey, M. et al. *Nature*, Vol. 209: 641, 642, 1966.
50	Institutional Mentally ill	Non-criminal				4	—	—	—	—	—	Casey, M. et al. *Lancet*, i: 859, 860, 1966.
24	Institutional	Criminal				2	—	—	—	—	—	Casey, M. et al. *Lancet*, i: 859, 860, 1966.
315	Security	Criminal	6 over 72	8 Subnormal 1 Schizophrenic		9	—	—	—	—	—	Price, W. et al. *Lancet*, i: 565, 566, 1966.
464	Institutional	Delinquent		Subnormal	Aggressive Grand mal	1	—	—	—	—	—	Welch, J. et al. *Nature*, Vol. 214: 500, 501, 1967.
19	Detention center	Criminal Sex crimes	74.1	IQ 83	Negro Acne	1	—	—	—	—	—	Telfer, M. et al. *Lancet*, i: 95, 1968.
129	Institutional	Criminal	+72			5	—	—	7	—	—	Telfer, M. et al. *Science*, Vol. 159: 1249, 1250, 1968.
34	Prison	Criminal	69-82½	2 Subnormal	Psychopathic	3	—	—	—	1	—	Wiener, S. et al. *Lancet*, i: 159, 1968.
1,021	Institutional Boys	Delinquent	Tall	IQs 77, 78, 91	Property offenses	3	—	—	1	—	—	Hunter, H. *Lancet*, i: 816, 1968.
200	Institutional	Criminal	+72		Aggressive Sex offenders	9	—	—	—	—	—	Vanasek, F. et al., Atascadero State Hospital, Calif., 1968.
1	Ordinary	Embezzle-ment	78	IQ 118	Not overtly aggressive Depressed	1	—	—	—	—	—	Leff, J. and Scott, P. *Lancet*, i: 645, 1968.
1	Ordinary	8 yrs. 7 mo.	57	IQ 95	Aggressive	1	—	—	—	—	—	Cowie, J. and Kahn, J. *British Medical Journal*, Vol. 1: 748, 749, 1968.
1	Ordinary	5 yrs. 6 mo.		IQ 85	Undescended testes Simian creases	—	—	—	—	—	1	Townes, P. *Lancet*, i: 1041–1043, 1965.
1	Ordinary	44 yrs.	72	Average	Trouble keeping jobs	1	—	—	—	—	—	Hauschka, T. et al. *American Journal of Human Genetics*, Vol. 14: 22–30, 1962.
1	Ordinary	12 yrs.		Average	Undescended testes	1	—	—	—	—	—	Sandberg, A. et al. *New England Journal of Medicine*, Vol. 268: 585–589, 1963.

However, in many of these cases only inmates 6 feet or more in height were selected for study, so care must be taken in interpreting the findings.

In a sample of 3,395 prison and hospital inmates, 56 individuals were XYY, nine others had supernumerary Ys in one combination or another. Only eight of the inmates were XXY. Supernumerary Y chromosomes in any other combination are only one-fifth as frequent as the XYY—a significant fact that suggests it is the YY complement in the presence of a *single* X chromosome that constitutes the most frequent anomaly.

However, the presence of an extra Y chromosome, in any combination, appears to increase the chances of trouble. It also seems that the presence of an extra X chromosome, no matter what the number of extra Y chromosomes may be, in no way reduces the chance of trouble.

The Y chromosome, so to speak, seems to possess an elevated aggressiveness potential, whereas the X chromosome seems to possess a high gentleness component.

It appears probable that the ordinary quantum of aggressiveness of a normal XY male is derived from his Y chromosome, and that the addition of another Y chromosome presents a double dose of those potencies that may under certain conditions facilitate the development of aggressive behavior.

Of course, as with any chromosome, this does not

NORMAL MALE MEIOSIS
(Formation of the sperm)

Primary Spermatocyte

FIRST MEIOTIC DIVISION

SECOND MEIOTIC DIVISION

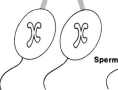

Sperm

SPERM	OVUM	NORMAL MALE	SPERM	OVUM	NORMAL FEMALE

NONDISJUNCTION OF SEX CHROMOSOMES IN MALE MEIOSIS

Primary Spermatocyte

Primary Spermatocyte

NONDISJUNCTION AT FIRST MEIOTIC DIVISION

FIRST MEIOTIC DIVISION

SECOND MEIOTIC DIVISION

NONDISJUNCTION AT SECOND MEIOTIC DIVISION

Sperm

MALE
(Klinefelter's
Syndrome)

MALE
(XYY Syndrome)

SPERM	OVUM		SPERM	OVUM	

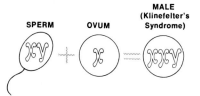 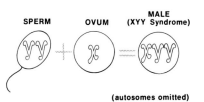

(autosomes omitted)

mean that the genes are directly responsible for the end effect. Rather, the genes on the sex chromosomes exercise their effects through a long chain of metabolic pathways. The final physiological or functional expression results from the interaction of the genes with their environments.

Genes do not determine anything. They simply influence the morphological and physiological expression of traits. Heredity, then, is the expression, not of what is given in one's genes at conception, but of the reciprocal interaction between the inherited genes and the environments to which they've been exposed.

Genes, chromosomes, or heredity are not to be interpreted, as so many people mistakenly do, as equivalent to fate or predestination. On the contrary, the genetic constitution, the genotype, is a labile system, capable of being influenced and changed to varying degrees.

Unchangeability and immutability are not characteristics of the genetic system. The genetic code for any trait contains a set of specific instructions. The manner in which those instructions will be carried out depends not only on those instructions but also upon the nature of their interaction with other sets of instructions as well as with their environments.

The phenotype, that is, the visible product of the joint action of genes and the environment, is variable. The idea of genetic or hereditary preformation is as incorrect and unsound as is the doctrine of hereditary predestination. In discussing the behavioral traits so frequently associated with the XYY type, these facts must be especially borne in mind.

How does the XYY chromosomal aberration originate? Most probably the double Y complement is produced during formation of the sperm. During the process of meiosis, in which chromosomes divide and duplicate themselves, normal separation of the sex chromosomes leads to two kinds of sperm—those with an X chromosome, and those with a Y chromosome. If an X sperm fertilizes a normal X ovum, an XX individual (normal female) will result. If the Y sperm fertilizes the ovum, a normal XY male will result.

Failure of the sex chromosomes to separate normally is called nondisjunction. There are two divisions during meiosis. If nondisjunction occurs during the first meiotic division in the production of sperm, this leads to two kinds of sperm cells—those with both the X and Y chromosomes, and those with no sex chromosomes. If an XY sperm fertilizes a normal ovum, an XXY individual will be the result. The XXY individual is a male (Klinefelter's Syndrome) but is usually sterile, lacking functional testes. About 80 percent of these males develop small breasts and at least 25 percent are of limited intelligence.

If nondisjunction occurs at the second meiotic division of the paternal germ cells, three types of sperm are produced: XX, YY, and those containing no sex chromosomes. Offspring resulting from fertilization of a normal ovum will be, respectively, XXX, XYY, and XO.

An XYY individual also could be produced if the sex chromosomes fail to separate normally in the early stages of division (mitosis) of a normal, fertilized XY ovum. However, in such an event, an individual with some type of mosaicism is more likely to occur.

Mosaicism refers to the existence of a different number of sex chromosomes in different tissues or parts of the body. For example, an individual may have only one X chromosome in some of his cells, and three chromosomes (XYY) in other cells. Such a mosaic would be designated XO/XYY. The O refers to the missing X or Y chromosome. If the single X chromosome is coupled with an isochromosome (I)—a chromosome with two identical arms—then the mosaic would be XI/XYY. Of course, other mosaics such as XY/XYY or XYY/XYYY occur.

Major physical abnormalities do not occur in XYY individuals for the reason that the Y chromosome carries relatively few genes. However, the physical abnormalities that do occur are interesting. As in most cases in which an extra sex chromosome is present, there is a high incidence of abnormal internal and external genitalia. Even in childhood, XYY individuals are usually strikingly tall, and as adults usually exceed six feet in height. Facial acne appears to be frequent in adolescence. Mentally, these individuals are usually rather dull, with IQs between 80 and 95. Abnormal electroencephalographic recordings, and a relatively high incidence of epileptic and epileptiform conditions, suggest a wide spectrum of brain dysfunction. Disorders of the teeth, such as discolored enamel, malocclusion and arrested development, also have been noted.

Allowing for the fact that in many cases tall prison inmates were selected for study of the XYY syndrome, and while a number of known XYY individuals fall several inches short of 6 feet, it is nonetheless clear that tallness usually characterizes the XYY individual.

This may be a significant factor in influencing the individual's behavioral development. Among children his own age, an XYY boy may be teased and taunted because of his height, and impelled either to withdrawal or aggression. As a juvenile, adolescent, or adult, he may find himself nurtured in environments that encourage physical aggression as a means of adaptation.

This should not be interpreted to mean that all tall men have an XYY constitution. Recently, Richard Goodman and his colleagues at Ohio State University examined the chromosomes of thirty-six basketball players ranging in height from 5 feet 11 inches to 6 feet 10 inches, and found no chromosomal abnormalities.

The resort to brawn rather than brain is not limited to individuals endowed with an extra Y chromosome. Most violent crimes are committed by chromosomally normal individuals. However, the high frequency with which individuals with XYY chromosomes commit crimes of violence leaves little doubt that in some cases the additional Y chromosome exerts a preponderantly powerful influence in the genesis of aggressive behavior.

In a maximum security prison in Melbourne, Australia, Saul Wiener and his colleagues found four XYY-type males in a study of thirty-four tall prisoners, all between 5 feet 9 inches and 6 feet 10.5 inches in height. A striking frequency of 11.8 percent! Of the three XYY inmates, one was charged with attempted murder, the second had committed murder, and the third, larceny. The fourth was an XYY/XYYY mosaic and had committed murder.

An interesting fact is that the tallest of the XYY murderers, 6 feet 10.5 inches tall, had a sister who was even taller. The tallness of the sister indicates that even though the X chromosome is not usually associated with excessive height in families where the males are extremely tall, a trait for tallness may be also carried in the X chromosome.

As a consequence of the discovery of what may be called the XYY syndrome, there now can be very little doubt that genes do influence, to some extent, the development of behavior.

It also appears clear, that, with all other factors constant, genes of the same kind situated at the same locus on the chromosomes of different people may vary greatly both in their penetrance and their expressivity.

Penetrance refers to the regularity with which a gene produces its effect. When a gene regularly produces the same effect, it is said to have complete penetrance. When the trait is not manifested in some cases, the gene is said to have reduced penetrance.

Expressivity refers to the manifestation of a trait produced by a gene. When the manifestation differs from individual to individual, the gene is said to have variable expressivity. For example, the dominant gene for allergy may express itself as asthma, eczema, hay fever, urticarial rash, or angioneurotic edema.

Hence, it would be an error to identify the XYY constitution as *predisposed* to aggressive behavior. Whatever genes are involved, they often fail to produce aggressive behavior, and even more often may be expressed in many different ways. In fact, the XYY phenotype, the product of the joint action of genes and environment, does vary from normal to various degrees of abnormality.

Some individuals, however, seem to be driven to their aggressive behavior as if they are possessed by a demon. The demon, it would seem, lies in the peculiar nature of the double Y chromosome complement. That the combined power of several Y chromosomes can be so great, in some cases, as to cause a man to become unrestrainedly aggressive is dramatically borne out by a case reported by John Cowie and Jacob Kahn of East Ham Child Clinic, London, in March 1968.

The first-born, wanted child of a mother aged twenty-three and a father aged twenty-five was referred at the age of four and a half years to a psychiatrist because he was unmanageable at home, destructive, mischievous, and defiant. He would smash his toys, rip the curtains, set fire to the room in his mother's absence, kick the cat, and hit his eight-month-old brother. He was over-adventurous and without fear. At two years of age, he began wandering away from home and was brought back by the police on five occasions. He started school at five years and at once developed an interest in sharp-pointed objects. He would shoot drawing compasses across the schoolroom from an elastic band and injured several children. In one incident, he rammed a screwdriver into a little girl's stomach.

At the age of eight years, seven months, he was 4 feet 9 inches tall, handsome, athletically proportioned, and of normal appearance. He is of average intelligence and often considerate and happy. His electroencephalogram is mildly abnormal. Both his parents and his brother have normal chromosomal complements, but the boy is of XYY constitution. His brother is a normally behaving child, and the parents are concerned, loving people.

As illustrated by this case, there is now an increasing amount of evidence that XYY individuals commence their aggressive and social behavior in early prepubertal years. In many cases, the offenses committed are against property rather than against persons. The XYY anomaly, therefore, should not be associated with one particular behavioral trait but rather regarded as an aberration characterized by a wide spectrum of behavioral possibilities ranging from totally normal to persistent antisocial behavior. The degree of aggressiveness varies and constitutes only one component of the highly variable spectrum of behavioral contingencies.

We have shown how the XYY chromosomal aberration can originate in nondisjunction during meiosis or during mitosis. But does an XYY male transmit the abnormality to his offspring? To this question the answer is: probably not. One report on an Oregon XYY man indicates the double Y chromosome complement may not be transmitted. The man has six sons, and all are of normal XY chromosomal constitution.

On the other hand, T. S. Hauschka of Roswell Park Memorial Institute and the Medical Foundation of Buffalo, and his colleagues, who discovered one of the first XYY individuals in 1961, suggest that there may be a hereditary predisposition to nondisjunction. The XYY individual they identified was a normal male who came to their attention because he had a daughter who suffered from Down's syndrome (mongolism). Since Down's syndrome, in most cases, also arises as a result of nondisjunction, this, coupled with other abnormalities in his offspring, suggested that he might be transmitting a hereditary tendency to nondisjunction.

The fact that the XYY complement is now known to be associated with persistent antisocial behavior in a large number of individuals raises a number of questions that the reasonable society, if not the Great Society, must consider seriously.

A first question, if not a first priority, is whether it would not now be desirable to type chromosomally all infants at birth or shortly after. At least 1 percent of all babies born have a chromosomal abnormality of some sort, and about one-quarter of these involve sex chromosome abnormalities. Some of these will be XYY. Forearmed with such information, it might be possible to institute the proper preventive and other measures at an early age. These measures would be designed to help the individuals with the XYY chromosomal constitution to follow a less stormy development than they otherwise might.

A second question is how society should deal with individuals known to be of XYY constitution. Such individuals are genetically abnormal. They are not normal and, therefore, should not be treated as if they were.

If the individual has the misfortune to have been endowed with an extra chromosome Number 21, he would have suffered from Down's syndrome (mongolism). He would not have been expected to behave as a normal individual. And why should the XYY individual be held any more responsible for his behavior than a mongoloid? Mongoloids are usually likeable, unaggressive individuals, and most sociable. The aggressive XYY individual is often the very opposite. Yet the unaggressive behavior of mongoloids is as much due to their genetic constitution as is, at least in part, the aggressive and antisocial behavior of the XYY individual.

Recognizing this fact, it becomes very necessary for us to consider how society and the law should deal with such individuals. We have learned how to identify and treat the hereditary defect of PKU (phenylketonuria), which can result in idiocy if not treated. Cannot we also develop measures to treat the XYY? Surgical intervention, such as sterilization, is totally inappropriate since it will not "cure" or alleviate the condition, nor will it reduce the frequency of XYY individuals in the general population. The XYY aberration, as far as we know, is not directly inherited and quite probably arises primarily from nondisjunction of the sex chromosomes in completely normal parents.

Although we are in no position to control the genetic inheritance of an individual, we can do a great deal to change certain environmental conditions that may encourage the XYY individual to commit criminal acts.

A society does not properly acquit itself of its responsibilities if it places the entire burden of caring for abnormal individuals upon the parents. What we are talking about here is not a program of eugenic control but a program of social therapy. There is every reason to believe that if we can successfully develop effective methods to help the aggressive XYY individual, then we will be moving in the right direction to control those social conditions that drive men to crime—regardless of their genotype.

The Hungry Fly

Vincent Dethier

In an elegant analysis of feeding behavior in the blowfly, Dethier integrates sensory function, neurophysiology, and behavior. What emerges is a fascinating picture of behavioral regulation in a single organism. This approach of analyzing a particular behavior in a single species is a good example of research in biological psychology.

Hyperphagia, overeating, is a comparative business. That which is overeating in one animal is normal in another. Animals that feed infrequently may appear to overindulge in the eyes of animals that feed frequently and regularly. The python that swallows the hog, the tick or leech that gorges itself on blood, human beings of certain tribes who eat themselves into a stupor when an elephant is killed and practically starve between slaughters—for all of these, "overeating" is a normal adaptation to particular environmental circumstances. Occasionally, in the normal course of events, some animals that eat normal-sized meals on a regular schedule become hyperphagic for limited periods. Certain migratory birds do precisely this prior to long flights with the result that considerable energy reserves are accumulated. Hibernating mammals overindulge seasonally in preparation for a long lean winter. Some animals, notably people, not uncommonly become abnormally or pathologically hyperphagic.

These cases, normal and abnormal alike, dramatically illustrate what we often take for granted—the fact that the vast majority of animals regulate their feeding within remarkably precise limits. The nature of the regulatory mechanism is one of the most fascinating problems in physiology and physiological psychology today.

Although the most direct path toward understanding man is formed through the study of man, there is always hope that the study of a basic phenomenon in a so-called lower or simple organism will assist us in locating the more direct pathway. Buoyed by this hope we have spent many years studying the feeding behavior of the black blowfly, *Phormia regina* Meigen (see Figure 1). The black blowfly is an unusually fine experimental animal for the study of feeding mechanisms because it is essentially an energy machine with few requirements. To live out its maximal life span of sixty days it requires only oxygen, water, and carbohydrate. Since it does not grow, it has no other needs that are not already bequeathed to it by its larval stage. The blowfly is, however, quite small—only 8 millimeters long.

We started our investigation with the simple assumption that feeding is influenced by oral factors (taste) and postingestion factors. If the characteristics and interactions of these factors could be understood, we felt that we would be able to construct a reasonably

Figure 1. Blowfly extending its proboscis (arrow) in response to chemical stimulation of a taste hair.

complete picture of the operation of normal feeding behavior. We approached the problem using behavioral, electrophysiological, and surgical techniques (including the induction of experimental hyperphagia).

Tasting with Their Feet

We first needed information about the physiology of the sense of taste in the blowfly. Although it had been known since the eighteenth century that insects could taste and smell, no one, up to the time when our work began, had ever knowingly seen a taste or olfactory receptor. There were, of course, many surmises and inspired guesses but no proof. The sequence of events that finally led to the discovery of taste receptors began about forty-five years ago with the observation of Dwight Minnich of the University of Minnesota that butterflies and flies could discriminate sugar from water merely by stepping in the solutions. After a long series of exquisitely controlled experiments Minnich concluded that these insects bore organs of taste on their feet. Many biologists were reluctant to accept the conclusion, and little came of the work at that time.

Ten years later Eltringham in England and Tinbergen in the Netherlands, examining butterflies and flies respectively, inferred from microscopic structure that certain delicate, transparent hairs were the taste organs of the legs. About the same time, Minnich himself arrived at similar conclusions regarding the taste organs of the fly proboscis. However, another lapse, nearly

thirty years, occurred before unequivocal proof was forthcoming. In 1953 Casmir Grabowski and I set out to settle the matter of identity once and for all. Examination of the legs of *Phormia* revealed that the only structures that could conceivably have a sensory function were the variously sized and shaped hollow hairs thickly clothing the legs. Remembering Minnich's observation that sugar applied to the whole leg elicited proboscis extension, we reasoned that stimulation of individual hairs might achieve the same result if indeed any of the hairs were gustatory organs. By the laborious method of counting all of the more than one hundred hairs on each leg, placing minute drops of sugar on the tips of individual hairs, and observing whether or not the proboscis extended, we discovered that the hairs described by Tinbergen and Minnich were in fact the taste organs of the legs and mouth, respectively.

Specific Receptors

By this time it was common knowledge that flies could distinguish between water, sugar, and salt. But did it follow that there were specific water, sugar, and salt hairs that were analogous to the different kinds of taste buds in the mammalian tongue? Again, by exploiting the behavioral criterion of proboscis extension, we were able to show that each chemosensory hair was sensitive to all stimuli, touch included. To demonstrate this, we treated a thirsty, hungry fly as follows. One hair on the proboscis was stroked gently with a dry needle; the fly responded by extending its proboscis. After stroking had been continued for several seconds, the response ceased. Waning of the response could have indicated sensory adaptation, central-nervous-system adaptation, or muscle fatigue. When a neighboring hair was stroked, however, the response resumed immediately, indicating that the earlier waning reflected sensory adaptation. Next, a hair adapted to touch was stimulated with a small drop of water rolled onto the tip. Proboscis extension occurred immediately, indicating that although the hair was adapted to touch, it was not adapted to water. Repeated stimulation with water eventually resulted in adaptation, which was again shown to be sensory. The adapted hair was then stimulated with sugar. The response occurred.

These behavioral experiments indicated that each hair is a complex organ possessing multiple specific receptors. Under appropriate circumstances the touch, water, and sugar receptors trigger proboscis extension, the first act in feeding. Without this oral stimulation the fly does not attempt to feed regardless of how hungry it may be.

Flies will not ingest sugar or water that has been adulterated with compounds of the sort that we ourselves find distasteful. Salts, acids, and hundreds of other compounds have been shown to inhibit proboscis extension and to shut off feeding if proboscis extension has already taken place. It was conceivable that unacceptable compounds like salt acted by interfering with

water and sugar receptors. Again, however, behavioral methods supplied evidence of the presence of a salt receptor in each hair. After proboscis extension was elicited by stimulating one hair with sugar, salt was applied to an adjacent hair. The result was proboscis retraction.

The experiments just described demanded that each hair possess a minimum of four receptor cells. Fortunately microscopic examination revealed that each hair is in fact multiply innervated. There are five bipolar neurons. The dendrites of four extend to a pore in the tip of the hair; the fifth dendrite terminates in the hair socket. This last is the mechanoreceptor; the others are the water, salt, and sugar receptors, and a fourth chemoreceptor whose sensory characteristics are not yet known (see Figure 2).

Electrophysiology of the Receptors

As is characteristic of all receptors, these labellar receptors generate electrical changes that can be detected with appropriate instruments. When a chemical stimulus reaches the terminal pore in the hair, it initiates a

Figure 2. Innervation of a taste hair; each is innervated by 5 bipolar neurons: 4 chemoreceptors (color) and a mechanoreceptor.

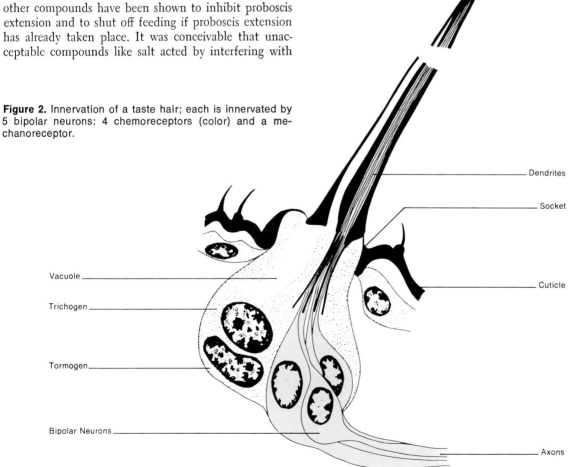

change in the permeability of the membrane of the dendrite. Depolarization of the membrane occurs. This depolarization spreads as a slow wave down to the underlying cell body. Here, repetitive, abrupt, all-or-none changes in potential are generated. These electrical volleys, the action potentials, travel along the nerve in both directions—along the axon to the central nervous system and back up the dendrite where the initial depolarization occurred. As early as 1937 I had attempted to record electrophysiological events in insect chemoreceptors, but equipment available at the time was unequal to the task. In 1955 Edward Hodgson, Jerome Lettvin, and Kenneth Roeder, working at Tufts University, devised a unique technique that made detection of action potentials possible. Independently, Hiromichi Morita and his associates at Kyushu University in Japan, who had been conducting with the admiral butterfly *Vanessa indica* a long series of experiments paralleling the blowfly studies, invented the same technique. These workers had discovered that action potentials generated by the chemoreceptors could be recorded through the tip of the hair.

The technique is ingeniously simple. An isolated blowfly head or proboscis is impaled on a fine silver wire or a small, salt-filled glass pipette into which a silver wire is inserted. This pipette serves as an indifferent electrode. Another glass pipette with a tip diameter of 4 to 10 microns, also salt-filled and connected with a silver wire, is slipped over the tip of a hair. This pipette serves simultaneously as a recording electrode and as a carrier for the stimulus.

Hodgson and his associates found that when the recording pipette contained salt solution alone, only one of the five neurons fired action potentials. These were of uniform amplitude and frequency. As the concentration of salt in the pipette was increased, the frequency of firing increased. When the pipette contained sugar in addition to salt, a second spike appeared on the record. It had a smaller amplitude than the first. Its frequency of firing was not appreciably affected by changes in salt concentration but did increase in an orderly fashion as sugar concentration was increased. Clearly then, there was one neuron sensitive to salt and another one sensitive to sugar.

In time, electrophysiological studies confirmed all of the behavioral findings. Myron Wolbarsht, working in our laboratory, demonstrated activity from the mechanoreceptor, and David Evans and Deforest Mellon found the water receptor. Finally, Edward Hodgson and Richard Steinhardt at Columbia University and Frank Hanson in our laboratory showed that behavioral rejection of nonelectrolytes (for example, alcohols) was not mediated by the salt receptor but occurred because the sugar and water receptors became temporarily inoperative. These discoveries were facilitated by Morita's development of a still more clever recording technique, which consisted of inserting an electrode through a minute hole bored through the side wall of the hair. This invention freed experimenters from the restriction of mixing stimulus and electrolyte since pure stimulus solutions could now be applied to the tip of the hair while the recording electrode was in the side.

There remained only one major gap in our understanding of the chain of peripheral events triggering and driving feeding. Once the fly has extended its proboscis, most of the chemoreceptive hairs of the labellum are no longer in contact with the solution because the oral lobes are spread. Inside on the oral surface there are minute papillae long suspected of being organs of taste. Because of their inaccessibility and extremely small size they had long defied experimental analysis. Electrophysiological recording was further complicated because the papillae are *inside* and are moist. After many failures Hanson and I finally succeeded in proving that a papilla, like a hair, contains specific receptors for touch, sugars, and salts. By squeezing the body of the fly between thumb and forefinger we were able to force enough blood into the head to cause eversion of the proboscis. A ligature tied at the base of the everted proboscis then prevented redistribution of the blood when squeezing ceased. The problem of the moisture on the papillae was met by adding agar to the test solution and, while the mixture was still boiling hot, forcing it into the recording pipette where it rapidly jelled.

Finding and Feeding

The factors inducing and driving ingestion are now well understood. In nature the food of the fly consists of nectar from flowers, honeydew secreted on leaves by aphids, sap from the wounds of trees, fermenting fruit, and many kinds of decaying material. For egg laying and ingestion of protein, flies assemble at carrion, offal, and feces. A fly locates its food by random searching or by orienting to odor. Flies are great explorers. They land on many surfaces and investigate. When food does possess an odor, as is the case with carrion and fermenting materials, the fly flies upwind to the source. Regardless of how the fly initially locates the food, it sooner or later steps in it, thus stimulating the taste hairs of the feet. This stimulation triggers proboscis extension causing the taste hairs of the labellum to be stimulated in turn. This sensory input results in eversion of the oral lobes. Now the papillae are stimulated and sucking commences. The whole process up to this point is completely under peripheral sensory control. A unique feature of ingestive behavior is the fact that the whole complex process of proboscis extension, oral-lobe spreading, sucking, and swallowing can be triggered and maintained by activity from a single neuron, the sugar cell of any hair.

Tests of the stimulating effectiveness of more than eighty carbohydrates, correlated with studies of the nutritional adequacy of these compounds, revealed that the effectiveness of sugars as taste stimuli bears no orderly relation to nutritional value. In fact, one of the more effective stimulating sugars is fucose, a methyl pentose, which is totally inadequate as a nutrient. In tests a fly will ingest nonnutritive, highly stimulating fucose in preference to poorly stimulating, highly nutritious mannose and starve to death.

What Stops Ingestion?

Ingestion obviously does not continue forever. What causes the blowfly to stop sucking? By analogy with human experience any number of factors might be involved in terminating feeding: a full gut, internal pressure against the body wall, rise in blood-sugar level, changes in hormonal levels. To understand how these might operate, it is necessary to follow the course of food within the fly. This can be accomplished by slitting the fly from end to end to expose the alimentary canal because a fly in this condition will still feed. It is even possible to remove surgically the entire alimentary canal and observe its operation in a saline bath.

The force of sucking drives food into the esophagus. Waves of peristalsis drive the food back to a point where the gut bifurcates (see Figure 3). One channel of the bifurcation is a thin duct leading into a dead-end,

impermeable storage sac, the crop. The other channel is the main course of the alimentary canal, the mid- and hindguts. Almost all absorption takes place in the midgut. During feeding, the food arriving in the esophagus is diverted into the crop by a synchronized system of valves. After ingestion has ceased, food is transferred from the crop to the midgut intermittently over a period of several hours. Churning and kneading motions in the crop cause food to be driven back into the esophagus every time the crop valve opens. When the crop valve closes, the midgut valve opens and peristalsis in the esophagus drives the slug of fluid into the midgut.

As time passes the crop becomes progressively more empty. Originally, rate of emptying was studied by feeding a large number of flies a known volume and concentration of sugar, sacrificing a few individuals periodically, removing the crop, and weighing it. Because the crop is like a tough little impervious plastic bag, precise values convertible to volume were obtained. A more ingenious method permitting continuous measurements in a living fly was subsequently perfected by George Green in our laboratory. He simply mixed an opaque material with the food, periodically x-rayed the flies in two planes, and calculated volume from area.

A close correlation was found to exist between the rate of crop emptying and the fly's acceptance threshold

Figure 3. Diagram of the blowfly's head, thorax, and anterior abdomen. The alimentary canal is shown as dark color; the stomatogastric nervous systems, as light color. The proboscis is fully extended.

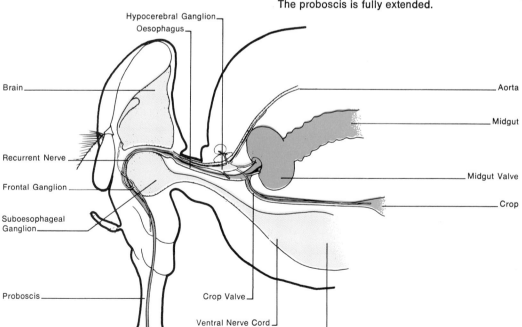

for food. For example, a newly fed fly may have an acceptance threshold for sucrose at concentrations in excess of two moles. Deprived for ninety hours the fly then has a threshold of 10^{-7} moles. Since electrophysiological studies have proved that there is no change in the threshold of the sense organs that drive feeding, we concluded that it is a central threshold that is changing. Some change associated with crop emptying results in central inhibition of chemosensory input.

We naturally suspected that fullness of the crop might provide the signal that results (in the central nervous system) in inhibition of sensory input. To test this idea we designed experiments in which the crop was either ligated, and thus functionally isolated, or removed entirely. A fly was placed on a wax block, ventral side up, held by two strips of plasticene, one across the thorax and one across the posterior abdomen. A small incision was made in the skin of the abdomen at the juncture of the thorax and abdomen, and the crop was carefully brought to the outside. A silk loop was slipped over the exposed crop and the duct tied. The crop was then pushed back through the wound. In some cases a second ligature was tied around the duct, a cut made between the two, and the crop removed.

When an empty crop was ligated or removed, sugar ingested by the fly filled the foregut and midgut. The acceptance threshold was elevated to the normal level. The crop need not contain sugar, therefore, to shut off feeding. Conversely, when full crops were removed, thresholds did not drop immediately as might have been expected if crop pressure were the inhibitory factor. The threshold did, however, drop after four to six hours. The same rapid decrease occurred if the full crop was ligatured. This acceleration in the drop in threshold was attributed to the fact that sugar in other regions of the gut could not be replenished after depletion. It was possible, therefore, that the presence or absence of sugar in the midgut was the critical factor shutting off ingestion.

Midgut Preparations

Surgery and manipulation of the midgut is extremely difficult; remember that the entire fly is only 8 millimeters long. However, Dietrich Bodenstein, now at the University of Virginia, had over the course of many years perfected exceptionally delicate surgical techniques applicable to insects. Together he and I conducted a series of experiments involving ligation, removal, and loading of the midgut. For ligation or removal a fly was placed dorsal side up in a depression in a wax plate. A small wedge of muscle tissue was removed from the prothorax. Removal of the wedge exposed the gut in the region of its bifurcation. A drop of physiological saline solution was placed in the wound. The cut-out wedge was also placed in solution. After the midgut was lifted into view, silk, roughly the diameter of baby hair, was slipped under it, brought around, and tied tightly. If the gut was to be cut, a second ligature was applied and a transection made between the two. The cut-out wedge was then replaced and the incision closed. After a period of recovery flies were fed.

Following feeding, the thresholds remained high for four hours. Obviously the presence of food in the midgut was not necessary to maintain elevated thresholds. In another experiment the midgut was loaded with sugar by giving flies enemas. Deprived flies with guts loaded via this route still acted hungry, so food in the midgut does not terminate feeding.

Parabiotic Flies

David Evans and I had shown earlier that blood-sugar levels rose rapidly after feeding. Could this rise play a role in the termination of feeding? One way of testing this hypothesis was to alter blood-sugar levels independently of feeding. We therefore prepared parabiotic flies. A small drop of paraffin was placed on the dorsal surface of the thorax. Here it was puddled with a hot needle so as to form a wax crater. Next, the floor of the crater together with the underlying cuticle was excised, exposing the hemocoele—the blood cavity. The crater was filled to the rim with saline. Another fly, similarly prepared, was placed against the first so that the rims of the two craters fit snugly together. The junction was sealed with a hot needle. The two flies now shared a common blood supply. After one was fed to repletion, the acceptance thresholds of both were tested. The fed fly refused food; its unfed partner sucked avidly. Not only did this experiment tend to rule out the direct influence of blood sugar in terminating feeding, it also weakened any hypothesis suggesting a role for hunger or feeding hormones. As a final check, some hungry flies received large quantities of sugar injected directly into the blood cavity (see Figure 4). Despite the fact that these flies were now metabolically satiated, they remained behaviorally hungry.

One small section of the alimentary canal had thus far escaped experimental scrutiny. This was the foregut, the region extending from the pharyngeal pump to the diverticulum. Does the presence or absence of food in this region, or the passage of food through this region, play a role in the termination of feeding? We could investigate this possibility by loading the foregut with food that had bypassed the mouth or by eliminating the foregut entirely. The foregut, however, lies within the fly's neck, a narrow corridor only 0.5 millimeter wide, crowded with many essential structures. Moreover, the foregut has so small a diameter (0.05 millimeter) that successful loading with food was never accomplished. The thought occurred to Bodenstein and myself that we could isolate the foregut physiologically by cutting its nerve supply.

The foregut, indeed the entire alimentary canal, is

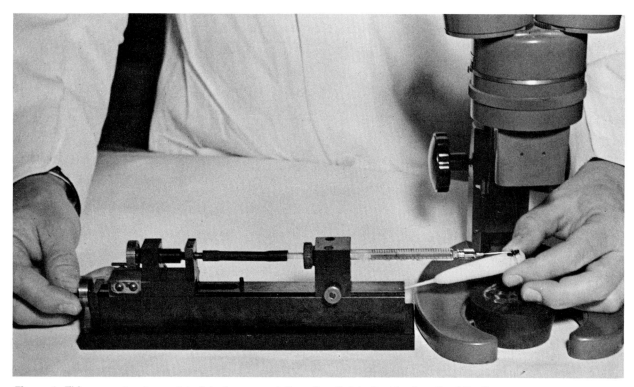

Figure 4. This apparatus is used to inject sugar solution directly into the blood cavity of the fly.

innervated by the stomatogastric nervous system, the analogue of the vertebrate autonomic system (see Figure 3). The stomatogastric system commences as a small ganglion, the frontal ganglion, situated anterior to the brain. Bilateral connectives join it to the brain. From the frontal ganglion a large trunk extends anteriorly for a short distance then reverses direction and passes posteriorly beneath the brain along the dorsal wall of the esophagus. This trunk is the recurrent nerve. Its diameter ranges from 5 to 10 microns. In the region of the bifurcation of the gut the recurrent nerve joins the hypocerebral ganglion. Here there are nerves serving the walls and valves of the alimentary canal, the aorta, the foregut itself, and the principal endocrine complex, the corpus allatum and the corpora cardiaca. If we could transect the recurrent nerve in the anterior region of the foregut, we would essentially have deprived the brain of all information originating in the area of the foregut.

After a large number of practice trials we perfected the surgical procedure. What at first was a very tricky undertaking has now become routine. Entrance is made through a dorsal slit in the neck. The exposed aorta is gently displaced to one side; adhesions supporting the two main tracheal trunks carrying the head's sole supply of oxygen are severed in order to free the esophagus; the superficial neck muscles are stretched apart. These manipulations expose the recurrent nerve, which can now be cut.

As a consequence of cutting the recurrent nerve, the feeding behavior of the fly undergoes an extraordinary change—the fly is unable to control its ingestion. We had produced surgical hyperphagia.

Until It Bursts

A hyperphagic fly continues to eat until the crop expands into the entire body, until all other organs are squashed into a thin mass pressed against the hind end of the body cavity, until the fly becomes so bloated that the thin intersegmental folds of cuticle separating the plates of the external skeleton stretch to a point where the fly becomes a turgid, spherical, transparent ball (see Figure 5). At this point the pharyngeal pump can no longer work effectively against the hydrostatic and elastic back pressure. Attempts at ingestion persist, but no fluid actually accumulates. If, however, the pump is made to work harder by increasing input from the oral receptors that drive it, by stimulating with a higher concentration of sugar, the fly actually bursts.

It is clear that transecting the recurrent nerve interferes with a mechanism that normally shuts off ingestion. Bodenstein and I proposed that there are receptors in the foregut that monitor postingestive transfer of fluid from crop to midgut and that information from these receptors counteracts input from the oral taste receptors. When the fly is deprived of this inhibitory feedback, there is no way to shut off oral stimulation. It is shut off temporarily when the sense organs adapt but is reinstated as soon as disadaption occurs. Since feeding

Cutting the recurrent nerve produces overeating—hyperphagia—and a bloated, fat fly. Sometimes the fly will eat so much it actually bursts.

in the operated fly is driven by unrestricted sensory input, it races out of control.

It is interesting to compare surgical hyperphagia in the fly with that which can be produced in the rat. In the rat a lesion in the lateral hypothalamus causes the animal to starve to death, whereas a lesion in the ventromedial hypothalamus results in tremendous overeating. These and other experiments suggest that there are excitatory and inhibitory areas in the central nervous system of the rat that play an important role in the regulation of feeding. In the fly there is no evidence for the existence of central feeding centers. Instead, there is a balance between two sensory systems. The peripheral oral system initiates feeding; the internal foregut system inhibits feeding.

The Inhibitory Receptors

Our interpretation was favored by the fact, known from previous operations for excision of crop and midgut, that merely cutting those branches of the recurrent nerve that served other regions of the gut failed to interfere with the normal pattern of ingestion. It did, however, suffer from two weaknesses: first, the recurrent nerve at the site of transection carries fibers from the endocrine complex to neurosecretory cells in the brain, and, despite the earlier evidence from experiments with parabiotic flies, might conceivably transmit some indication of endocrine change associated with ingestion; second, no receptors had been found in the walls of the foregut.

It was not long before both of these weak points were shored up by experiment. It will be recalled that the recurrent nerve takes its origin from the frontal ganglion anterior to the brain. At this point it does not contain fibers from the endocrine glands because these enter the posterior part of the brain. If the recurrent nerve could be cut anteriorly, the point would be settled. After many false starts the operation was perfected. I lifted a skin flap between the eyes, went in through the fat body obscuring the frontal ganglion, and cut the recurrent nerve there. After the skin flap was returned to normal position, the fly was permitted to feed. The outcome was the same spectacular hyperphagia that had occurred after the posterior cut. The endocrine system is not involved.

An intensified search for receptors in the foregut finally turned up two likely candidates. In precisely the region indicated by hypothesis there is a pair of large multipolar neurons in the gut wall that resemble in appearance known stretch receptors found elsewhere in the body. In the meantime, Alan Gelperin demonstrated by an elaborate series of experiments that the postulated receptors must monitor stretch in the foregut

as food is transferred through the region. It remains for us only to consolidate the conclusion electrophysiologically.

The Complete Picture

Our understanding of the regulation of feeding in the blowfly seemed to be in tidy order until the recent appearance of a report by Nuñez demonstrating that hyperphagia can also be produced in flies by transecting the ventral nerve cord, the analogue of the vertebrate spinal cord, in the region of the neck. We were soon able to confirm this report. It occurred to Gelperin and myself that even though both recurrent-nerve section and ventral-cord section resulted in hyperphagia, the pattern of hyperphagia might be different. And indeed it is. A fly lacking information from the foregut takes a normal size initial meal, but, instead of gradually reducing further feeding to zero as the normal fly does, it continues to take many short meals over the next few hours. A fly with its ventral cord interrupted takes one interminable first meal. Thus, although sensory adaptation normally shuts off feeding when reinforced by central inhibitory feedback, it is unable to accomplish braking alone. Part of the contribution of the central nervous system is information regarding the extent of distension of the body wall because when nerves to the body wall are cut the fly overeats in much the same way as it does following ventral-cord transection.

The picture that emerges, therefore, of feeding regulation in the blowfly is one of balance and imbalance between fluctuating chemosensory input and fluctuating inhibitory input from foregut and body-wall stretch receptors. Chemosensory input varies as levels of adaptation and disadaptation in the taste receptors rise and fall. Inhibitory input varies as the rate of fluid transfer from crop to midgut decreases with deprivation and increases with feeding, and as distension of the body wall varies accordingly. When inhibitory feedback predominates, feeding ceases; when oral excitation predominates, feeding commences.

We see in the fly a relatively simple system operating by means of antagonistic sensory systems, one chemical and peripheral and the other mechanical and internal. Somewhere in the central nervous system the incoming information is integrated. At the moment there is no need to postulate, nor is there any evidence for, feeding centers of the sort found in the hypothalamus of vertebrates. The fly system is primitive in the sense that it is not tied in directly with nutritive values and metabolic changes. Yet the fact that in the fly's world high sensory stimulating value and nutritive value are normally correlated, and metabolic state and distension (gut and body wall) are normally correlated ensures that energy needs are met efficiently.

Figure 5.

Copulation in Rats

Gordon Bermant

In a series of precise behavioral experiments Bermant was able to generate a model of the control of copulatory behavior in rats. These experiments not only help us understand the specific mechanisms controlling a specific behavior pattern but show how psychologists can combine data with theory to produce an elegant analysis of behavior.

The musings of poets aside, animals do not languish for lack of love and sexual union. If an animal fails to eat, he rapidly deteriorates and dies. If he fails to drink, he dies even sooner. But if an animal repeatedly fails to copulate, he neither gets sick nor dies. As far as life-sustaining functions are concerned, copulation fulfills no physiological need and is not necessary for the survival of the animal. Why, then, do animals copulate?

Whenever we ask *why* a behavior occurs, there are really two different questions we could have in mind: *What for?* or *How come?* To the question *What for?* we expect an answer in terms of the function or purpose that the behavior serves; to *How come?* we want a description of the events that cause the behavior.

The *What for?* of copulation is simple. It serves the function of transmitting sperm cell to ovum, thereby playing a crucial role in the continuation of animal species. We might at first imagine that we could answer the question "Why do animals copulate?" by saying that they do it with the intention of reproducing. However, this explanation of copulation would certainly be incorrect if we applied it to subhuman species. Only man has developed the skills in thought and language that are required to comprehend and express the relation between copulation and reproduction. Whereas men and women may copulate with the intention of producing offspring, nonhuman animals do not. Therefore, when we ask why animals copulate, we are really searching for the *How come?*, for the *determinants* of the behavior: the physiological and environmental conditions that cause the complex postures and motions of copulation. For the past several years I have been investigating some of these determinants of copulation in a number of animal species, primarily the laboratory rat.

Why Study Rats?

Rats have been the favorite experimental subjects of American animal psychologists for many years, and hence we know a great deal about their behavior. In addition, the study of rats has contributed much of what we know about the physiology of reproduction, particularly the roles played by the gonadal and pituitary hormones. And finally, certain rather unique features of the rat's copulatory pattern allow us to perform experiments that would be impossible with other species. These advantages make the small, inexpensively maintained rat an ideal subject for experimental investigation of copulatory behavior.

A word about definitions: I shall use the term *copulatory behavior*, not *sexual behavior*. Sexual behavior is best defined as any behavior that distinguishes males from females; copulatory behavior refers specifically to activities directly associated with the transfer of sperm.

Behavioral Description: The Male

The first stage in an investigation of this sort is a careful description of the behavior and its temporal organization. Social behaviors such as copulation are intricate nonverbal dialogues. There is a continuous interchange of action and reaction between the animals. In describing the behavior we must pay close attention to the reciprocating effects that the behavior of each animal has on the other.

In the copulatory behavior of the rat, the male usually appears to take the initiative. It is therefore convenient to organize the behavioral description around the responses of the male.

Suppose that a male rat, with previous copulatory experience, and a receptive female are placed together in a small enclosure. Within a minute or less, the male normally begins the preliminaries that lead to copulation. This often involves nothing more than a brief nuzzling of the female's flank or genital area. Such stimulation produces in the highly receptive female a short, jerky forward motion and a lordosis response (see Figure 1). The male may then move behind the female and mount her. He grasps her flanks with his forelegs and begins a series of rapid, shallow, pelvic thrusting movements. At this point two possibilities arise: either he will penetrate the female or he won't. If after several rapid thrusts he fails to penetrate, he dismounts by pushing away rather slowly and turning at a slight angle to the female. But if penetration occurs, the male makes a single deep thrust and immediately thereafter pushes vigorously up and away from the female. Under normal conditions the duration of penile insertion during the single deep thrust and withdrawal is between two- and three-tenths of a second (200 to 300 milliseconds). The energetic, almost acrobatic dismount following the single deep thrust is one of the most consistent features of the copulatory sequence. Unless special (electronic) methods of detection are used, the form of this dismount is the only reliable indication that the male has achieved penetration.

So far we have seen two of the male's responses: a mount without penetration, which is called simply a *mount*; and a brief penetration, which is called an *intromission*. The male does not emit semen during these brief intromissions. When, then, does the male ejaculate?

After his initial intromission the male withdraws from the female and engages in genital grooming and other noncopulatory behavior for twenty to sixty seconds. Then he reapproaches the female and either mounts or achieves another intromission. This pattern of brief copulatory responses separated by relatively long periods of inactivity usually continues until the male has achieved from eight to fifteen intromissions. Then his behavior shows a dramatic change.

Now, after mounting and penetrating, the male does not throw himself off but thrusts deeply as many as five times. The last of these thrusts is accompanied by an orgasmic spasm of the male's hindquarters at the moment of deepest penetration. Only now does he ejaculate. For a few seconds following the ejaculation, the male clutches his partner, often so tightly that they do

not separate if the experimenter tries to lift them from the cage. This time the male dismounts very slowly, usually within five seconds after the ejaculation.

Following ejaculation, the male does not approach the female for about five minutes (five to ten times longer than after each of his previous brief penetrations). Then the male mounts again to achieve an intromission—and begins his second ejaculatory series. In this series the male makes fewer mounts and intromissions, and ejaculates sooner than in the first series.

If the male is allowed to remain with the original female for several hours, he may ejaculate five times or more. However, the period of time between an ejaculation and the next intromission (the *postejaculatory interval*) rapidly increases in length, suggesting that the male is becoming tired (see Figure 2). Later we shall see that physical fatigue is only partially responsible for this waning of copulatory activity.

This description highlights four basic questions that need to be answered:

1. What prompts the male to approach and mount the female for the first time?
2. What determines whether a male will succeed in achieving penetration?
3. Why does the male require so many intromissions before ejaculating?
4. What causes the male to slow down and eventually stop his copulatory responding?

Much of my research has centered around the last three of these questions.

Sensory Feedback: The Primary Determinant of Intromission

In order to determine what factors facilitate penetration by the male, we analyzed intromission further and then performed some experiments.

The intromission response itself is divided into two stages or components: (1) a series of rapid shallow thrusts followed by (2) a single vigorous deep thrust and withdrawal. The distinction between shallow and deep thrusting was first studied in detail in 1940 by Calvin Stone and Leonard Ferguson of Stanford University. On the basis of high-speed photography, they made estimates of the duration of penetration. It seemed to them that penetration took place even during the early portions of the shallow thrusting stage. This is important because it determines the duration of penetration, and hence the amount of genital sensory feedback. To be sure of the answer, I refined Stone and Ferguson's experiment in 1963, in Frank Beach's laboratory. The refinement consisted of small electrodes attached to each animal so that direct genital contact, with the aid of an electronic circuit, illuminated a lamp that was photographed along with the animals.

My films generally confirmed Stone and Ferguson's findings but with one crucial exception: The males

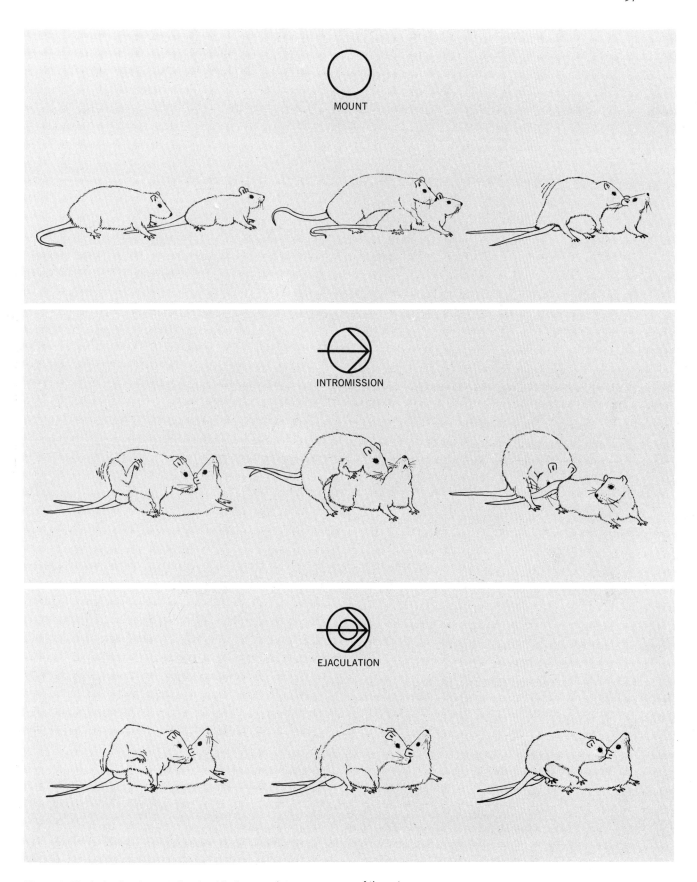

Figure 1. The behavioral events involved in the copulatory sequence of the rat.

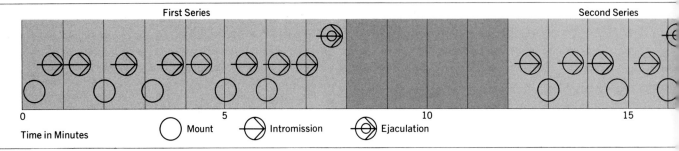

Figure 2. The time course of normal copulatory behavior in the rat involves about 5 ejaculatory series, of which 3 are shown here. The pauses between the ejaculation and the beginning of the next series become progressively longer.

made very little if any direct genital contact during their shallow thrusting. Whenever the lamp lighted to indicate successful penetration, the male ceased his shallow thrusting and executed the single deep thrust. This meant that shallow thrusting did not contribute substantially to the stimulation of the penis but served to orient the male properly for executing the deep thrust. It seems, therefore, that shallow thrusting is the detection component of the response, and deep thrusting the stimulation component.

I went on to test this conclusion by experiment. Norman Adler and I reasoned that if feedback from the penis is required for the release of the deep-thrust response, then by preventing feedback by anesthetizing the penis we should be able to block the response. Sure enough, a topical anesthetic applied to the male abolished the deep thrust without interfering with mounting and shallow thrusting. Sven Carlsson and Knut Larsson of Goteborg University have obtained identical results using a liquid local anesthetic.

The necessity for feedback prior to full penetration is not restricted to the rat. Madeline Cooper and Lester Aronson of the American Museum of Natural History have shown that male cats surgically deprived of feedback from the penis are incapable of successfully penetrating a female. As with rats, these males continue to mount, but their orientations are inadequate for penetration. In these cases the motivation to perform remains unaffected but the capacity for successful performance is hampered.

The Ejaculatory Mechanism

What is the relation between intromissions and ejaculation? The most obvious suggestion is that one produces the other. The series of intromissions preceding each ejaculation somehow changes the internal state of the male so that the ejaculatory response becomes more and more likely. But how to discover the physiological mechanisms producing these changes?

In 1956 Frank Beach suggested a model for the underlying mechanism, which was later further developed by the Swedish psychologist Knut Larsson. The basic idea is that the stimulating effects of each short intromission are not immediately forgotten but are stored somewhere in the nervous system. Because some

of the excitation aroused by each intromission stays with the rat, the total level of excitation increases during the series of intromissions. When the amount of accumulated excitation reaches a critical level, the next penetration results in enough additional excitation to produce ejaculation.

Larsson suggested that the level of stored excitation increases spontaneously for several minutes following a single intromission, even if the male does not achieve another intromission during that time. This spontaneous growth becomes progressively slower and eventually declines unless the male augments the process by achieving another intromission (see Figure 3).

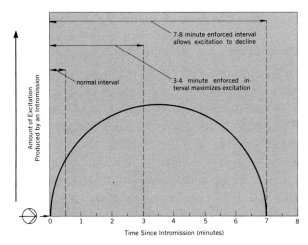

Figure 3. Time relationship between intromission and excitation in rats.

Larsson arrived at his theory by observing the behavior of males who were experimentally separated from the female after each intromission. (Normally, when the animals were not separated by the experimenter, the males achieved an intromission every twenty to thirty seconds and ejaculated after ten to twelve intromissions.) When a separation of between two and three minutes was enforced, the males ejaculated after only four or five intromissions. When the separation was seven minutes or more, the number of intromissions needed to achieve ejaculation became very large. Indeed, some males failed to ejaculate even after several

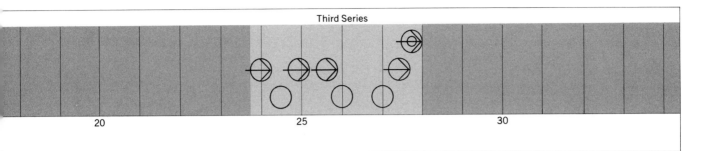

dozen intromissions. Larsson concluded that the short, enforced separations of three minutes had allowed the excitation from each intromission to grow spontaneously to its maximum. Therefore the total number of intromissions required to reach the ejaculatory level of excitation had been reduced to a minimum. Longer enforced separations allowed a decline in excitation. (See Figure 4.)

This "accumulating excitation" model has achieved partial support from the results of several experiments. For example, I showed in 1964 that if the male were separated from the female only once during an ejaculatory series, then he ejaculated after fewer intromissions than when no interval was enforced. Yet the number of intromissions required was greater than when separation occurred after each intromission. This is the result predicted by the theory.

The basic assumption of this model of the ejaculatory mechanism is that the number of intromissions preceding ejaculation is determined only by the time interval between the intromissions (see Figure 5). However, I believe this model is oversimplified. It would be sur-

prising if nothing more were involved in the control of such a complex sequence of behavior, and in fact, the results of several experiments have shown that it does oversimplify the picture. We are forced to acknowledge that other factors must be involved in determining the number of intromissions required for ejaculation.

Our understanding of how these factors operate has been aided by physiological data collected by Benjamin Hart of the University of California, Davis. Hart has shown that male rats whose spinal cords have been separated from their brains are still capable of showing strong reactions similar to ejaculation. This means that the neural machinery associated with ejaculation is organized in the spinal cord. It may be, as Hart suggests, that these responses are normally checked or inhibited by higher brain centers, and the function of genital excitation is simply to release them.

This physiological information can be incorporated into the original excitation model in a straightforward way. Earlier we assumed that the critical level of excitation for ejaculation was always the same. Now we can see that this level may increase or decrease as more or

Figure 4. Effect of intervals of enforced separation of male and female during copulatory sequence.

Result

Normal Pattern	10-12 Intromissions
Several Enforced Intervals of 2-3 Minutes	4 or 5 Intromissions
Several Enforced Intervals of 7-8 Minutes	Very Large Number of Intromissions
One Enforced Interval of 2-3 Minutes	7 or 8 Intromissions

Intromission   Ejaculation

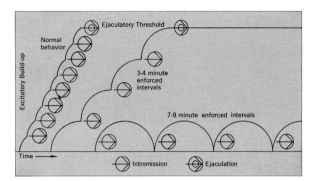

Figure 5. Larsson's theory of excitatory buildup accounts for the effects of enforced intercopulatory intervals (see Figure 4): The number of intromissions needed to produce an ejaculatory excitation level depends upon the amount of excitatory buildup after each intromission.

less inhibition is impressed on the spinal ejaculation reflex by the brain. The amount of inhibitory influence at any time can be expected to change with many changes in the environment; therefore, we need to do experiments that will tell us in detail how the environment controls inhibitory influence on ejaculation.

Cessation of Copulation: Exhaustion or Boredom?

In 1956 Frank Beach and Lisbeth Jordan allowed twelve male rats to copulate with single females until the males appeared exhausted (that is, until thirty minutes passed without the occurrence of a copulatory response). After each exhausted male was allowed from twenty-four hours to two weeks of rest, the males were placed with new receptive females and again allowed to copulate until exhausted. The experiment showed that a twenty-four-hour rest period was not enough: only one of the twelve males ejaculated again, and only three achieved intromission. In fact, ten to fifteen days of rest seemed necessary for the males to regain original levels of copulatory performance.

Then, in 1958, Allen Fisher of the University of Pittsburgh reported a startling and paradoxical finding. Fisher found that if he replaced the original female with a new one immediately after the male reached exhaustion, the "exhausted" male began to copulate immediately and could achieve ejaculation with no difficulty; moreover, if the male were continually supplied with new females at regular intervals, he could double or triple his total number of ejaculations before exhaustion.

This dramatic restoration of copulatory behavior established beyond doubt that the gradual cessation of copulation with the first female is not produced simply by physical exhaustion or by the inability to copulate further. "Copulatory exhaustion" is now seen to be at best a relative term. The male simply does not exhaust himself with only one female. Instead he becomes progressively more disinterested in the stimuli she pro-

vides—until they no longer elicit his copulatory behavior. Another female provides a novel set of stimuli capable of rekindling the male's interest. And so does still another female after that.

Fisher's result is puzzling in the light of the findings of Beach and Jordan. It appears that male rats are potentially more active copulators immediately after prolonged copulation than after twenty-four hours of rest. How to resolve this paradox?

As a first step toward understanding this, Dale Lott, Linn Anderson, and I did the following experiment. We first allowed males to "exhaust" themselves with single females. Then we introduced a second female immediately, or after periods of rest ranging up to twenty-four hours. The males were allowed to copulate with the second female for as long as they had with the first. The design of this experiment permitted us to trace the time course of changes in copulatory behavior. When the second female was introduced immediately after the removal of the first, the male would mount her virtually immediately. However, after a twenty-four-hour delay, males took substantially longer to begin copulation. (See Figure 6.) In fact, some of the males refused to mount at all. Although the males in this experiment were more likely to copulate after a twenty-four-hour delay than the males in Beach and Jordan's

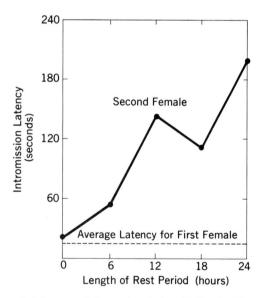

Figure 6. After copulating extensively with the first female, a male takes longer to begin copulating with a second female as the amount of rest between females is *increased.*

experiment, they were certainly slower to begin copulation after this period of rest than when they had been given no rest at all.

We saw that a substantial number of rats copulated to ejaculation with the new female. We now look at the period of time that elapsed from this ejaculation to the next intromission. Do these postejaculatory intervals also show evidence of recovery? Does changing females affect the male's ability to recover from ejaculation? It turns out (see Figure 7) that the intervals are always

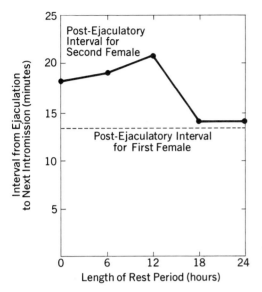

Figure 7. The introduction of a second female does not permit the male to recover from ejaculation more rapidly; he shows recovery only after a rest of about 24 hours.

greater with the second female than with the first: Changing females did not improve the male's ability to recover from ejaculation. In fact, even following the twenty-four-hour rest period the postejaculatory interval is only beginning to return to its original value.

Here, then, is a partial resolution of the paradox. We can see that the "novelty" produced by the introduction of the second female immediately after prolonged contact with the first causes the male to approach her promptly and commence copulation. But this novel stimulation does not reestablish the male's original ability to recover rapidly from ejaculation. This recovery comes only with time. It is not complete even after twenty-four hours. Also, it is clear that the ability of the second female to arouse the male to achieve intromission dwindles substantially within twenty-four hours; the immediacy of the change in females is a part of the novelty that induces the male to copulate. Males copulate with the second female not *in spite* of her immediate introduction but *because* of it.

The Female's Motivation

We have so far concerned ourselves exclusively with the male's behavior. But the success of the male in achieving intromission and ejaculation also depends on the response of the female to his attempts—the female must be properly receptive. What are the characteristics of the female's receptivity?

Female rats, like the females of many other mammalian species, are receptive to copulatory behavior only at the time they are capable of reproducing—that is, the time of ovulation. Under normal laboratory conditions, female rats ovulate once every four or five days. For approximately nineteen hours during this time, the female will allow the male to mount and achieve penetration.

The most characteristic response of the receptive female is *lordosis*: an arching of the back that produces a pronounced elevation of the hindquarters and genital area. Lordosis and a sideward deflection of the tail permit the male to achieve penetration.

The lordosis response is not under voluntary control in the female. It is a reflex response that usually occurs only when the male grasps the female's flanks. The female rat does not spontaneously present herself to the male in her copulatory posture, as, for example, female monkeys do. Instead she is dependent upon the male for the elicitation of this response. But it is only in this one sense that the female rat is the passive member of a copulating pair.

When a receptive female is placed with a vigorous male, she does not appear to have much to do with the selection of intercopulatory or postejaculatory intervals. The male seems to control the pace of copulation. Receptive females will occasionally approach sluggish males and circle them or perhaps nuzzle them a little. But this sort of approach is exceptional. It is, in itself, insufficient evidence that the female is positively motivated for copulation. In fact, considering both the reflexive nature of the lordosis response and the male's predominant role in determining when the events will occur, it is clearly possible that the female might not have positive copulatory motivation at all. How could this problem be put to a direct experimental test?

One method is to attempt to train the female to perform some arbitrary response (for example, to press a lever) in order to be exposed to a vigorous male. If a female can be trained to seek copulation, then we can safely state that she has positive copulatory motivation.

In 1960, at Harvard University, I discovered that female rats would press a lever in order to receive a single copulatory contact (mount, intromission, or ejaculation) from a male. The training procedure was essentially the same as that used to teach animals to press levers for food. Each time the female pressed the lever, I placed a male in the cage and allowed him to achieve one contact. I then removed him and waited to see if the female would press the lever again. Under these conditions females would usually maintain their lever-pressing behavior until they had received five ejaculations. Clearly the female is motivated.

Complications appeared immediately, though, for at this same time Trevor Pierce and Ronald Nuttall of the Social Relations Department at Harvard demonstrated that female rats would work not only to achieve copulatory contact but also to avoid it. They placed a receptive female in a small arena containing several vigorous males. At one end of the arena was an elevated platform. The female was allowed to jump onto this "balcony" at any time, but the males were forced to remain in the arena below. The presence of several males in the arena ensured that the female would be under almost continuous invitation to copulate.

Under these conditions the female made regular trips to and from the balcony. Immediately upon jumping down she would be approached by a male who would mount, intromit, or ejaculate. The attempt of a second male would usually follow very shortly thereafter. The female rarely accepted the second male but instead dodged her way through the other animals to the balcony, where she remained for a period of time before jumping down again. The female was clearly motivated both to achieve copulation and to prevent repeated copulations from occurring within brief intervals. Each female established a set of "preferred intervals" for copulation.

A careful examination of the behavior in the lever-pressing and balcony situations reveals that the amount of time a female chooses to wait between copulatory episodes is consistently related to the kind of stimulation she has just received from the male (see Figure 8).

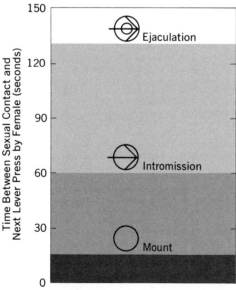

Figure 8. When a receptive female is allowed to control the time between sexual contacts by pressing a lever, the time between copulatory episodes is consistently related to the kind of stimulation she has just received from the male: she will press the lever sooner after a mount than after an intromission, and sooner after an intromission than after an ejaculation.

Whenever a female was mounted without penetration, she would press the lever again (or return to the arena) after a pause of twenty seconds or less. If she received an intromission, she was likely to wait about one minute before seeking the next contact, and if the male had

ejaculated, the female would usually delay her next contact for between two and five minutes.

This close relation between the type of copulatory contact and the female's subsequent pause allows us to conclude that females can detect the difference between mounts, intromissions, and ejaculations. More important, it suggests that the more genital stimulation a female receives from a single contact, the longer she will wait before responding again.

In 1963, William Westbrook and I began a series of three experiments to obtain more exact information on how changes in the quantity of copulatory stimulation affected the female's tendency to initiate further contact. Our hypothesis was that if we reduced the amount of stimulation afforded by copulatory contact, the females would seek subsequent contacts earlier. In all three experiments, we used the lever-pressing technique. In the first experiment we concentrated on the effect of ejaculation.

When the male rat ejaculates, his seminal fluid coagulates almost immediately to form a viscous plug in the female's vagina. Sometimes this "vaginal plug" falls out of the female within a few minutes. At other times it is pulled out during subsequent copulation. In any case, the presence of the plug in the vagina seems an obvious place to look for a substantial contribution to the prolongation of the female's postejaculatory intervals. Following up this reasoning with experimentation, we injected males with a drug that prevented the emission of seminal fluid at the time of the ejaculatory response. With this treatment, males showed all the behavioral signs of ejaculation. But no semen was emitted. When females received no vaginal plugs, they recovered from ejaculation sooner than they did when plugs were deposited. The plug plays a functional role in determining the female's postejaculatory interval. It appears to contribute quite a bit to the amount of vaginal stimulation.

In our next experiments we attempted to reduce the amount of available stimulation one step further. First we partially anesthetized the females' vaginas and external genital areas and noted that they then responded more rapidly after all three types of contact than they did while unanesthetized. Finally, we reduced copulatory stimulation to a bare minimum by placing the females with males whose penises had been anesthetized. This treatment, we said earlier, prevents full intromission as well as ejaculation. Under these conditions, receptive females actively sought copulatory stimulation at extremely short intervals throughout a full hour.

The basic determinant of copulatory receptivity in female rats is the hormonal state of the animal around the time of ovulation. Without this, she will not permit copulation. Our experiments indicate that superimposed on this basic receptivity are short-term changes in responsiveness caused by the amount of genital stimulation the female receives.

These experiments show that both male and female rats impose on copulatory activities their own sets of temporal limitations, each set largely determined by the amount of sensory feedback afforded by previous contact. The temporal requirements of each partner mesh neatly and naturally together so that effective copulation and reproduction proceed efficiently from generation to generation. This is yet another of nature's wise prearrangements of compatible connections between animals. The experimental psychologist seeks to explicate these relationships, and in so doing concludes by admiring them.

The Young Monkeys
Harry and Margaret Harlow

Dethier and Bermant analyzed motivated behavior—feeding and copulation—on a simple, almost reflex level. The Harlows are concerned with more complicated patterns of social behavior. In this article, they discuss their extensive research on the role of mother and peers in the development of monkey social behavior.

When we watch a newborn rhesus monkey with its mother, the infant seems to display signs of affection almost at once, clinging to the mother's body and climbing into her arms. The slightly older infant cries piteously when separated from its mother. Still later, as the maternal bond weakens, the young monkey reaches out to others its own age for companionship and, finally, for sexual satisfaction.

These examples illustrate the three basic social responses of primates—affection, fear, and social aggression. In fact, the responses usually emerge in that order as the infant monkey matures.

Affection, the reaction to cuddling, warmth, and food, comes first in these broadly based and sometimes even overlapping categories. Then comes fear, as the infant begins to explore a sometimes dangerous world. And finally, there is social aggression when the monkey is older, more exploratory, and better able to handle itself.

These responses obviously are not the simple component behavior patterns that B. F. Skinner has described, nor are they like Pavlovian reflex reactions. Rather, they are highly complicated and built-in patterns of behavior that can be modified by learning. Under certain circumstances, normal development can be blocked, and the patterns disrupted. When this is done under experimental conditions, we can learn more about the sensitive, vital process of socialization.

Certainly monkeys are not people, but they are the next highest form of animal life, and we can perform complex experiments with them, manipulating their environment with a freedom not possible when using people as subjects. For example, we can put monkeys into isolation as they develop, we can add to or take away from their basic emotional needs. And as we learn more about the basic emotions of monkeys, we can profit from this knowledge in our ever-active search to find out more about ourselves in the world.

The Beginnings of Affection

The first sign of affection by the newborn rhesus monkey is a reflex action that facilitates nursing. The infant grasps its mother's fur and moves upward on her body until restrained by her arms. This brings the baby monkey's face close to the mother's breast, and the infant begins to nurse. Throughout the first two or three weeks of life, the response of infant to mother continues to be based on reflexes, although the baby gradually gains voluntary control of its motor behavior. But even after the young monkey is skilled enough to walk, run, and climb by itself, it continues to cling to its mother. The bond of affection between infant and mother continues to grow stronger instead of weaker during the next few months.

The mother monkey warmly returns her infant's affection, and this reciprocal affection operates in a way that helps prepare the young monkey for participation in a more complex social environment. The mother shows her fondness by cradling, grooming, caressing, and protecting her baby. At first, this affection is primarily reflex behavior and is stimulated by the touch, sound, and sight of the baby. Interestingly, the baby need not be the female monkey's own, for preadolescent, adolescent, and adult females are attracted to all the infants in their group. Given the opportunity, even females who have not recently borne young will adopt infants, and this indicates that hormonal changes associated with parturition are not essential to the establishment of maternal affection.

Fear

Fear responses show themselves after the young rhesus has matured intellectually and has had enough experience to recognize objects that are strange and dangerous. In its first two months a young rhesus shows little or no fear. But by the third or fourth month of life, unfamiliar places, persons, and objects as well as loud or unusual noises make the infant screech and cling to its mother. Young monkeys separated from their mothers will cry frequently and clasp themselves. An infant that has previously known only its mother can be frightened by other monkeys, but if the young rhesus has previously been part of a group, it will be afraid of other monkeys only when threatened by them, or actually hurt.

Making Friends

By the time they are two months old, young monkeys that have been allowed to live in groups show an interest in other monkeys, especially infants. First contacts are usually brief, beginning with physical exploration, which can be one-sided or mutual. From these early experiences come more complex play behavior and the development of affection for other young monkeys. Emotional attachment to monkeys of the same age usually appears before the emergence of fear. However, if such attachments are not permitted to develop—if, for instance, the young monkey is kept apart from his peers—there is some possibility that this friendly emotion will not emerge at all. Nevertheless, the infant that has received a good deal of maternal affection can sometimes make friends even when the normal age for doing so has passed.

Emotional bonds among those of the same age usually grow stronger as the maternal relationship begins to ebb. The infant's first emotional experience, the attachment to its mother, is quite distinct from later

emotional ties. For example, the peer relationship originates in and develops through play. Young monkeys that have not been permitted to establish relationships with other infants are wary of their playmates when finally allowed to be with them, and these deprived monkeys often fail to develop strong bonds of affection. Yet monkeys that have been deprived of mother love but provided with early contacts *can* develop ties with their peers that seem comparable to the bonds formed by mother-reared infants.

Affection of age mates for one another is universal within the entire primate kingdom. It starts early in all species of monkeys and apes, and it is evident throughout the life span. The beginnings of human sociability, however, are more variable because children's opportunities to contact their age mates differ from family to family and from culture to culture. Four decades ago, research by Charlotte Buhler and her associates in Vienna showed that human infants in their first year of life generally are responsive to one another. This can be confirmed informally by anyone who looks in on a pediatrician's waiting room where healthy young children contact one another quickly. If held, they strain toward one another, and if close together, they reach out to one another. They smile at each other, and they laugh together.

Sex Roles

In early infancy, the child's sex is relatively unimportant in social interactions: Human boys and girls, like male and female monkeys, play together indiscriminately at first. Though this continues for several years in humans, behavioral differences begin to appear in monkeys by the third or fourth month and increase steadily until the animal is mature.

Male monkeys become increasingly forceful, while the females become progressively more passive. A male will threaten other males and females alike, whereas females rarely are aggressive toward males. During periods of play, males are the pursuers, and the females retreat. As they grow older, increasing separation of the sexes becomes evident in friendship and in play.

During their juvenile period, one to two years of age, and even after, rhesus monkeys as a rule form pairs and clusters of friends of the same sex. Only in maturity when the female is in heat does the pattern change, and then only temporarily. Male-female pairs dominate until the mating period ends. And then the partners return to their own sex groups. With humans, too, friendships with those of the same sex predominate in childhood, adolescence, and maturity. Even when men and women attend the same social event, men often cluster together with other men, while women form groups by themselves. Clubs for men only, or for women only, further demonstrate this sexual split.

At both the human and subhuman levels, this separation is undoubtedly based on common interests, which in turn are based on anatomical and physical differences between the sexes. For example, male primates of most species are larger and stronger than the females and better equipped physiologically for feats of strength and physical endurance. This probably leads the male to more large-muscle activities. Culture influences do not create differences in behavior between the sexes, but they do mold, maintain, and exaggerate the natural differences. Thus boys, not girls, are encouraged to become athletes, and women boxers and shot-putters are generally regarded as oddities.

The importance of peer relationships in monkeys cannot be overemphasized. All primates that live in groups achieve much of their communal cohesiveness and adult sexual social behavior through affectionate relationships with others of the same age. Monkeys learn their sex roles through play. By the third or fourth month of life, male and female sexual behavior are beginning to be different. By the time they are a year old, most monkeys who have been reared in groups display mature and specialized sexual behavior, except that male intromission and ejaculation do not occur until puberty, at about four years of age.

Social Aggression

Sexual differentiation usually is learned by monkeys before social aggression appears. After numerous and varied studies at the University of Wisconsin, we have concluded that unless peer affection precedes social aggression, monkeys do not adjust; either they become unreasonably aggressive or they develop into passive scapegoats for their group.

Rhesus monkeys begin to make playful attacks on one another almost as soon as they are old enough for actual contact, and their aggression increases steadily throughout the first year of life. The young monkeys wrestle and roll, pretend to bite one another, and make threatening gestures. But they do not hurt each other, even though their teeth are sharp enough to pierce a playmate's skin.

If the young rhesus has had normal group contact during infancy, it will show restraint toward both friends and strangers. Only if threatened, or to protect weaker members of its group, will it fight.

While in the group the young try to find a place in the hierarchy, and as dominance is established, a relative peace ensues. In contrast, monkeys who have been socially deprived may seriously injure one another when placed together at this stage.

Isolation Breeds Fear

One experimental rearing condition that throws much light on the problems of aggression and peer affection is total social isolation. At birth, the monkey is enclosed in a stainless steel chamber where light is diffused, temper-

ature controlled, air flow regulated, and environmental sounds filtered. Food and water are provided, and the cage is cleaned by remote control. During its isolation, the animal sees no living creature, not even a human hand. After three, six, or twelve months, the monkey is removed from the chamber and placed in an individual cage in the laboratory. Several days later it is exposed for the first time to peers—another monkey who has been reared in isolation and two who have been raised in an open cage with others. The four are put in a playroom equipped with toys and other apparatus designed to stimulate activity and play (see Figure 1); they spend usually half an hour a day in the room five days a week, and these sessions go on for six months.

Fear is the overwhelming response in all monkeys raised in isolation. Although the animals are physically healthy, they crouch and appear terror-stricken by their new environment. Young that have been isolated for only three months soon recover and become active in playroom life; by the end of a month they are almost indistinguishable from their control age mates. But the young monkeys that had been isolated for six months adapt poorly to each other and to the control animals. They cringe when approached and fail at first to join in any of the play. During six months of play sessions, they never progress beyond minimal play behavior, such as playing by themselves with toys. What little social activity they do have is exclusively with the other *isolate* in the group. When the other animals become aggressive, the isolates accept their abuse without making any effort to defend themselves. For these animals, social opportunities have come too late. Fear prevents them from engaging in social interaction and consequently from developing ties of affection.

Monkeys that have been isolated for twelve months are very seriously affected. Although they have reached the age at which true aggression is normally present, and they can observe it in their playmates, they show no signs of aggression themselves. Even primitive and simple play activity is almost nonexistent. With these isolated animals, no social play is observed and aggressive behavior is never demonstrated. Their behavior is a pitiful combination of apathy and terror as they crouch at the sides of the room, meekly accepting the attacks of the more healthy control monkeys. We have been unable to test them in the playroom beyond a ten-week period because they are in danger of being seriously injured or even killed by the others.

Our tests have indicated that this social failure is not a consequence of intellectual arrest. In the course of thirty-five years of experimentation with and observation of monkeys, we have developed tests of learning that successfully discriminate between species, between ages within species, and between monkeys with surgically-produced brain damage and their normal peers. The tests have demonstrated that the isolated animals are as intellectually able as are monkeys of the same age raised in open cages. The only difference is that the isolates require more time to adjust to the learning apparatus. All monkeys must be adapted to testing, but those coming from total isolation are more fearful, and so it takes longer for them to adjust to the situation.

From Apathy to Aggression

We continued the testing of the same six- and twelve-month isolates for a period of several years. The results were startling. The monkeys raised in isolation now began to attack the other monkeys viciously, whereas before they had cowered in fright. We tested the isolates with three types of strangers: large and powerful adults, normal monkeys of their age, and normal one-year-olds. The monkeys that had been raised in the steel isolation cages for their first six months now were three years old. They were still terrified by all strangers, even the physically helpless juveniles. But in spite of their terror, they engaged in uncontrolled aggression, often launching suicidal attacks upon the large adult males and even attacking the juveniles—an act almost never seen in normal monkeys of their age. The passage of time had only exaggerated their asocial and antisocial behavior.

In those monkeys, positive social action was not initiated, play was nonexistent, grooming did not occur, and sexual behavior either was not present at all or was totally inadequate. In human terms, these monkeys, who had lived unloved and in isolation, were totally unloving, distressed, disturbed, and delinquent.

Sexual Inadequacy

We have found that social deprivation has another long-term effect that is particularly destructive—inadequate sexual behavior. This is found in all males and most females reared in total or semi-isolation. Whereas some of the females that had been in semi-isolation still show a certain amount of sexual responsiveness, this is probably due to their easier role in copulation. The separate actions required for copulation begin to appear in young infants, but these actions are not organized into effective patterns unless early social play—particularly of a heterosexual nature—is allowed. Monkeys that fail to develop adult sexual patterns by the time they are twelve to eighteen months old are poor risks for breeding when they are mature.

For example, we found in one study that semi-isolated females that are placed with breeding males avoid social proximity and do not groom themselves. They often engage in threats, aggression, and autistic be-

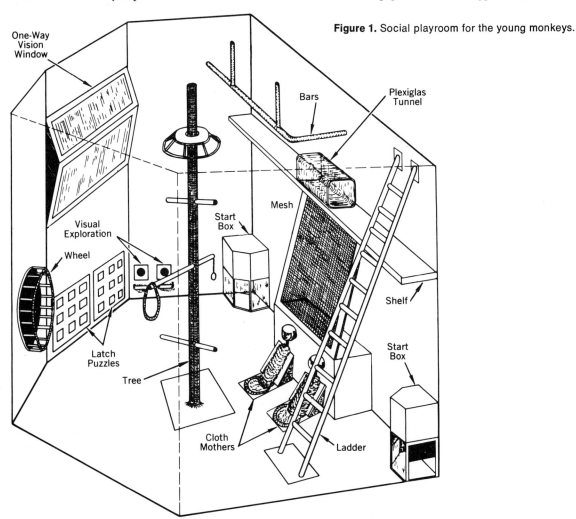

Figure 1. Social playroom for the young monkeys.

One-Way Vision Window

Bars

Plexiglas Tunnel

Visual Exploration

Wheel

Mesh

Start Box

Latch Puzzles

Tree

Shelf

Start Box

Cloth Mothers

Ladder

havior such as clutching and biting themselves, and they frequently fail to support the male when mounting occurs. In contrast, normal females seldom threaten males, are not aggressive, and do not engage in autistic behavior; they maintain social proximity, groom themselves, and provide adequate support for the mounting male.

Parallel tests with males show that socially deprived males are even more inadequate than their female counterparts. Compared to the normal males, they groomed less, threatened more, were more aggressive, rarely initiated any sexual contact, engaged in unusual and abnormal sexual responses, and—with one exception—never achieved intromission.

The sexual inadequacies of the socially deprived monkeys did not come from a loss of biological sex drive. High arousal was often seen, but it led to inappropriate responses—autistic behavior, masturbation, and violent aggression—all in a frenetic sequence lasting only a few seconds.

Monkeys Without Mothers

In another series of experiments on the emotional bases of social development in monkeys, we raised some infants with continuous peer experience and no mothers. Two, four, and six monkeys were reared together in groups. The groups of two tended to cling together in the first few weeks, chest to chest, and this behavior persisted long after normally raised infants would have stopped clinging to their mothers. The two young monkeys moved about like Siamese twins joined at the chest. When some external force turned up to break the two apart, or one rhesus attempted to explore an object, the other quickly tried to resume the clinging posture. This immature behavior continued until the animals were put in separate cages, although we found that it could be drastically reduced if the pairs were reared together for a fixed period of time, separated for another specified time, and then subjected to alternate togetherness and separation.

We also found that four or six infant monkeys living together in one cage tend very soon to form a line in which one rhesus leans forward and the others get behind him in a single file, each clinging to the back of the animal in front of him. If the first monkey moves without breaking loose, the whole group usually moves in unison with it, but if the lead rhesus frees itself, the pattern breaks up, to be re-formed shortly.

While monkeys reared in pairs play very infrequently —the tight clasp they have on one another restricts movement—the infants raised in larger groups play extensively. In one respect, the monkeys that have been raised in the larger groups are quite precocious: Their sexual behavior is perfected at an early age and as adults they breed readily. This is in sharp contrast with the absence or insufficiency of sexual activity in male and female isolates.

Throughout our studies, we have been increasingly impressed by the alternative routes monkeys may take to reach adequate social behavior, which by our criteria includes affection toward peers, controlled fear and aggression, and normal sexual behavior. In protected laboratory conditions, social interaction between peers and between mother and child appear to be in large part interchangeable in their effect on the infant's development. A rhesus can surmount the absence of its mother if it can associate with its peers, and it can surmount a lack of socialization with peers if its mother provides affection. Being raised with several age mates appears to compensate adequately for a lack of mothering, although it is likely that animals reared in this way would be at a disadvantage if confronted by monkeys that had had a mother and early experience with others their age as well.

From an evolutionary point of view, there is an advantage to the animal in having two independent sources of affection—mother and peers. Each in part compensates for the deficiencies of the other. Mothers vary considerably in the depth and type of their attachment to their children. A rhesus mother denied normal affection in her early life may be so detached from her infant and, in many cases, may be so brutal that the effects could be devastating for her infant unless there were companions available for play. Human mothers may also exhibit detachment and physical abuse, which pediatricians refer to as the "battered baby" syndrome —a much more prevalent phenomenon than police and court records indicate.

Isolation studies that begin at birth and continue until some specified age provide a powerful technique for the analysis of maturational processes without interference from an overlay of learning. Indeed, the isolation experiment is one of the few methods by which it is possible to measure the development of complex behavior patterns in any pure or relatively pure form. While it is commonly thought that learning shapes preestablished, unlearned response patterns, this is barely half the picture, at least as far as social learning is concerned.

One of the most important functions of social learning in primates—and perhaps in all mammals and many other classes of animals as well—is the development of social patterns that will restrain and check potentially asocial behavior. These positive, learned social patterns must be established before negative, unlearned patterns emerge. In this sense, social learning is an anticipation of later learning: The inappropriate exercise of negative behavior can be checked within the social group while the same behavior is permitted toward intruders threatening from without.

It's All in Your Mind

Frank Beach

One of the pioneers in the field of hormones and behavior, Beach surveys the biological and social factors controlling sex behavior in mammals and analyzes aspects of sex behavior in a large number of species. He is not as concerned with the precise neurochemical control of a single behavior pattern as he is with the broad evolutionary picture of mammalian sexuality.

The sex glands begin secreting hormones in the human fetus well before birth. Until puberty, boys and girls produce male hormones (androgens) and female hormones (chiefly estrogens) in small and roughly equal amounts. Early in adolescence, however, the amount of androgen secreted by the boy's testicles and the amount of estrogen produced by the girl's ovaries rise sharply.

Similar changes take place in the hormone levels of all male and female mammals when they reach sexual maturity. But the changes in sexual behavior that occur in mammals as they mature differ markedly from species to species, and between male and female in the same species. Something other than hormones, then, must be at work in at least some cases.

Mating and Reproduction

For around nineteen hours every four or five days, at about the time of ovulation, the female rat is in estrus. During those nineteen hours she and the male rat pay a great deal of attention to each other. The rest of the time they do not, because rats, like most mammals, mate only when the female is in heat and fertilization can take place. When the female is infertile, the male is not attracted and the female is not receptive.

In rats, mating and reproduction are blood brothers; in human beings, they are less intimately related. The human female, alone among mammals, has no easily identifiable period of estrus, and it is clear that human sexual relations take place for a variety of nonreproductive reasons. The break between human and subhuman sexual behavior is not, however, as sharp as it might appear. Apes and monkeys sometimes mate when the female is not in estrus, although neither appears to enjoy sex as much under those conditions as when the female is in heat.

As one moves up the evolutionary scale, there is a gradual loosening of the tie between mating and reproduction. The explanation for this lies partly in parallel physiological changes. The sexual behavior of lower mammals like the rat is very strongly controlled by hormones from the ovaries and testes, whereas that of higher mammals is less dependent upon chemical products of the sex glands. In higher mammals, the balance of power shifts toward the central nervous system—and especially, it seems, toward the neocortex. That part of the brain, relatively small in rats but very large in human beings, is responsible for the most flexible, least stereotyped aspects of behavior, including memory and learning.

Hormonal Versus Cortical Control

Some of the most convincing evidence concerning the hormonal control of sexual behavior comes from ontogenic studies that examine correlations between changes in hormone level and changes in sexual behavior (at puberty, for instance), and from castration studies, in which the hormone-producing sex glands are surgically removed and the effects on mating behavior noted. Evidence of control by the neocortex comes from surgical studies in which the cortex is wholly or partly removed, and from observations of learned sexual behavior.

In all these matters there are differences between species, and also between males and females of the same species.

In rodents, which are relatively simple mammals, hormonal control is very strong. When a female rat ovulates and goes into estrus for the first time, she also displays sexually receptive behavior for the first time. She approaches the male, runs away, and then arches her back in a lordosis response when the male follows and mounts. Her sexual behavior requires no practice before puberty, and it is not modified by later experience. It simply begins, complete, when her ovaries mature.

In the male rat, the situation is only slightly different. The difference is that the young male does practice some elements of the adult mating pattern well before his testicles begin secreting large amounts of androgen. Young males often do a great deal of playful chasing, wrestling, and mock fighting, in the course of which one rat will sometimes mount another briefly and perhaps perform a few pelvic thrusts (though without signs of sexual excitement).

Since young rats castrated at birth behave the same as normal rats, prepubertal behavior cannot be attributed to the traces of androgen in the immature rat's body. It seems, then, that hormonal control of the male rat's sexual behavior is slightly less complete than hormonal control of the female's.

Immature male dogs are more inclined to sex play than young rats, but in general the full copulatory pattern in male and female carnivores also appears suddenly at puberty, when the level of hormone secretion rises. In monkeys and apes, puberty is marked by

an upsurge in erotic responsiveness and in the capacity for coitus. It is difficult to make comparisons between primates and subprimates, however, because there has been much more early experimentation with primates.

Chimpanzees of both sexes, for example, often make exploratory attempts to mate before puberty.

Human children in many societies, if not all, engage in sex play a lot. Further, genital stimulation in young infants of both sexes sometimes elicits motor responses like those of adult orgasm. The hormonal changes that take place in our species at puberty are analogous to those that take place in the rat, but the behavioral changes are far less sudden and less complete.

When human reproductive life ends, as it does in women at the menopause, the effects of the reduced hormone level vary widely. Some women say that their sexual desires and capacities are just as great after menopause as before; some say they decline; a few even say they increase. In men, both the level of androgen production and the level of sexual performance seem to decline gradually with age. Some very old men remain potent; some younger men become impotent even though hormone production has not stopped. Given this rather tenuous relation between hormones and sexual activity, it is hardly surprising that the results of hormone injections are undependable as far as behavior is concerned.

| CASTRATION STUDIES | The clearest findings on the hormonal control of mating behavior in subprimates come from castration studies. One thing such experiments confirm is the vital importance of hormones to the sex life of the female rat. When her ovaries are removed, she becomes immediately and totally unresponsive;

when hormones are administered artificially, the full mating pattern reappears. Hormone injections also cause full estrus behavior in immature females, or in females that are between estrus periods.

In female dogs, too, removing the ovaries abolishes sexual receptivity promptly and permanently, and estrus behavior can be fully restored by hormone therapy.

Males are less consistent in their response to castration. Male rats lose their copulatory ability totally and permanently (unless they are given hormones), but it does not vanish nearly as fast as it does in female rats. Also, some male rats retain sexual responsiveness much longer than others.

In an experiment with male dogs, I found that castration had different results, depending on the dog's age and prior experience with mating. Dogs castrated before puberty never copulated successfully, even after receiving hormone injections. In some mature, experienced males, potency began to decline shortly after surgery, but it could be fully restored by hormones; in others, sexual behavior continued without benefit of hormone therapy for more than five years.

There are only a few scattered reports on castration in primates. The behavior of female apes and monkeys whose ovaries have been removed is much like that of females who are not in estrus. That is, they are generally unreceptive but occasionally permit copulation, especially if an aggressive male seems to threaten physical injury. Male apes castrated in infancy develop a vigorous sexual pattern nonetheless, and castrated adults seem to retain their potency, though neither group is capable of ejaculation and orgasm.

The information we have on castration in human beings is fragmentary, subjective, and of dubious reliability. About all one can say is that the effects of removing testicles and ovaries surgically seem to be similar to those of menopause and aging: highly variable from individual to individual.

The marked freedom from hormonal control of erotic responsiveness in our species is, I believe, a direct consequence of the extreme dependence of human behavior upon the complex and intricately organized neocortex. Fish and amphibians have no neocortex, and reptiles and birds have only a rudimentary one. In rats the cortex is well defined but small. In monkeys and apes it is much larger and more specialized; in man it constitutes 90 percent of the brain's volume.

Destruction of a primate's neocortex will greatly incapacitate the animal, and partial damage can seriously disrupt sexual behavior. It is difficult to draw more specific conclusions than this from the available evidence, which often omits information that one can get only from careful and repeated teaching both before and after brain injury.

| CORTICAL LESION STUDIES | In some lower mammals, the higher parts of the brain can be totally removed or separated from lower centers without fatal results. Fe-

male rats and dogs submit to copulation after extensive brain surgery, though their reactions are not as well integrated as those of normal animals. Male rats and dogs immediately become sexually inactive if the cortex is removed. In male rats, smaller cortical lesions do not rule out the motor pattern of coitus but do reduce the animal's capacity for sexual arousal; in cats, whose cortices are more highly specialized, the effects of the lesion vary according to its location.

It appears that the cortex is essential for mating in males of lower species but dispensable for females. Additional evidence on this score comes from a study of sexual inversion in female rats. Many female rats show malelike responses when they confront estrus females. They mount and clasp the other female and sometimes execute pelvic thrusts. These females are not abnormal—they also respond receptively when approached by a male. If their cortexes are removed, all the masculine responses stop, though the feminine responses remain, just as those of other decorticated females do.

Male-Female Cortical Differences

The fact that the sexual behavior of female subprimates seems to be controlled more strongly by hormones and less strongly by the neocortex than that of males has considerable theoretical significance, but it must be interpreted with caution. For one thing, coitus requires more complex behavior of the male rat (or dog) than it does of the female. He, for example, must note and follow up on several sensory cues, whereas she need respond only to the tactile stimulus of the male's clasp. In addition, since female subprimates show no external signs of orgasm, the essential element in their sexual pattern is receptivity, but it is not known whether receptivity and the key element in the male pattern, ejaculation, are truly comparable.

In the sexual behavior of men and women, there are also suggestive differences, though they, too, must be interpreted with great caution. What they suggest is not a difference in the *extent* of cortical control but possibly a difference in kind. As is well known, more men than women report that they are erotically aroused by so-called psychological stimuli—books, pictures, the sight of the opposite sex, and so on. Men also seem to be more prone to sexual fantasies than women; for example, Kinsey, Pomeroy, and Martin found that 89 percent of the men in their sample fantasized during masturbation, as compared to 64 percent of the women. And women are more susceptible than men to distraction during coitus (leading men to complain that women do not put their minds to it); Kinsey relates this to women's greater reliance on continuing physical stimulation for continuing erotic arousal.

It seems fairly clear that female brains differ from male brains, and that at least part of the difference can be traced to the influence of hormones—specifically to male hormones produced by the testicles before and shortly after birth. Recent experiments have shown that the brains of female guinea pigs, rats, dogs, and monkeys can be made more masculine if the female is exposed to male hormones at the appropriate state. The precise timing of this sensitive stage differs in various species, but for some animals and probably for human beings as well it occurs well before birth. Female guinea pigs and rats are affected by the treatment when their mothers are injected with male hormones during pregnancy, and they are born with brains that are neither completely masculine nor entirely feminine. In maturity, these modified females (pseudohermaphrodites, as they are sometimes called) react to injections of male hormone by displaying masculine mating responses; at the same time they are less responsive than normal females to feminine hormones produced by the ovaries. They are never therefore fully receptive to males.

Learned Behavior

In a very general fashion it is correct to say that mammalian species whose cerebral cortex is large and complexly organized are more susceptible to the effects of learning and personal experience than are species with simpler and smaller cortices. In almost all mammals, sexual behavior is open to some modification by experience (that is, to some control by the neocortex). In primates, the animal's individual history can be crucial.

Studies of animals reared in isolation confirm this difference between lower and higher species. Male rats reared without contact with other animals copulate effectively at their first opportunity. Male dogs reared in isolation have trouble, though they are not completely incapacitated. Such a dog may mount estrus females as readily and as often as other males do, but his orientation frequently is poor. He tends to mount the head, side, or flank of the female, with the result that he is only half as likely to achieve intromission as are dogs reared normally.

For monkeys, the effects of isolation are similar but more severe. Harry Harlow reports that when a male and a female raised in isolation are brought together after puberty, they react with excitement to sexual stimuli but cannot achieve coitus: the female's presentation is too high, or the male's thrusts are misdirected, or the pair cannot integrate their activities. As Harlow writes: "It is not a motor deficit, but a lack of knowledge of what to do." The deficiencies tend to persist despite numerous and lengthy opportunities for trial-and-error learning.

Sexual Preference and Boredom

Whereas one rat acts more or less the same as another during mating, human beings differ radically in their sexual behavior—from individual to individual, from culture to culture, and in the same person over a period of time. The increasingly individualized behavior of same-sexed members of different species as control by the hormones grows weaker is another sign of increasing control by the neocortex.

Members of higher species not only show more individual differences than members of lower species but also more sensitivity to individual differences in the opposite sex. Take the matter of boredom.

If a male rat is placed with an estrus female and allowed to mate freely, he eventually seems to tire, and the interval between ejaculations becomes longer and longer. But if the exhausted male is offered a new estrus female, he immediately approaches her and for a while resumes copulation—though this does not last long (see the article by Gordon Bermant in this section).

In higher mammals, the invigorating effects of novelty are even more noticeable. Male rhesus monkeys show a clear increase in sexual activity when new females in the troop go into estrus. An early student of animal behavior, G. V. Hamilton, noted that a male monkey caged with the same female for a considerable time required long periods of foreplay before ejaculation but that if the females in two such pairs were interchanged, the males usually mounted and ejaculated without delay.

In a South Sea community studied by William Davenport, the men bitterly lamented the outlawing of concubinage on the grounds that it made them old before their time. In our own society, men often report dramatic increases in sexual ability when they change partners, and three-fourths of the husbands interviewed by Kinsey and his colleagues admitted at least an occasional desire for extramarital intercourse.

Females also differ more and more from each other within species as they ascend the evolutionary ladder. And, like males, they tend increasingly to show different responses to different members of the opposite sex.

Near the bottom of the mammalian scale is the female rat who is equally receptive to all males who approach her. In several studies of mating preferences in female dogs, however, I found that nearly every bitch showed clear-cut preferences for particular males as sexual partners. There was also some agreement among the females as to which males were attractive. In one experiment one male dog was never rejected by three females and rarely rejected by the other two. Another was consistently unpopular with four females out of five, and even the fifth rejected him sometimes.

Some female apes show marked reluctance to mate with certain males but accept other partners eagerly. R. M. Yerkes tells of an ape named Wendy who eagerly accepted Bokar but rejected Pan. When Pan first solicited coitus, Wendy came down from the wall of her cage and assumed the coital position. Then, as Pan approached, she sprang up and attacked him. Yerkes suggests that she was temporarily dominated by her physiological condition but then became overcome by her negative feelings toward Pan.

Many women have sexual intercourse with only one man in a lifetime; many others, in our own society as well as in less restrictive ones, have coitus with a great many different men. That is to say, not only is the average woman more selective than the average female of lower species, but the extremes are farther apart.

Women who do have sexual relations with more than one partner often report different degrees of responsiveness to each. When the women in Kinsey's sample who had had extramarital affairs were asked to compare husband and lover, 42 percent said they reached orgasm more frequently with their lovers, and 24 percent said they responded more fully to their husbands. Only 34 cent said the frequency of orgasm was about the same with both men.

In stressing the greater tendency of higher mammals to react differently to different partners and to become bored, I would not want to create the impression that cortical control means less, or less satisfying, sexual behavior. Consider the experience of an anthropologist, reported by Paul Gebhard of the Institute for Sex Research. The anthropologist was accustomed to having intercourse about once a week. During a certain field trip, however, he found it expedient to meet the daily demands of a native woman. Though it took some time to get used to the new rhythm, within a few months he found himself as happy with the daily schedule as he had been with the weekly one. When the field trip was over, he readjusted (with some difficulty) to his original frequency. What this anecdote shows, among other things, is that neocortical control can have a facilitating as well as an inhibiting effect on sexual behavior.

Overview of Stress

Hans Selye

There are a few major concepts from biology that have strongly influenced the behavioral sciences. The concept of physiological homeostasis, for example, facilitated the study of behavior regulation, especially of hunger and thirst (see Dethier's article in this volume). Another major concept from physiology is stress. Hans Selye is a leader in this field. His work on stress and the general adaptation syndrome has influenced areas as diverse as human emotionality, psychosomatics, social behavior, and population regulation in animals. In this article Selye discusses the origins of his research and the effect it has had on physiological theory.

We can get high on our own stress hormones. Stress stimulates our glands to make hormones that can induce a kind of drunkenness. Who would consider it prudent to check his conduct as carefully during stress as he does during the cocktail hour? He should. I venture to say that this sort of drunkenness has caused much more harm to society than the other kind.

The concept of stress is very old. It must have occurred even to prehistoric man that there was something in common between the loss of vigor and feeling of exhaustion that overcomes us after hard labor, prolonged exposure to cold or heat, loss of blood, agonizing fear, or any kind of disease.

Man also must have found out long ago that we experience every unaccustomed task—be it swimming in cold water, lifting rocks, or going without food—in three stages: at first it is a hardship, then we get used to it, and finally we can't stand it any longer.

But it was not until some thirty years ago that we found that stress causes certain changes in the structure and chemical composition of the body, which can be accurately appraised. Some of these changes are merely signs of damage; others are the body's attempts to restore itself to normal, its mechanism of defense against stress.

Back in 1926, when stress was still a mystery and I was a second-year medical student, I first came across this stereotyped response. I wondered why the most diverse diseases produced so many common signs and symptoms. Whether a man suffers from severe blood loss, an infection, or advanced cancer, he loses his appetite, strength, and ambition; usually he also loses weight, and even his facial expression betrays his illness. I felt sure that the syndrome of just being sick, which is essentially the same no matter what disease we have, could be analyzed and expressed scientifically.

This possibility fascinated me and, with the enthusiasm of youth, I wanted to start work right away. But, my background as a second-year medical student didn't reach far enough, and I got no further than the formulation of an idea. And the more I learned about the details of medicine, the more I forgot my broad but imprecise plan to tackle the syndrome of being sick.

Years later, under auguries more auspicious for research, I encountered the problem again. I was working as a young assistant in the biochemistry department of McGill University in Montreal, trying to find a new sex hormone in extracts of cattle ovaries. I injected the extracts into rats to see if their organs would show changes that could not be attributed to a known hormone.

Much to my satisfaction, the first and most impure extracts changed the rats in three ways: (1) the adrenal cortex became enlarged; (2) the thymus, spleen, lymph nodes, and all other lymphatic structures shrunk; and (3) deep, bleeding ulcers appeared in the stomach and upper gut.

Because the three types of change were closely interdependent, they formed a definite syndrome. The changes varied from slight to pronounced depending on the amount of extract I injected.

At first I ascribed all these changes to a new sex hormone in my extract. But soon I found that all toxic substances—extracts of kidney or spleen or even a toxin not derived from living tissue—produced the same syndrome. Gradually my classroom concept of the syndrome of just being sick came back to me. I realized that the reaction I had produced with my impure extracts and toxic drugs was an experimental replica of the syndrome of just being sick. Adrenal enlargement, gastrointestinal ulcers, and thymicolymphatic shrinkage were the omnipresent signs of damage to the body under disease attack. Thus the three changes became the objective indices of stress and the basis for the development of the entire stress concept.

My first paper on the syndrome of stress was published in the British journal *Nature* under the title, "A Syndrome Produced by Diverse Nocuous Agents."

In this paper, I suggested the name *alarm reaction* for the animal's initial response because I thought that the syndrome probably represented a general call to arms of the body's defensive forces.

However, the alarm reaction evidently was not the entire response. My very first experiments showed that continuous exposure to any noxious agent capable of setting off this alarm reaction is followed by a stage of adaptation or resistance.

Homeostasis

Apparently disease is not just suffering, but a fight to maintain the homeostatic balance of our tissues when they are damaged. No living organism can exist continuously in a state of alarm. An agent so damaging that continuous exposure to it is incompatible with life causes the organism to die within hours or days of the alarm reaction. However, if survival is possible, the alarm reaction gives way to what we call the stage of resistance.

What happens in the resistance stage is, in many instances, the exact opposite of events in the alarm reaction. For instance, during the alarm reaction, the adrenal cortex discharges into the bloodstream secretory granules that contain hormones. Consequently the gland depletes its stores. In the resistance stage, the cortex accumulates an abundant reserve of secretory granules. Again, in the alarm reaction, the blood volume diminishes and body weight drops, but during the stage of resistance the blood is less concentrated and body weight returns to normal.

Curiously, after prolonged exposure to any noxious agent, the body loses its acquired ability to resist and enters the stage of exhaustion. This third stage always occurs as long as the stress is severe enough and is applied long enough because the adaptation energy or adaptability of a living being is always finite.

General Adaptation Syndrome

All these findings made it necessary to coin an additional all-embracing name for the syndrome. I called the entire response the *General Adaptation Syndrome* (G.A.S.: *general*, because it is produced only by agents that have a general effect upon large portions of the body; *adaptive*, because it stimulates defense and thereby helps inure the body to hardship; *syndrome*, because its signs are coordinated and partly dependent on each other). This whole syndrome then evolves through three stages: (1) the alarm reaction, (2) the stage of resistance, and (3) the state of exhaustion.

An important part of the defense mechanism in the resistance stage is the pituitary, which secretes the so-called adrenocorticotrophic hormone (ACTH) that in turn stimulates the adrenal cortex to produce corticoids. Most important of these adaptive hormones are the glucocorticoids, such as cortisone, which inhibit tissue inflammation, and the mineralocorticoids, which promote inflammation. These hormones allow the body to defend its tissues by inflammation or to surrender them by inhibiting inflammation.

Various derangements in the secretion of adaptive hormones in the resistance stage lead to what I call diseases of adaptation. These diseases are not caused by any particular pathogen but are due to a faulty adaptive response to the stress induced by some pathogen. For example, the excessive production of a proinflammatory hormone in response to some mild local irritation could damage organs far from the original site of an injury. In this sense, the body's faulty adaptive reactions seem to initiate or encourage various maladies. These could include emotional disturbances, headaches, insomnia, sinus attacks, high blood pressure, gastric and duodenal ulcers, certain rheumatic or allergic afflictions, and cardiovascular and kidney diseases.

Over the years, we overcame two other obstacles to the concept of a single stereotyped response to stress. One obstacle was that qualitatively different types of stressors of the same stressor potency do not elicit exactly the same overall syndrome. For example, cold causes shivering, heat produces sweating, adrenaline increases blood sugar and insulin decreases it. All of these stressors have different specific effects. But their nonspecific effects are essentially the same: they all elicit the G.A.S., that is, adrenal cortex enlargement, shrinking of the thymus, deep bleeding ulcers.

The second obstacle was that the same stressor appeared to have different effects on different individuals. But we traced this difference to conditioning factors that can selectively enhance or inhibit a particular stress effect. This conditioning may be internal—genetic predisposition, age, sex—or external, resulting from certain hormone treatments, drugs, or diet. Because of such conditioning, a normally tolerable degree of stress can adversely affect a predisposed region upon which a biologic agent acts, causing a disease of adaptation.

There is ample evidence that nervous and emotional stimuli (rage, fear, pain) can act as stressors, eliciting the G.A.S. Animals conditioned with corticoids and natrium salts undergo heart failure when we expose them to purely nervous stimuli. On the other hand, pretreatment with neurogenic stressors protects an animal's heart under nervous stimuli that otherwise prove fatal. Neurogenic stressors can also protect against inflammatory and hypersensitivity reactions, mainly through the pituitary-adrenocortical axis.

Psychosomatic Reactions

Psychosomatic medicine shows that mental attitudes can produce bodily changes. Common examples are stomach ulcers or a heightened blood pressure caused by emotional upsets.

In a series of experiments, the Medical Research Group of the Swedish Army sought to determine whether psychological stimuli can provoke biochemical and physiological reactions that lead to internal disorders. The Swedish experimenters subjected thirty-two senior officers (average age fifty-six) to the stress of alternating for seventy-five hours between staff work and three-hour sessions at an electronic shooting range. The officers were not allowed to relax or sleep, use stimulants, smoke or go for walks. Although the experiment provoked emotional actions of only moderate intensity, the subjects underwent significant biochemical changes.

In a similar, considerably more trying experiment, thirty-one soldiers stayed at the shooting range for the entire seventy-five hours. Although their average age was only twenty-nine, their emotional and biochemical reactions were much more pronounced. One officer experienced temporary claustrophobia and panic. His adrenaline excretion was very high; he suffered headache, blurred vision, and palpitation; and his pulse exceeded 100 beats per minute.

In both experiments about 25 percent of the subjects developed pathological electrocardiographic patterns. Only after several days of rest did their electrocardiographs return to normal. The experiments prove that relatively brief stints of stress can provoke pathological changes in our body. If they are repeated often or are allowed to persist for long periods, they might cause disease.

Dealing with Stress

On the opposite question of whether bodily changes and actions affect mentality, we have almost no systematic research. Of course, I do not refer to the potential psychological effects of physical brain damage. But it is a fact that looking fit helps us to be fit. A pale, unwashed, unshaven tramp in dirty rags actually resists physical or mental stresses more effectively after a shave, some sun, a bath, and a change into crisp new clothes.

My grandmother first introduced me to these truths when I was six. I no longer remember what I was so desperately crying about, but she looked at me with a particularly benevolent and protective look that I well remember and said, "Anytime you feel *that* low, just try to smile with your face, and you'll see . . . soon your whole being will be smiling." I tried it. It works.

None of this is new. Man has long been aware of physical and mental strain, the relationships between bodily and mental reactions and the importance of defensive-adaptive responses. But stress first became meaningful to me when I found that we can dissect it by modern research methods and identify the components of the stress response in chemical and physical terms. Then I was able to use the concept of stress to solve purely medical problems as well as problems of everyday life.

Everyone knows how it feels to be keyed up by nervous tension. It prepares us for peak accomplishment. On the other hand, the tingling sensations and jitteriness of being too keyed up impair our work and even prevent rest.

When we are overly alerted, tension has stimulated our adrenals to overproduce adrenaline and corticoids. We know that by injecting adrenaline or corticoids, we can excite a person. A patient who takes large doses of cortisone for an allergy or rheumatism often cannot sleep. He may slip into euphoria, or feel something closely akin to mild drunkenness. A sense of deep depression may follow.

It has long been known that mental excitement causes an initial excitement that is followed by depression. Examples include being caught up in a mob or an individual act of violence, as well as physical stressors—being burned or having an infectious fever. We can now narrow the cause down to the hormones produced during the acute alarm-reaction phase of the G.A.S. They can stimulate us for action and then put us into a depression. This is of great practical value for the body: it is necessary to be keyed up for peak accomplishment and equally important to be let down—to let depression prevent us from carrying on too long at top speed. Of course hormones are not the only regulators of our emotional level, but knowing more about them may one day allow us to regulate our emotions.

What has stress research taught us about reaching a healthy balance between rest and work? Of course, all work and no play harms anyone at any age. The best advice, based on objective physiological facts, is not to get more excited than is necessary to gain the momentum you need for your best self-expression. When we get excessively stimulated, especially late in the day, our stress reaction may carry over into the night.

Nature likes variety. Our civilization forces people into highly specialized occupations that may become monotonous. We must remember that stress is the great equalizer of biological activities. If we use the same parts of our bodies or minds over and over, nature has only stress with which to force us out of the rut.

The Psychopharmacological Revolution

Murray E. Jarvik

Science, like all intellectual disciplines, is not unrelated to society. Just as the past and present intellectual climates influence the kinds of inquiry scientists undertake, so do the results of this inquiry influence society and its future. Murray Jarvik here discusses the origins and mode of action of the new behavior-modifying drugs. He also speculates on the use to which these agents may be put.

We conclude with this article because the issue of the "new drugs" is as relevant to social concern as it is of importance to science. While scientists do not, and perhaps should not, determine social policy, psychology today is becoming increasingly involved with the future of man.

One hot August evening in 1955, Helen Burney sat listlessly on her bed in the violent ward of the large Texas hospital where she had been confined for the past four months. During most of that unhappy time, Helen had been highly vocal, abusive, and overactive. Only the day before she had tried to strike a ward aide, but immediately several burly attendants had grabbed her, roughly tying her into a straitjacket and pinioning her arms against her chest. But today Helen's behavior was very different. Her incessant talking and shouting had stopped; all day long she spoke only when spoken to; most of the time she lay on her bed with her eyes half closed, moving little, and looking rather pale. However, she was unusually cooperative with the nursing personnel, got out of bed when told to, and went to the dining room without resisting. What had happened to bring about this remarkable change?

That morning she had received an injection of a new synthetic drug, chlorpromazine, which had been discovered a few years earlier in France. On the same day thousands of mental patients throughout the world were receiving the same drug, many of them for the first time. News of the drug's usefulness had spread rapidly in the preceding months, and it was being tried in mental hospitals throughout the world. Few of those taking or administering the drug realized that they were participating in a revolution in psychiatric treatment. In fact, many psychiatrists felt that this drug would be no more effective in treating schizophrenia than the other drugs that had previously been tried with little success. But they were wrong—and luckily, too—for there was little else they could offer the masses of impoverished patients who clogged the mental institutions all over the world. Soon it would be difficult to find a psychotic patient who was not receiving a drug of some kind for the treatment of his illness. The era of clinical psychopharmacology had begun, and the new drugs were hailed as the first real breakthrough in the treatment of one of man's most serious and mysterious afflictions—psychosis.

Until it was discovered that drugs could help the severely disturbed, almost the only recourse in the management of such patients was physical restraint. Philippe Pinel, the famous French psychiatrist, campaigning for humane treatment of the insane at the end of the eighteenth century, freed the inmates of the grim

Bicêtre mental hospital from their iron chains. Unfortunately, other physical restraints had to be substituted when patients became assaultive or destructive, and though the padded cell and the camisole, or straitjacket, may have been softer than chains, they allowed no greater freedom. Not until the mid-1950s did drugs finally promise total emancipation from physical restraint for most patients. Despite the fears of some psychiatrists, psychologists, and social workers that the social and psychological factors contributing to mental illness would be ignored, the use of psychopharmaceuticals radically improved the treatment of the mentally ill within and without the hospital. Indeed, only with their use has it been possible for some families to be held together, for some individuals to be gainfully employed, and for some patients to be reached by psychotherapy.

Since 1955, psychopharmacology has burgeoned as an important scientific discipline in its own right. In the past fifteen years, many new chemical agents have been developed for the treatment of each major category of mental illness. These drugs include phenothiazines, rauwolfia alkaloids, butyrophenones, propanediol and benzodiazepine compounds, monoamine oxidase (MAO) inhibitors, dibezazepine derivatives, and many more. They have been found useful in the treatment of psychoses, neuroses, and depressions. Even autistic behavior, psychopathy, sexual deviation, and mental retardation have been attacked with drugs, but clinical psychopharmacologists feel that the surface has only been scratched in these areas. The search continues, though presently on a smaller scale than in the past, for more effective agents.

Folk Psychopharmacology

Although as a full-fledged scientific discipline, psychopharmacology is less than fifteen years old, the psychological effects of drugs have piqued the curiosity of occasional researchers for almost a hundred years. Indeed, it is surprising that interest was so slow in developing, for man's empirical knowledge of the effects of drugs on behavior is both ancient and widespread.

The records of mankind, going back thousands of years, are filled with anecdotal and clinical reports of the psychological action of drugs obtained from plants. Though we can be sure that most of these folk remedies were merely placebos, a few have demonstrable medicinal properties and are still in use today. The cuneiform tablets of ancient Assyria contain numerous references to medicinal preparations with psychological effects. For more than 5,000 years, the Chinese have used the herb Ma Huang (yellow astringent), which contains the potent stimulant, ephedrine, and in the earliest writings of China, Egypt, and the Middle East there are references to the influence of various drugs on behavior.

In the first century before Christ, the Roman poet Horace wrote lyrically of the psychological effects of alcohol: "What wonders does not wine! It discloses secrets; ratifies and confirms our hopes; thrusts the coward forth to battle; eases the anxious mind of its burthen; instructs in arts. Whom has not a cheerful glass made eloquent! Whom not quite free and easy from pinching poverty!" And "In vino veritas" was already a familiar Roman adage when it was cited by Pliny.

Opium, an effective folk remedy, is mentioned in the Ebers papyrus, and Homer tells us that Helen of Troy took a "sorrow-easing drug" obtained from Egypt—probably opium. Although the analgesic and sedative properties of opium were extensively described in classical literature, little was said about its addictive properties until Thomas de Quincey hinted at them, early in the nineteenth century, in his Confessions of an English Opium Eater. And while the chemical isolation of morphine and the invention of the hypodermic needle, in the middle of the nineteenth century, made profound addiction truly feasible, morphine is still considered by many physicians the most essential drug they use—"God's own remedy."

Morphine and its derivatives and analogues (for example, heroin) are self-administered by countless thousands of people throughout the world, although in many countries, especially in the West, such use is illegal. The practice persists, nevertheless, perhaps for the reasons given by the French poet, Jean Cocteau, who was himself an addict: "Everything that we do in life, including love, is done in an express train traveling towards death. To smoke opium is to leave the train while in motion; it is to be interested in something other than life and death."

Like morphine, cocaine is another vegetable product discovered by primitive man. It is clearly not a placebo, and its use is illegal. The Indians of Peru have chewed coca leaves for centuries, and still do, to relieve hunger, fatigue, and the general burdens of a miserable life. The alkaloid cocaine was isolated in 1859, and its systematic use was not only practiced but advocated by such respected figures as Sigmund Freud and William Halsted, as well as by the legendary Sherlock Holmes. It is highly doubtful that the continued use of cocaine produces a physiological dependence. Today, cocaine-taking is relatively uncommon in the northern hemisphere.

On the other hand, an ancient drug that remains exceedingly popular, though its medical uses today are nil, is marijuana, the dried leaves of the hemp plant Cannabis sativa. Cannabis is so ubiquitous, and grows so easily, that its widespread use is not surprising. Marco Polo is credited with bringing the "Green Goddess" to the Occident, although Herodotus tells us that the Scythians inhaled the vapor, obtained by heating hemp seeds on red-hot stones, and then "shouted for joy." To this day, cannabis is almost always smoked; this allows its active ingredients to be absorbed into the pulmonary blood circulation and, avoiding the liver, to be promptly carried to the brain. Similarly, the active ingredients of opium and tobacco are usually self-administered by inhalation of the vapors from heated plant products.

Hashish, derived from *cannabis*, and smoked, chewed, or drunk, has been widely used for centuries throughout the Middle East. The Arabic term for a devotee of hashish is "hashshash"; from the plural, "hashshashin," comes the English word "assassin," for at the time of the Crusades, the Hashshashin were a fanatical secret Moslem sect who terrorized the Christians by swift and secret murder, after having taken hashish to give themselves courage. Richard Burton, the famous traveler, adventurer, and writer, described his experiences with hashish during a pilgrimage to Mecca at the end of the nineteenth century. About fifty years earlier, Moreau de Tours suggested that physicians should take hashish in order to experience mental illness and thereby understand it better. Claude Bernard, the great French physiologist, is said to have declared that "hashish is the curare of the mind." Today we know a great deal about the mode of action of curare and almost nothing about that of hashish, but Bernard suggested a working hypothesis. Perhaps *cannabis*, like curare, blocks some vital neurohumor in the brain.

Quantitative, objective studies of *cannabis* are rare, even today. However, a recent report by Carlini indicates that *cannabis* facilitates maze-learning in rats. In the absence of comparative studies, it is difficult to say how *cannabis* resembles or differs from other drugs; anecdotal reports suggest that it resembles lysergic acid diethylamide (LSD).

Another drug with a long history of use is *mescaline* or *peyote*, which the Aztecs are credited with having used five centuries ago, and which has been and still is used by certain Indians of Central America and the southwest United States. Its effects resemble those of marijuana and LSD; they have also been compared with those of *psilocybin*, a drug that the Aztecs derived from a psychotogenic mushroom they called "teonanacatl," or "God's flesh."

The Chemical Era

Until the nineteenth century, the only drugs known to affect behavior were those derived from plants and long familiar to mankind. With advances in chemistry during the first half of the nineteenth century, however, the general anesthetics, including nitrous oxide, diethyl ether, and chloroform were discovered and brought into widespread use; and by the time Emil Kraepelin began his psychopharmacological investigations in the 1880s, a few new sedatives, including the bromides and chloral hydrate, were available.

Nitrous oxide, an artificially prepared inhalation anesthetic, was investigated by Sir Humphrey Davy, who described its effects thus in 1799: "I lost all connections with external things; trains of vivid images rapidly passed through my mind and even connected with words in such a manner as to produce perceptions perfectly novel. I existed in a world of newly connected and newly modified ideas."

Inhaling nitrous oxide soon became a favorite student diversion, and enterprising showmen charged admission for public demonstrations of its effects; the popular interest in this gas reminds one very much of the current preoccupation with LSD. But though nitrous oxide was beguiling to thrill seekers, it never became as popular as LSD, perhaps because the gas is difficult to transport.

Although *diethyl ether* was originally prepared in 1543 by Valerius Cordus when he distilled alcohol with sulfuric acid, its potential as an anesthetic remained unknown for 300 years until Crawford Long and William Morton first used it clinically in the 1840s. Ether parties subsequently became popular among students, although the drug's extreme flammability probably discouraged more widespread popular use. *Chloroform* was introduced about the same time as ether, but its toxic effects upon the heart, recognized almost immediately, discouraged its nonmedical use. It was not known for many years that the liver, also, is severely damaged by this drug.

Chloral hydrate, a powerful sleep-producing drug, was introduced into medicine in 1869 but has been generally ignored by experimental psychologists—though not by the underworld where, in the form of "knockout drops" mixed with alcohol, it has been the active ingredient of the "Mickey Finn." *Paraldehyde*, first used in 1882, has similarly been eschewed by psychological investigators, perhaps because of its extremely unpleasant odor; nevertheless, it has been used extensively for many years in mental institutions for producing temporary narcosis in dangerously violent patients, especially those with delirium tremens from alcohol withdrawal.

Bromides, particularly potassium bromide, slowly gained popularity during the nineteenth century to the point where millions of people were taking them as sedatives. Unlike the barbiturates however, the bromides produce psychoses involving delirium, delusions, or hallucinations, as well as a variety of neurological and dermatological disturbances. For a time, chronic toxicity resulting from continued use of these compounds became a leading cause of admission to mental hospitals. Bromide is still a common ingredient in headache remedies, "nerve tonics," and over-the-counter sleeping medications.

The Antipsychotic Drugs

With the antipsychotic drugs, as happens more often than is supposed, use preceded research. The ancient preparation, Indian snakeroot powder, mentioned more than 2,500 years ago in the Hindu Ayurvedic writings, deserves at least as much credit for ushering in the era of clinical psychopharmacology as does the modern synthetic drug, chlorpromazine. According to the ancient doctrine of signs, since the roots of the plant *Rauwolfia serpentina* were snakelike, they were administered for snakebite. Snakeroot was also used for insomnia and insanity—quite rational uses, in view of modern findings—as well as for epilepsy and dysentery, which it actually aggravates, and for a host of other conditions for which its value is questionable.

The first scientific intimation that Indian snakeroot might be useful in mental illness came in 1931 when Sen and Bose published an article in the *Indian Medical World* entitled *"Rauwolfia serpentina*, a New Indian Drug for Insanity and High Blood Pressure." But this suggestion was not confirmed for almost a quarter of a century. *Rauwolfia* began to attract the attention of the Western world only in 1949, when Rustom Valkil advocated it for hypertension, and the Swiss pharmaceutical firm, Ciba, subsequently isolated the active ingredient, which they named *reserpine*. In 1953 a Boston physician, Robert Wilkins, confirmed that reserpine was effective in the treatment of hypertension, and a year later a New York psychiatrist, Nathan Kline, announced that he had found reserpine useful in the treatment of psychotic disorders. Soon numerous psychiatrists in other parts of the world corroborated Kline's results, and the use of reserpine spread with amazing speed. When Frederick Yonkman at Ciba used the term "tranquilizing" to describe the calming effect of reserpine, the word "tranquilizer" entered all modern languages to designate a drug that quiets hyperactive or anxious patients.

The subsequent clinical history of reserpine is a strange one. Reserpine and chlorpromazine were twin heralds of the dawn of psychopharmacological treatment, but the popularity of reserpine in the treatment of mental disease has dwindled until today, a decade and a half later, its use has been practically abandoned for such therapy while chlorpromazine is still the leading antipsychotic drug. Yet there are many studies that attest to the efficacy of *rauwolfia* and its derivatives in the treatment of psychiatric disorders; probably its tendency to produce depression was one of the chief reasons for its near demise. Furthermore, chlorpromazine has spawned scores of offspring-phenothiazines, widely used for the mentally ill.

Like reserpine, *chlorpromazine*'s usefulness as an antipsychotic drug was discovered more or less by accident. In the early 1950s the French surgeon, Henri Laborit, introduced chlorpromazine into clinical anesthesia as a successor to promethazine, known to be a sedative antihistamine capable of heightening the effect of other drugs. It was noticed that chlorpromazine reduced anxiety in surgical patients and enabled them to face their ordeal with indifference. This led to its trial with agitated psychotics, whom it calmed with dramatic effectiveness. In 1954 the drug was released

commercially in North America by Smith, Kline and French as an antiemetic, but shortly thereafter it was tried with psychiatric patients. Large-scale controlled studies by the United States Veterans' Administration and by the Psychopharmacology Service Center of the National Institute of Mental Health showed chlorpromazine and the related phenothiazines to be useful in the treatment of acute schizophrenia. Other studies show that phenothiazines help discharged mental patients to stay out of the hospital. A drug with ubiquitous actions on all body systems, chlorpromazine has been used in the treatment of anxiety and tension, depression, mental retardation, senility, drug addiction, pain, nausea and vomiting, and spasticity. Since its mechanisms of action are still not known, it is difficult to delimit the validity of these applications.

Antianxiety Drugs

Anxiety is such a common experience that everyone reading this article has a subjective understanding of the term. It may be defined as an unpleasant state associated with a threatening situation, and is closely allied to fear. Sedative hypnotic drugs including alcohol, barbiturates, bromides, and chloral hydrate, have frequently been employed for the treatment of anxiety. In 1955 a number of new drugs with properties common to the sedative hypnotics were introduced for the treatment of anxiety, but the most successful of these, by far, was *meprobamate*, popularly known as Miltown or Equanil. Many of the arguments concerning the uniqueness of meprobamate revolve around its similarity or dissimilarity to the barbiturates. But since the properties of the various barbiturates differ from one another, it is not easy to compare the whole class to meprobamate. All, however, tend to produce sleep when used in large doses, to produce effects reported as pleasant, and to produce convulsive seizures as a consequence of sudden withdrawal after the prolonged administration of large doses. Giving meprobamate to a patient suffering from neurotic anxiety is not quite the same as inserting a nail into a broken bone to hold it together, or giving insulin to a diabetic. In giving meprobamate, we are employing a drug with a poorly defined action to treat a poorly defined condition. But the condition is widespread and demands action, and the drug seems to help.

In any case, meprobamate's standing as the most popular tranquilizer was soon usurped by *chlordiazepoxide* (Librium). This compound strongly resembles meprobamate and the barbiturates, but there do appear to be differences the experimentalist can measure. For example, Leonard Cook and Roger Kelleher recently reported an experiment in which rats could postpone a punishing shock by pressing a lever. Cook and Kelleher found that at some doses chlordiazepoxide will produce an increase in the rate of lever pressing whereas meprobamate does not. Also it has been shown with a Lashley jumping stand that rats will sometimes become "fixated" if the discrimination problem is made insoluble. Chlordiazepoxide seems to eliminate this fixated behavior whereas meprobamate does not. The possible differences in the behavioral effects of sedative hypnotic drugs have not yet been fully explored, and the study of these differences should tell us a great deal about the drugs themselves.

Antidepression Drugs

While depression, at least in a mild form, is an experience perhaps as common as anxiety, it can also constitute a severe disease (formerly called melancholia), which sometimes leads to suicide. Psychiatrists are far from unanimous in their definitions of this complicated entity, but during the past decade they have found two classes of drugs helpful in combating it—the *monoamine oxidase* (MAO) *inhibitors*, and their successors, the *dibenzazepine* compounds. As with reserpine and chlorpromazine, their usefulness as antidepressants was discovered by accident when iproniazid (a MAO inhibitor) was given to tubercular patients and found to elevate their mood, and when imipramine (a dibenzazepine derivative related to chlorpromazine) was found to relieve depressed psychotics.

In attempting to understand the etiology of depression, it is ironic that biochemists have not hesitated to rush in where experimental psychologists fear to tread. What has emerged, based on a combination of clinical observations and animal studies, is the *catecholamine theory* of depression. Broadly interpreted, the theory says that a state of well-being is maintained by continuous adrenergic stimulation of certain receptors in the brain by catecholamines like norepinephrine and dopamine (hormones produced in the brain). For example, reserpine's so-called tranquilizing effect—indifference to surroundings, lack of appetite, and apparent lassitude—is attributed to depletion of catecholamines. Another compound, alphamethyltyrosine, which decreases the synthesis of catecholamines, has been found to produce "depression" in animals. On the other hand, some compounds have been found that produce an increase in the level of brain catecholamines. Administration of MAO inhibitors, which inactivate MAO and thus prevent catecholamine from being destroyed, produce increased levels of catecholamines and greater alertness, activity, and degree of electrical self-stimulation (in animals implanted with electrodes in "reward" areas of the brain). Administering the precursors of catecholamines—for example, dihydroxyphenylalanine (DOPA)—or MAO inhibitors will prevent or reverse the depression caused by reserpine (see Figure 1).

The dibenzazepine compounds, typified by *imipramine* (Tofranil), do not change the level of brain catecholamines in animals, yet they are effective antidepressants. However, the mode of action of these compounds may be compatible with the theory. Studies show that the catecholamine level in the brain is reduced, not only by enzymatic destruction, (for example, by MAO), but also by reabsorption of the catecholamines into the neurons. It has been hypothesized that the dibenzazapine compounds potentiate the action of normally present catecholamines by preventing this reabsorption.

LSD

LSD shares the responsibility with reserpine and chlorpromazine for ushering in the psychopharmacology era. Albert Hofmann's accidental discovery of this substance at Sandoz Pharmaceuticals in Basel, Switzerland in 1943 is now well known. LSD is a semisynthetic compound of plant origin, a derivative of ergot (a fungus that infects rye). Although its effects are similar to those of marijuana and mescaline, its outstanding characteristic is its extreme potency and its ability to pro-

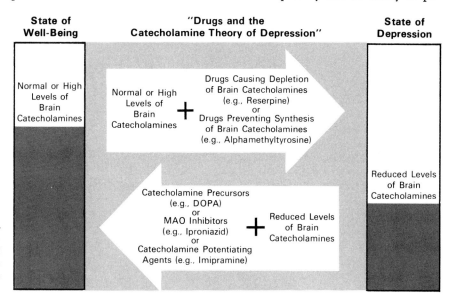

Figure 1. The relationships between drug-produced changes in brain catecholamine levels and changes in mental states provide evidence for the "catecholamine theory of depression."

duce bizarre mental states picturesquely described by Humphrey Osmond as psychedelic or "mind-expanding." The ability of LSD to block 5-hydroxytryptamine (another amine resembling the catecholamines in some respects, abbreviated 5HT) and thus to change brain levels of 5HT, has excited interest. More recently Maimon Cohen has reported the frightening finding that LSD can damage chromosomes. The role of LSD in producing a psychotic state has not been established. Despite thousands of papers dealing with this substance, we have very little idea of what LSD does, and we don't know how it does it. It is unfortunate that legal restrictions and the manufacturers' understandable diffidence make this fascinating chemical inaccessible for research.

There is something in the use or action of psychotogenic or "hallucinogenic" drugs that appeals to certain towering if unconventional figures in literature and the arts. From the time of Toulouse-Lautrec through the era of the expatriates (Gertrude Stein, James Joyce, Ernest Hemingway), bohemian Paris was not exactly abstemious, nor did it restrict itself to alcohol for thrills or new sensations. Though the virtues of illicit drugs do not appear in paid advertisements in the public press, nevertheless very talented "copywriters" have turned out glowing testimonials to promote the use of these drugs. Thomas de Quincey and Samuel Coleridge, at the beginning of the nineteenth century, recommended opium, and Paolo Mantegazza in 1859 gave highly colored accounts of the beatific effects of coca. Freud also approved of cocaine and advised his fiancée to take it. Charles Baudelaire, called the "De Quincey of hashish," was supported by Arthur Rimbaud and Paul Verlaine in acclaiming the beneficence of this drug; more recently Aldous Huxley declared that the "doors of perception" could be opened by mescaline and LSD. Many jazz, swing, bop, and other musicians claim that marijuana and other stimulant drugs enhance their playing or composing.

Whether drugs truly enhance creativity is a moot point. Artists, poets, scientists, and inventors will testify that LSD or marijuana or amphetamine inspired them to produce works of value, but controlled experiments to test these claims are lacking. Who would not like to find a magic drug that would turn an ugly frog into a handsome prince, or a Cinderella into a princess? Drugs can sometimes seem to have magic powers, but they do not ordinarily instill beauty, wisdom, and virtue into the taker. Yet estrogens can change a skinny, adolescent girl into a beauty queen and, if one can extrapolate from cases of precocious puberty (or infant Hercules), superandrogens must be responsible for Clark Kent's transformation into Superman.

Drugs do change our perception of the world, and when this perception becomes unbearable, as in terminal cancer, drug use is clearly justified. The question is whether it is justified for the relief of unhappiness,

dissatisfaction, or boredom. The religious uses of wine and peyote for sacramental purposes have, in part, inspired Timothy Leary to found a new religion, the League for Spiritual Discovery (LSD), which advocates the use of LSD and other so-called psychedelic drugs. The legal difficulties of this organization have spurred city, state, and federal legislative and enforcement bodies to enter the field of psychopharmacology in order to control the distribution and use of behavior-affecting drugs. But the government is trying to make rules about substances that are still poorly understood, and it rests with psychopharmacologists to clarify the action of psychotogenic drugs so that such rules can be made on a more rational basis.

The Birth of Scientific Psychopharmacology

Without the spur of clinical success, it is doubtful that basic research in the effects of drugs on behavior could have advanced very rapidly. During the first half of the twentieth century, drugs were seldom used in the treatment of mental illness, since morphine, cocaine, barbiturates, and other sedative hypnotics had already been tried and proven generally ineffective. Other more physical approaches to therapy, including hydrotherapy, occupational therapy, and psychosurgery had been employed with varying results. Only electroconvulsive shock (ECS) seemed to be very successful, but its administration required considerable skill. Psychiatrists depended chiefly, therefore, on psychological methods (primarily communicative interactions), which, unfortunately, were usually inefficient and ineffective for the majority of severely psychotic individuals.

Experimental psychologists showed only an intermittent and desultory interest in the effects of drugs on behavior. A handful of drugs had already been investigated, but the results were of very little interest to the most influential psychologists, who were busy, in the 1930s and 1940s, building their own psychological systems or attacking rival systems.

In fact, however, psychopharmacology had already been born more than half a century earlier. In 1879 the first laboratory of experimental psychology had been established at Leipzig by Wilhelm Wundt. One of Wundt's most famous students was Emil Kraepelin, sometimes called the father of modern psychiatry because he invented a widely used system for classifying mental disorders. Kraepelin might also be called the father of scientific psychopharmacology, for he applied Wundt's new experimental methods to investigate the influence of drugs on psychological functions. Kraepelin studied pharmacology at Tartu in Estonia, then a center of research in this field. During his stay there he demonstrated that alcohol, morphine, and other drugs impair reaction time and the mental processes involved in associational learning. It is an ironic coincidence that Kraepelin was interested in the two areas that finally

Drug Group	Example	Trade or Common Name	Natural or Synthetic	Usage	How Taken	First Used	Evidence of Addiction?
PSYCHOTHERAPEUTICS							
Antipsychotic							
Rauwolfia alkaloids	reserpine	Serpasil	natural	greatly diminished	injected, ingested	1949	no
Phenothiazines	chlorpromazine	Thorazine	synthetic	widespread	injected, ingested	1950	no
Antianxiety							
Propanediols	meprobamate	Miltown	synthetic	widespread	ingested	1954	yes
Benzodiazepines	chlordiazepoxide	Librium	synthetic	widespread	ingested	1933	yes
Barbiturates	phenobarbital	see SEDATIVES					
Antidepressant							
Monoamine oxidase inhibitors	tranylcypromine	Parnate	synthetic	diminished	ingested	1958	no
Dibenzazepines	imipramine	Tofranil	synthetic	widespread	ingested, injected	1948	no
Stimulant	amphetamine	see STIMULANTS					
PSYCHOTOGENICS							
Ergot derivative	lysergic acid diethylamide	LSD, Lysergide	synthetic	widespread?	ingested	1943	no
Cannabis sativa	marijuana	hemp, hashish	natural	widespread	smoked	?	no
Lophophora williamsii	mescaline	peyote button	natural	localized	ingested	?	no
Psilocybe mexicana	psilocybin		natural	rare	ingested	?	no
STIMULANTS							
Sympathomimetics	amphetamine	Benzedrine	synthetic	widespread	ingested, injected	1935	yes
Analeptics	pentylenetetrazol	Metrazol	synthetic	rare	ingested, injected	1935	no
Psychotogenics	lysergic acid diethylamide	see PSYCHOTOGENICS					
Nicotinics	nicotine		natural	widespread	smoked, ingested	?	yes
Xanthines	caffeine		natural	widespread	ingested	?	yes
SEDATIVES AND HYPNOTICS							
Bromides	potassium bromide		synthetic	widespread	ingested	1857	no
Barbiturates	phenobarbital	Luminal	synthetic	widespread	ingested, injected	1912	yes
Chloral derivatives	chloral hydrate		synthetic	rare	ingested	1875	yes
General	alcohol		natural	widespread	ingested	?	yes
ANESTHETICS, ANALGESICS, AND PARALYTICS							
General anesthetics	nitrous oxide	laughing gas	synthetic	rare	inhaled	1799	no
	diethyl ether		synthetic	greatly diminished	inhaled	1846	no
	chloroform		synthetic	rare	inhaled	1831	no
Local anesthetics	cocaine	coca	natural	widespread	applied, ingested	?	yes
Analgesics	procaine	Novocaine	synthetic	widespread	injected	1905	no
	opium derivatives	morphine, heroin	natural	widespread	injected, smoked	?	yes
Paralytics	d-tubocurarine	curare	natural	widespread	injected	?	no
NEUROHUMORS (NEUROTRANSMITTERS)							
Cholinergic	acetylcholine		natural synthetic	laboratory	injected	1926	no
Adrenergic	norepinephrine		natural synthetic	laboratory	injected	1946	no
Others (?)	5-hydroxytryptamine	5-HT, serotonin	natural synthetic	laboratory	injected	1948	no

coalesced seventy-five years later—basic, quantitative, experimental psychopharmacology, and the treatment of mental disease.

Though psychopharmacology had little scientific status at the beginning of the twentieth century, Kraepelin's early work was continued by a few psychologists who studied the effects of alcohol, caffeine, cocaine, strychnine, and nicotine. In 1908 the Englishman W. H. R. Rivers reported on the influence of drugs on fatigue; in 1915 the Americans Raymond Dodge and Francis Benedict, and Harry Hollingsworth examined the effects of drugs on motor and mental efficiency. In 1924 even Clark Hull, one of the most influential psychologists of the mid-twentieth century, studied the effect of pipe smoking and coffee drinking on mental efficiency, before he turned his attention to building theoretical systems.

Psychopharmacological research was spurred in the 1930s and 1940s by the imminence and advent of World War II, which aroused military interest in the applications of drugs, particularly the amphetamines, and concern about the psychological consequences of anoxia, severe oxygen deficiency. Both allied and German soldiers were given amphetamines to combat sleeplessness and fatigue; these drugs were found to diminish fatigue, but whether they could raise performance above normal levels was an open question that is still not fully answered. Insufficient supply of oxygen to the brain was shown to adversely affect reasoning, memory, and sensory functioning; for example, it renders the subject less sensitive to visual stimuli and prolongs the time needed for the eyes to adapt to the dark. Such impairment was particularly serious in military pilots for whom the loss of judgment and sensory function resulting from lack of oxygen at high altitudes could be disastrous.

More recently a number of factors have converged to make psychopharmacology a popular field for research. During the mid-1950s, Europe and the United States were prospering, and governmental support for health services and medical research began to expand at an unprecedented rate. Spurred by therapeutic success and the possibilities of large profits, and as yet unencumbered by severe governmental restrictions concerning drug safety and efficacy, pharmaceutical companies were eager to discover new drugs prescribable to millions of waiting patients. Support for research on new psychotherapeutic drugs became big business. In addition, the Psychopharmacology Service Center, established within the National Institute of Mental Health, contributed millions of dollars for research on the psychological effects of drugs.

With the rise of psychopharmacology, clinical psychologists immediately began to devise methods, such as rating scales and questionnaires, to evaluate the effects of the new drug therapies. However, some of the psychotherapeutic achievements credited to the action of drugs may also be attributed to reforms in mental hospitals and better programs of community mental hygiene.

Psychological Methods in Psychopharmacological Research

To screen potentially useful drugs and characterize their action, psychopharmacologists have used a variety of procedures in studies carried out with rats and mice. Measures of spontaneous motor activity are widely employed, as are other observational and rating techniques. Among the most favored procedures are those based on operant conditioning, because they are objective, automatic, generally quite reliable, and permit extended investigation of a single animal. The chief apparatus is the Skinner box, a cage containing a lever-pressing mechanism. Depending on the experimental conditions, depression of this lever can produce either a positive reinforcement (food) or a negative reinforcement (electrical shock). Some investigators feel that the schedule, and not the kind or amount of reinforcement, determines a particular drug susceptibility. Some schedules require that the animal respond quickly, or slowly, or in certain patterns, in order to obtain food or avoid shock. On the other hand, even before the phenothiazines and reserpine appeared on the market, it was shown that these drugs seemed to selectively impair conditioned responses controlled by aversive consequences (that is, punishing shock) but had less effect upon unconditioned responses. It appears that the strength of the stimulus and the nature of the motor response required are vital factors determining the relative susceptibility to different drugs.

Many psychopharmacologists not trained in the Skinnerian approach use discrimination boxes and mazes to study the effects of drugs, and a number also use classical conditioning procedures; maze-learning was used in a recent study, which demonstrated that analeptics (such as strychnine) facilitate learning. Similarly, work on the amnesia produced by intracerebral antibiotics was based on results obtained with mazes and shuttle-boxes. Even single-trial learning procedures are being increasingly used to study the effects of drugs. Psychological research has not yet reached a point at which any one method of measuring behavior can be considered superior to any other.

Chemistry and the Brain

Psychologists have subdivided behavior in different ways, but they are in general agreement about certain broad categories of functions. If different psychological functions depend upon discrete chemical substances, then we might expect to find specificity of drug action—that is, that certain drugs selectively affect certain functions. If the localization of psychological functions involves a grosser type of organization—if it depends, say, on complex neural connections—then we would not necessarily expect to find such specific relations between drug action and psychological function.

Certain sensory structures are clearly chemically coded. Taste and smell receptors obviously are, and respond to specific drugs. Sodium dehydrochlorate and saccharin, even when injected into an antecubital vein, respectively produce a characteristic bitter or sweet taste on reaching the tongue and are used for measuring blood circulation time. Streptomycin and dihydrostreptomycin selectively, though not exclusively, attack the eighth nerve; visual effects are produced by santonin, digitalis, and LSD. Haptic sensations are said to be produced by cocaine ("cocaine bug"), but there is no good evidence that somesthetic sensory pathways are selectively affected by any chemical substance. Histamine and polypeptides, such as substance P or bradykinin, will at times produce itch or pain, and hint that sensory chemical specificity is a possibility.

Motor structures are also chemically coded and enable curariform drugs to have a selective paralyzing action. Similarly, autonomic ganglia can be affected selectively by different drugs, and the vast field of peripheral neuropharmacology rests on such specificity.

We are beginning to learn how the central nervous system is organized neuropharmacologically. Histochemical, radioautographic, and fluorescent techniques are making such mapping possible. For example, it is known that the central nervous system pathways that control motivational mechanisms such as hunger, thirst, and sex are susceptible to cholinergic, adrenergic, and hormonal substances. Further mapping of this kind is bound to result in better understanding of the relationship between drug action and functional localization in the central nervous system.

One can inhibit activity with a wide variety of depressant drugs or activate animals with stimulant drugs. No simple role can be ascribed to acetylcholine, norepinephrine, or 5-hydroxytryptamine (serotonin) in the control of behavior. What part, if any, these substances play in learning is even more mysterious. Some theorists have proposed an inhibitory cholinergic system balanced by an excitatory adrenergic system, and the facts seem to fit thus far. Of course, the brain is full of all species of chemicals that are waiting to be investigated by psychologists. Nucleic acids and particularly ribonucleic acid (RNA) have been assigned a special role in learning by some, but evidence is conflicting. Proteins seem a more likely candidate, and such inhibitors of protein synthesis as puromycin and cyclohexamide do interfere

with both memory and learning. The production of retrograde amnesia and the posttrial facilitation of learning by drugs provide evidence for a consolidation process. But the experiments are difficult to perform, and many unspecified sources of variability will have to be identified before general mechanisms can be revealed.

The Future of Psychopharmacology

Ever since Loewenhoek's invention of the microscope, scientists have tended to believe that in the "ultrafine structure" of an organism lie the explanations for its functioning. Hence it is not surprising that attempts to explain drug action are couched in terms of chemical binding to specific molecular receptors. However, behavior can no more be seen in a test tube full of brain homogenate than can the theme of a mosaic be determined from an analysis of its stones. The Gestalt principle that the whole is something more than the sum of its parts is not always recognized by physical scientists who tend to be very analytical, to look at "parts" in their approach to explanation. The psychologist has an increasingly important role to play in psychopharmacology, for he must determine whether the particular sedative, antidepressant, psychotogenic, or facilitating drug that the biochemists and neurophysiologists want to study really has the behavioral properties they think it does.

In the future it should be possible to say in what ways each important psychopharmaceutical influences behavior, and thus to characterize it by a behavioral profile, just as we can now describe a chemical in terms of its chromatographic pattern. Ultimately, it ought to be possible to look at the chemical structure of any new drug and predict whether it will be useful as an antipsychotic, an antifatigue agent, an appetite stimulant, and so forth. By the same token, the physiological determinants of behavior will be so well worked out that we will understand why a drug that causes alertness also depresses hunger, or why one that causes difficulty in doing arithmetic also causes peculiar sensations in the skin. One can envisage the day when drugs may be employed not only to treat pathological conditions (reduce pain, suffering, agitation, and anxiety) but also to enhance the normal state of man—increase pleasure, facilitate learning and memory, reduce jealousy and aggressiveness. Hopefully such pharmacological developments will come about as an accompaniment of, and not as a substitute for, a more ideal society.

Biographies

ADLER   AZRIN   BAKAN   BEACH   BERMANT   BLOCK   BURGHARDT

NORMAN T. ADLER, contributing editor, graduated with high honors in psychology from Harvard, where he engaged early in the study of instinctive behavior; he successfully trained fighting fish to fight their own image in a mirror and demonstrated the functional role of the mirror image in regulating the behavior of the fish. He was awarded a Sheldon Travelling Fellowship from Harvard and spent 1962–1963 traveling around the world, visiting international laboratories. Adler holds the Ph.D. from the University of California, Berkeley, where he worked with the distinguished physiological psychologist, Frank Beach. His scientific interests range widely these days in his position as assistant professor in the Psychology Department, University of Pennsylvania.

NATHAN AZRIN ("Pain and Aggression") is director of research at the Anna State Hospital's Behavior Research Laboratory in Anna, Illinois, and is a professor at the Rehabilitation Institute at Southern Illinois University. In 1956 Azrin received his Ph.D. in psychology from Harvard, where he studied under B. F. Skinner. Since then he has published widely in the field of behavioral research and has edited the *Journal of the Experimental Analysis of Behavior*. Though his initial training was in social psychology and personality at Boston University, he transferred to Harvard, not as the result of a change of interest, but rather because he felt that the problems of personality and social psychology could be handled most effectively within the behaviorist framework.

DAVID BAKAN ("Is Phrenology Foolish?") received his B.A. from Brooklyn College, his M.A. from Indiana University, and his Ph.D. in 1948 from Ohio State University. Since 1961 he has been a professor of psychology at the University of Chicago; before that time, he taught at

Ohio State, the University of Missouri, and Harvard. He is the author of many articles and several books, including *The Duality of Human Existence* and *On Method: Toward the Reconstruction of Psychological Investigation*.

FRANK BEACH ("It's All in Your Mind"), before getting his Ph.D. at the University of Chicago, tried free-lance magazine writing. Starting in 1932 as a fellow in clinical psychology at Kansas State Teachers College, he moved to high-school English and drama teacher to museum curator to several other jobs in research and teaching to Sterling Professor at Yale University and finally, in 1958, to a psychology professorship at the University of California at Berkeley.

In 1951, Beach won the Warren Medal for Excellence in Scientific Experimentation, given by the Society of Experimental Psychologists, for his research on hormones and behavior. From 1956 to 1959 he headed the psychology section of the National Academy of Sciences; from 1957 to 1965 he was chairman of the academy's Committee for Research on Problems of Sex; and he has been a member of the Panel on Psychobiology of the National Science Foundation.

Books bearing his signature are *Hormones and Behavior* (Hoeber, 1948), *Patterns of Sexual Behavior* (Harper & new journal, *Hormones and Behavior* (Wiley, 1965). Also he helps edit a new journal, *Hormones and Behavior* (Academic Press, New York), whose birth he says reflects the rapid growth of his field of research.

GORDON BERMANT ("Copulation in Rats"), a professor of psychology at the University of California, Davis, is a Harvard Ph.D. who studied the behavior of chickens during his postdoctoral days at Harvard. A former student of Frank Beach, Dr. Bermant is critical of psy-

chologists "who are so involved in looking at intrinsically uninteresting behavior in ecologically invalid surroundings that the basic fact of the evolution of behavior to meet environmental demands escapes their attention." He sticks to the behavior of animals because he believes this approach maximizes the chances for results that will merge with the advances in knowledge in the biological sciences. His interests are the determinants of species-specific behavior, primarily reproductive behavior.

HENRY DAVID BLOCK (coauthor, "The Psychology of Robots") did his undergraduate work at City College New York before receiving his Ph.D. in mathematics from Iowa State College. He currently is a professor of applied mathematics at Cornell University and has published articles on topics ranging from eigenvalues and isoperimetric inequalities to learning in some simple nonbiological systems. "The original impetus for this article," he reports, "came from a demonstration at a friend's home where I tried to show their 12-year-old son how a simple machine made from paper cups could learn to beat us all at some games. From the discussion that followed, I became aware that many of the difficulties blocking the way to more sophisticated robots were closely related to current difficulties in theoretical psychology."

GORDON M. BURGHARDT ("Chemical Perception in Newborn Snakes") is an assistant professor of psychology at the University of Tennessee, Knoxville. He began college as a chemistry major, but the lure of animal behavior became irresistible, especially after he studied with Eckhard Hess at Chicago.

Dr. Burghardt, who spent the summer of 1963 with Konrad Lorenz and his associates at the Max-Planck Institute in Seewiesen, West Germany, feels that the

CHOMSKY   DETHIER   DEUTSCH   FANTINO   GELDARD   GINSBURG   THE HARLOWS   HEBB

time is ripe for an experimental evolutionary and ethological approach to human behavior.

NOAM CHOMSKY ("Language and the Mind") holds the Ferrari P. Ward Professorship of Modern Languages and Linguistics at the Massachusetts Institute of Technology. He received his Ph.D. in linguistics at the University of Pennsylvania, where his dissertation was on transformational analysis. He is the author of books and articles not only on linguistics but on philosophy, intellectual history, and contemporary issues.

VINCENT DETHIER ("The Hungry Fly") is a professor of biology at Princeton. He received his Ph.D. in biology in 1939 from Harvard and since that time has published widely in the field of physiology and behavior, "with side jaunts into ecology and classification"—and fiction. His *To Know a Fly*, a humorous, cartoon-illustrated paperback about the life of a scientist who studies flies, was described by *Science* magazine as a minor classic.

Dr. Dethier was in Africa during World War II, and in 1951–52 returned to the Belgian Congo on a Fulbright Scholarship to study sleeping sickness and learn about how the tse-tse fly locates its host. Flies are excellent experimental animals, he says: "They have a simple nervous system, they are hardy, year-round, and rich in behavioral forms—all in all, our best bet."

J. ANTHONY DEUTSCH ("Neural Basis of Memory") is a professor of psychology at the University of California, San Diego, and is an active researcher in the area of physiological psychology. His work has dealt mainly with the mechanism of thirst, intracranial self-stimulation, and the physical basis of memory and learning. He did his undergraduate and doctoral studies at Oxford University, where he spent eight years on the

faculty before coming to the Center for Advanced Study in the Behavioral Sciences at Stanford University in 1959. After spending some time on the faculty at Stanford and as a visiting associate professor at UCLA, he moved to New York University in 1964. He returned to California in 1966 to take up his present post at UCSD.

Dr. Deutsch's first book, *The Structural Basis of Behavior*, which dealt with his behavior theory, was published in 1960. More recently, he coauthored a textbook, *Physiological Psychology* (1966), with his wife, Diana.

EDMUND FANTINO ("Of Mice and Misers"), an assistant professor of psychology at the University of California, San Diego, teaches courses in learning and motivation and in the control of behavior. For three years before coming to UCSD he was an assistant professor at Yale.

A native of New York City, Dr. Fantino did his undergraduate work at Cornell, majoring in mathematics. He went to Harvard for his graduate work in psychology and received his Ph.D. in 1964.

His research at present concerns choice in the pigeon (supported by National Science Foundation grants), conditioned reinforcement, and escape and avoidance conditioning in the rat.

FRANK A. GELDARD ("Body English") received his Ph.D. from Clark University in 1928; in that year he went to the University of Virginia, where he founded the Psychological Laboratory in 1929. In 1960 he became Dean of the Graduate School of Arts and Sciences at Virginia; since 1962 he has been Stuart Professor of Psychology at Princeton.

His books include *Fundamentals of Psychology* (Wiley, 1962), and *Communications Processes* (Pergamon Press, 1965).

HERBERT GINSBURG (coauthor, "The Psychology of Robots") did undergraduate work at Harvard, then received his Ph.D. in 1965 from the University of North Carolina. His thesis was on Jean Piaget. For the past several years Ginsburg has been on the faculty of the Department of Child Development and Family Relations at Cornell University. His major research interest is in the cognitive development and education of children.

HARRY and MARGARET HARLOW ("The Young Monkeys") are famous for their work with surrogate mothers, both wire and cloth. During the last ten years the Harlows have discovered a variety of affection ties in monkeys. They have experimentally produced social and asocial monkeys, good and bad mothers, as well as sexually adjusted and maladjusted monkeys.

Dr. Harlow, a past president of the American Psychological Association, received his Ph.D. from Stanford and went to the University of Wisconsin in 1930 to "enrich the literature on rodents." When he arrived, he found that the university had demolished its animal laboratory to make room for a building finally erected thirty years later. In desperation, he turned to the Madison Zoo—and to the monkeys. "For better or worse," he says, "I became forever a monkey man."

Mrs. Harlow came to the university as a specialist in human development but soon broadened her interests to include other primates.

DONALD O. HEBB ("The Mind's Eye") has been a professor of psychology at McGill University since 1947. Much of his work has been with brain-injured patients and with animals. Dr. Hebb is the author of the popular *Organization of Behavior* (1949) and his *Textbook of Psychology* is widely used.

JARVIK   JULESZ   KAMIYA   MEHRABIAN   MONTAGU   ROCK   SELYE   SIMMONS   VERHAVE

MURRAY E. JARVIK ("The Psychopharmacological Revolution") is a professor of pharmacology at the Albert Einstein College of Medicine in New York City. He received his M.D. and his Ph.D. from the University of California, Berkeley. Dr. Jarvik's chief professional interests are the actions of drugs on behavior and the physiological basis of memory.

BELA JULESZ ("Experiment in Perception") is head of the sensory and perceptual processes department at the Bell Telephone Laboratories in Murray Hill, New Jersey. He is noted for his research in visual perception using computer-generated patterns.

Born in Budapest, he received his diploma in communication engineering from the Technical University there in 1950 and was graduated from the Hungarian Academy of Sciences in 1956. His doctoral thesis on the encoding of television signals presaged his later interest in analyzing and processing pictorial information.

In the spring of 1969 he was visiting professor of experimental psychology at MIT, teaching and writing a book on the foundations of Cyclopean perception —a technique of tracing the information flow in the visual system by psychological means.

JOSEPH KAMIYA ("Conscious Control of Brain Waves") is a lecturer in medical psychology at the Langley Porter Neuropsychiatric Institute of the University of California Medical Center in San Francisco.

His doctoral studies were completed at the Berkeley campus of the University of California, and he went on to teach social psychology at the University of Chicago. It was there that he became interested in sleep and dream research and made his first studies of alpha waves.

ALBERT MEHRABIAN ("Communication Without Words") was born in Tabriz, Iran, in 1939. He received his high school education in the preparatory section of the American University of Beirut, Lebanon, and then moved to the United States. He studied mechanical engineering at MIT, where he received his B.S. and M.S. degrees. He continued his graduate work at Clark University, which awarded him a Ph.D. in psychology in 1964. Since that time he has been at UCLA.

ASHLEY MONTAGU ("Chromosomes and Crime"), noted anthropologist and social biologist, was born in England and came to the United States in 1930. He received his Ph.D. from Columbia University in 1937. He has written extensively on race, genetics, and human evolution and was responsible for drafting the UNESCO statement on race. Among his 31 books are *The Human Revolution, Human Heredity,* and *The Natural Superiority of Women.*

IRVIN ROCK ("Perceptual Adaptation") is a professor at the Institute for Cognitive Studies, Rutgers University. After completing his B.S. and M.A. at City College of New York, he received his Ph.D. from the New School for Social Research.

HANS SELYE ("Overview of Stress"), in addition to his three earned doctorates (M.D., Ph.D., D.Sc.), has received honorary degrees from universities in Argentina, Austria, Canada, Czechoslovakia, Chile, Germany, Guatemala, Italy, Japan, and the United States.

After having been at McGill University for many years, he is currently professor and director of the Institute of Experimental Medicine and Surgery at the University of Montreal.

Dr. Selye is the author of approximately 1,200 publications; twenty-two of these are books, including the *Textbook of Endocrinology,* regarded as the most complete work on the subject. He is presently working on a multivolume study about inflammation and wound-healing.

JAMES A. SIMMONS ("The Sonar Sight of Bats") studied under E. G. Wever at the Princeton Auditory Research Laboratories. Much of his undergraduate work was in chemistry and he hopes someday to study behavior from the point of view of chemical events in the central nervous system.

THOM VERHAVE ("The Inspector General is a Bird") was born in Amsterdam, the Netherlands, and immigrated to New York City in 1949. He received his Ph.D. in psychology from Columbia in 1956, after which he spent six years as a psychopharmacologist. In 1963 he joined the faculty of Arizona State University.

Bibliographies

I. Philosophical and Historical Basis of Psychology

Is Phrenology Foolish?

A HISTORY OF EXPERIMENTAL PSYCHOL-
OGY. 2nd ed. E. G. Boring. Appleton-
Century-Crofts, 1950, pp. 50–60.
HUMAN NATURE IN AMERICAN THOUGHT;
THE AGE OF REASON AND MORALITY,
1750–1860. M. Curti in *Political Sci-
ence Quarterly*, Vol. 48, pp. 354–375,
1953.
THE INFLUENCE OF PHRENOLOGY ON
AMERICAN PSYCHOLOGY. D. Bakan in
*Journal of the History of the Behav-
ioral Sciences*, Vol. 2, pp. 200–220,
1966.
PHRENOLOGY. J. G. Spurzheim. Lippin-
cott, 1908.
PHRENOLOGY; FAD AND SCIENCE: A 19TH
CENTURY AMERICAN CRUSADE. J. Da-
vis. Yale University Press, 1955.

The Psychology of Robots

BRAINS, MACHINES, AND MATHEMATICS.
M. A. Arbib. McGraw-Hill, 1964.
CYBERNETICS. N. Wiener. Wiley, 1961.
CYBORG: EVOLUTION OF THE SUPERMAN.
D. S. Halacy, Jr. Harper & Row,
1965.
DESIGN FOR A BRAIN: THE ORIGIN OF
ADAPTIVE BEHAVIOR. W. R. Ashby.
Wiley, 1967.
LEARNING IN SOME SIMPLE NON-BIOLOGI-
CAL SYSTEMS. H. D. Block in *Ameri-
can Scientist*, March 1965.
SIMULATION OF STATISTICALLY COMPOS-
ITE SYSTEMS—SELF-REPRODUCING MA-
CHINES. H. D. Block in *Prospects for
Simulation and Simulators of Dy-
namic Systems*. G. Shapiro, M.
Rogers, eds. Spartan Press, 1967.
THEORY OF SELF-REPRODUCING AUTOM-
ATA. J. Von Neumann. Edited and
completed by A. W. Burks. Uni-
versity of Illinois Press, 1966.

The Mind's Eye

A HISTORY OF EXPERIMENTAL PSYCHOL-
OGY. 2nd ed. E. G. Boring. Appleton-
Century-Crofts, 1950.
A HISTORY OF INTROSPECTION. E. G. Bor-
ing in *Psychologist at Large*. Basic
Books, 1961.
PRINCIPLES OF PSYCHOLOGY. W. James.
Dover, 1950.
SENSORY DEPRIVATION. P. Solomon, P.
Kubzansky, *et al.*, eds. Harvard Uni-
versity Press, 1961.
THINKING. G. Humphrey. Wiley, 1963.

II. Perception and Cognition

Language and the Mind

ASPECTS OF THE THEORY OF SYNTAX.
N. Chomsky. M.I.T. Press, 1965.
CARTESIAN LINGUISTICS. N. Chomsky.
Harper & Row, 1966.
GRAMMATICAL STRUCTURE AND THE IM-
MEDIATE RECALL OF ENGLISH SEN-
TENCES. H. Savin, E. Perchonock in
*Journal of Verbal Learning and
Verbal Behavior*, Vol. 4, pp. 348–
353, 1965.
THE PHILOSOPHY OF LANGUAGE. J. Katz.
Harper & Row, 1966.
THE PSYCHOLOGICAL REALITY OF LIN-
GUISTIC SEGMENTS. J. Fodor, T.
Bever in *Journal of Verbal Learning
and Verbal Behavior*, Vol. 4, pp.
414–420, 1965.
SOUND PATTERN OF ENGLISH. N. Chom-
sky, M. Halle. Harper & Row, 1968.
STRUCTURE OF LANGUAGE: READINGS IN
THE PHILOSOPHY OF LANGUAGE. J.
Fodor, J. Katz, eds. Prentice-Hall,
1964.

Communication Without Words

THE COMMUNICATION OF EMOTIONAL
MEANING. J. Davitz, ed. McGraw-Hill,
1964.
EXPRESSION OF THE EMOTIONS IN MAN.
P. Knapp, ed. International Univer-
sity Press, 1963.
LANGUAGE WITHIN LANGUAGE: IMMEDI-
ACY, A CHANNEL IN VERBAL COMMUNI-
CATION. M. Wiener, A. Mehrabian.
Appleton-Century-Crofts, 1968.
THE SILENT LANGUAGE. E. Hall. Double-
day, 1959 (in paperback, Fawcett,
1961).
SIGNIFICANCE OF POSTURE AND POSITION
IN THE COMMUNICATION OF ATTITUDE
AND STATUS RELATIONSHIPS. A. Mehra-
bian in *Psychological Bulletin*, Vol.
71, pp. 359–372, 1969.

Experiment in Perception

BINOCULAR DEPTH PERCEPTION WITHOUT
FAMILIARITY CUES. B. Julesz in *Sci-
ence*, Vol. 145, pp. 356–362, 1964.
EXTENSION OF PANUM'S FUSIONAL AREA
IN BINOCULARLY STABILIZED VISION.
D. Fender, B. Julesz in *Journal of
the Optical Society of America*, Vol.
57, pp. 819–830, 1967.
THE SUPPRESSION OF MONOCULARLY PER-
CEIVABLE SYMMETRY DURING BINOCU-
LAR FUSION. B. Julesz in *Bell System
Technical Journal*, Vol. 46, No. 6,
pp. 1203–1221, July–August, 1967.
TEXTURE AND VISUAL PERCEPTION. B.
Julesz in *Scientific American*, Vol.
212, No. 2, pp. 38–48, February,
1965.

Conscious Control of Brain Waves

EEG CORRELATES OF SLEEP: EVIDENCES
FOR SEPARATE FOREBRAIN SUB-
STRATES. M. Sterman, W. Wrywicka
in *Brain Research*, Vol. 6, Pt. 1, pp.
143–163, 1967.
AN ELECTROENCEPHALOGRAPHIC STUDY
ON THE ZEN MEDITATION (ZAZEN).
A. Kasamatsu, T. Hirai in *Fol. Psy-
chiat. Neurol. Japon.*, Vol. 20, pp.
315–336, 1966.
ELECTROPHYSIOLOGICAL CORRELATES OF
SOME YOGI EXERCISES. B. K. Bagchi,
M. A. Wenger in *EEG Clinical
Neurophysiology*, Supplement No. 7,
pp. 132–149, 1957.
ELECTROPHYSIOLOGICAL STUDIES OF
DREAMING AS THE PROTOTYPE OF A
NEW STRATEGY IN THE STUDY OF CON-
SCIOUSNESS. J. Stoyva, J. Kamiya in
Psychological Review.
TRAINED SELF-CONTROL OF THE EEG
ALPHA RHYTHM. J. Kamiya in *Altered
States of Consciousness*. C. Tart, ed.
Wiley (in press).

The Sonar Sight of Bats

ACOUSTIC SIGNALS FOR AUTO-INFORMA-
TION OR ECHOLOCATION. F. Vincent
in *Acoustic Behavior of Animals*. René
Busnel, ed. Elsevier, 1963.
ECHOLOCATION: AUDITORY CUES FOR
RANGE PERCEPTION BY BATS. J. Sim-
mons in *Proceedings, 76th Annual
Convention, American Psychological
Association*.
LISTENING IN THE DARK. D. Griffin. Yale
University Press, 1958.
MECHANISMS OF ANIMAL BEHAVIOR. P.
Marler, W. J. Hamilton. Wiley, 1966.

Chemical Perception in Newborn Snakes

CHEMICAL CUE PREFERENCES OF INEX-
PERIENCED SNAKES: COMPARATIVE AS-
PECTS. G. M. Burghardt in *Science*,
1967.
ETHOLOGY: AN APPROACH TOWARD THE
COMPLETE ANALYSIS OF BEHAVIOR.
E. H. Hess in *New Directions in Psy-
chology*. Holt, Rinehart and Winston,
1962, pp. 157–266.
LIVING REPTILES OF THE WORLD. R. F.
Inger, K. P. Schmidt. Doubleday,
1957.
THE NATURAL HISTORY OF NORTH AMERI-
CAN AMPHIBIANS AND REPTILES. J. A.
Oliver. Van Nostrand, 1955.
THE SCIENCE OF SMELL. R. H. Wright.
Allen and Unwin, 1964.
STIMULUS CONTROL OF THE PREY ATTACK
RESPONSE IN NAIVE GARTER SNAKES.
G. M. Burghardt in *Psychonomic Sci-
ence*, Vol. 4, pp. 37–38, 1966.

Body English

THE AMERICAN SCIENTIST: MAN OR SUPERMAN? M. Gunther in *Saturday Evening Post*, December 16, 1967.

CUTANEOUS CHANNELS OF COMMUNICATION. F. A. Geldard in *Sensory Communication*. W. A. Rosenblith, ed. Wiley, 1961. Chap. 4.

CUTANEOUS CODING OF OPTICAL SIGNALS: THE OPTOHAPT. F. A. Geldard in *Perception and Psychophysics*, Vol. 1, pp. 377–381, 1966.

MULTIPLE CUTANEOUS STIMULATION: THE DISCRIMINATION OF VIBRATORY PATTERNS. F. A. Geldard, C. E. Sherrick in *Journal of the Acoustical Society*, Vol. 37, pp. 797–801, 1965.

PATTERN PERCEPTION BY THE SKIN. F. A. Geldard in *The Skin Senses*. D. Kenshalo, ed. Charles C Thomas, 1968. Chap. 13.

SOME NEGLECTED POSSIBILITIES OF COMMUNICATION. F. A. Geldard in *Science*, Vol. 131, pp. 1583–1588, 1960.

Perceptual Adaptation

ADAPTATION, AFTEREFFECT, AND CONTRAST IN THE PERCEPTION OF CURVED LINES. J. J. Gibson in *Journal of Experimental Psychology*, Vol. 16, pp. 1–31, 1933.

THE FORMATION AND TRANSFORMATION OF THE PERCEPTUAL WORLD. I. Kohler in *Psychological Issues*, Vol. 3, No. 4, pp. 1–173, 1964.

GESTALT PSYCHOLOGY. W. Köhler. Liveright, 1947.

PLASTICITY IN SENSORY-MOTOR SYSTEMS. R. Held in *Scientific American*, Vol. 213, No. 5, pp. 84–94, 1965.

VISION AND TOUCH. I. Rock, C. Harris in *Scientific American*, Vol. 216, No. 5, pp. 96–104, 1967.

VISION WITHOUT INVERSION OF THE RETINAL IMAGE. G. Stratton in *Psychology Review*, Vol. 4, pp. 341–360, 463–481, 1897.

III. Learning, Memory, and the Modification of Behavior

The Inspector General Is a Bird

THE COMPLEX DISCRIMINATED OPERANT: STUDIES OF MATCHING-TO-SAMPLE AND RELATED PROBLEMS. W. W. Cumming, R. Berryman in *Stimulus Generalization*. D. I. Mostofsky, ed. Stanford University Press, 1965.

FROM GENERATION TO GENERATION. S. N. Eisenstadt. Free Press, 1956.

INTERMITTENT REINFORCEMENT OF MATCHING-TO-SAMPLE IN THE PIGEON. C. B. Ferster in *Journal of the Experimental Analysis of Behavior*, Vol. 3, pp. 259–272, 1960.

THE PIGEON AS A QUALITY-CONTROL INSPECTOR. T. Verhave in *American Psychologist*, Vol. 21, pp. 109–115, 1966.

SOCIAL ORGANIZATION. C. H. Cooley. Schocken Books, 1962.

SOME OBSERVATIONS ON EXTINCTION OF A COMPLEX DISCRIMINATED OPERANT. W. W. Cumming, R. Berryman, L. R. Cohen, R. N. Lanson in *Psychological Reports*, Vol. 20, pp. 1328–1330, 1967.

TRANSMISSION OF LEARNED BEHAVIOR BETWEEN RATS. R. M. Church in *The Journal of Abnormal and Social Psychology*, Vol. 20, pp. 163–165, 1957.

WILL. R. J. Herrnstein in *Proceedings of the American Philosophical Society*, Vol. 108, No. 6, pp. 455–458, 1964.

Of Mice and Misers

FUNCTIONAL AUTONOMY OF MOTIVES AS AN EXTINCTION PHENOMENON. D. C. McClelland in *Psychological Review*, Vol. 49, pp. 272–283, 1942.

THE MEASUREMENT OF NERVOUS HABITS IN NORMAL CHILDREN. W. Olson. University of Minnesota Press, 1929.

MOTIVATION, PERFORMANCE AND EXTINCTION. R. W. Earl in *Journal of Comparative and Physiological Psychology*, Vol. 50, pp. 248–251, 1957.

ON THE PERSISTENCE OF AN EAR-SCRATCHING RESPONSE IN THE RAT. W. Datel, J. P. Seward in *Journal of Abnormal and Social Psychology*, Vol. 47, pp. 58–61, 1952.

PATTERN AND GROWTH IN PERSONALITY. G. W. Allport. Holt, Rinehart and Winston, 1961.

PROBLEMS PRESENTED BY THE CONCEPT OF ACQUIRED DRIVES. J. S. Brown in *Current Theory and Research in Motivation: A Symposium*. University of Nebraska Press, 1953.

THE STRUCTURE OF FUNCTIONAL AUTONOMY. J. P. Seward in *American Psychologist*, Vol. 18, pp. 703–710, 1963.

Pain and Aggression

ATTACK, AVOIDANCE, AND ESCAPE REACTIONS TO AVERSIVE SHOCK. N. H. Azrin, R. R. Hutchinson, D. F. Hake in *Journal of the Experimental Analysis of Behavior*, Vol. 10, pp. 131–148, 1967.

EXTINCTION-INDUCED AGGRESSION. N. H. Azrin, R. R. Hutchinson, D. F. Hake in *Journal of the Experimental Analysis of Behavior*, Vol. 9, pp. 191–204, 1966.

REFLEXIVE FIGHTING IN RESPONSE TO AVERSIVE STIMULATION. R. E. Ulrich, N. H. Azrin in *Journal of the Experimental Analysis of Behavior*, Vol. 5, pp. 511–520, 1962.

Neural Basis of Memory

THE HUMAN BRAIN: ITS CAPACITIES AND FUNCTIONS. Isaac Asimov. Houghton Mifflin, 1964.

PHYSIOLOGICAL PSYCHOLOGY. J. A. Deutsch and D. Deutsch. Dorsey Press, 1966.

THE STRUCTURAL BASIS OF BEHAVIOR. J. A. Deutsch. University of Chicago Press, 1960.

IV. Motivation and Biological Psychology

Chromosomes and Crime

HUMAN HEREDITY. A. Montagu. World Publishing, 1964.

THE GENETIC CODE. I. Asimov. Grossman, 1963 (in paperback, Signet).

GENETICS. *Biology and Behavior Series*. David C. Glass, ed. Rockefeller University Press and Sage Foundation, 1968.

HUMAN POPULATION CYTOGENETICS. W. M. C. Brown. Wiley, 1967.

THE YY SYNDROME. *Lancet*, March 12, 1966.

The Hungry Fly

INSECTS AND THE CONCEPT OF MOTIVATION. V. G. Dethier in the *Nebraska Symposium on Motivation*, pp. 105–136, 1966.

Tell us what you think

All over the country today students are taking an active role in the quality of their education. They're telling administrators what they like and what they don't like about their campus communities. They're telling teachers what they like and what they don't like about their courses.

This response card offers you a unique opportunity as a student to tell a publisher what you like and what you don't like about his book.

EVALUATION QUESTIONNAIRE

1. **Your school:**_____

_____

2. **Your year:** ☐ Freshman ☐ Sophomore ☐ Junior ☐ Senior
☐ Graduate student

3. **Title of course in which READINGS was assigned:**_____

_____

4. **Course level:** ☐ First year ☐ Second year ☐ Third year
☐ Fourth year ☐ Graduate

5. **Length of course:** ☐ Quarter ☐ Trimester ☐ Semester ☐ Year

6. **How many articles were you assigned to read?**_____

7. **How many articles did you read that weren't assigned?**_____

8. **Did you find the majority of the articles:**
☐ Very interesting ☐ Fairly interesting ☐ Not interesting

9. **If you think there's a gap between what you're studying and what's going on in the world today, did you find that the articles in READINGS helped bridge that gap?** ☐ Yes ☐ No

If yes, how?
☐ Shed light on events in the news.
☐ Offered insight into personal problems and gave me ideas about solving them.
☐ Discussed the problems of individuals in ways that helped explain people I know.
☐ Offered insight into social problems and gave me ideas about solving them.
☐ Gave me information and arguments for attacking ideas I disagree with.
☐ Presented information and arguments that changed my own ideas.
☐ Other:_____

_____

If no, why?
☐ Seemed irrelevant to events in the news.
☐ Didn't identify personal problems important to me or suggest ways to solve them.
☐ Didn't make discussion of individual problems relevant to people I know.
☐ Didn't identify social problems important to me or suggest ways to solve them.
☐ Discussed individual and social problems but didn't make them important to me personally or show ways to deal with them.
☐ Didn't cause me to change my ideas about any important topic.
☐ Other:_____

10. **How interesting were the materials used in your course? How do you rate them?**
Rating: 1 = Most interesting   7 = Least interesting
Materials used:

	1	2	3	4	5	6	7
READINGS	☐	☐	☐	☐	☐	☐	☐
Textbook	☐	☐	☐	☐	☐	☐	☐
Lectures	☐	☐	☐	☐	☐	☐	☐
Films	☐	☐	☐	☐	☐	☐	☐
Laboratory work	☐	☐	☐	☐	☐	☐	☐
Paperbacks	☐	☐	☐	☐	☐	☐	☐
Other_____	☐	☐	☐	☐	☐	☐	☐

11. **How helpful were the introductions to each article?**
☐ Very helpful   ☐ Sometimes helpful
☐ Not helpful   ☐ Did not read them

12. **Would additional materials printed with each article have been helpful?** ☐ Yes ☐ No
If yes, what kind?
☐ Marginal outlines of key points.
☐ Review questions.
☐ Glossaries of themes and concepts.
☐ Other:_____

13. **What textbook did you use?**
Author(s):_____

    Title:_____
How would you rate it?

Content:
☐ Covered each area fully.
☐ Too much on some topics, not enough on others.
☐ Seemed up to date.
☐ Seemed out of date.

☐ Other:_____

_____

Level:
☐ Easy to read and generally interesting.
☐ Hard to read: explanations too complicated.
☐ Quality of writing not interesting.

☐ Other:_____

_____

Illustrations:
☐ Easy to understand, attractive, informative.
☐ Inadequate: hard to understand.
☐ Unclear, unattractive.
☐ Didn't help in understanding.

☐ Other:_____

_____

14. **Are laboratory experiments part of your course work?**
☐ Yes ☐ No
If no, would you have liked to have had the equipment and opportunity to do psychological experiments as part of your course work? ☐ Yes ☐ No

15. **Comments on course, text materials, etc.:**_____

_____

_____

_____

_____

16. **What do you think of this questionnaire?**_____

_____

_____

_____

_____

_____

THIS FLAP IS GUMMED | JUST FOLD, SEAL, AND MAIL | NO STAMP NECESSARY

MICROSCOPIC BRAINS. V. G. Dethier in *Science*, Vol. 143, pp. 1138–1145, 1964.
TO KNOW A FLY. V. G. Dethier, Holden-Day, 1962.

Copulation in Rats

CHARACTERISTICS OF MASCULINE "SEX DRIVE." F. A. Beach in *Nebraska Symposium on Motivation*. M. Jones, ed. University of Nebraska Press, pp. 1–31, 1956.
CONDITIONING AND SEXUAL BEHAVIOR IN THE MALE ALBINO RAT. K. Larsson. Almqvist and Wiksell, 1956.
SEX AND BEHAVIOR. F. A. Beach, ed. Wiley, 1965.

The Young Monkeys

AFFECTION IN PRIMATES. M. K. Harlow, H. F. Harlow in *Discovery*, Vol. 27, pp. 11–17, 1966.
BEHAVIORAL ASPECTS OF REPRODUCTION IN PRIMATES. H. F. Harlow, W. Danforth Joslyn, M. G. Senko, A. Dopp in *Journal of Animal Science*, Vol. 25, pp. 49–67, 1966.
LEARNING TO LOVE. H. F. Harlow, M. K. Harlow in *American Scientist*, Vol. 54, pp. 244–272, 1966.
LOVE IN INFANT MONKEYS. H. F. Harlow in *Scientific American*, June, 1959.
MATERNAL BEHAVIOR OF RHESUS MONKEYS DEPRIVED OF MOTHERING AND PEER ASSOCIATION IN INFANCY. H. F. Harlow, M. K. Harlow, R. O. Dodsworth, G. L. Arling, in *Proceedings of the American Philosophical Society*, Vol. 110, pp. 329–335, 1967.

It's All in Your Mind

ANIMAL RESEARCH AND PSYCHIATRIC THEORY. Frank Beach in *Psychosomatic Medicine*, Vol. 15, No. 5, pp. 374–389, 1953.
CEREBRAL AND HORMONAL CONTROL OF REFLECTIVE MECHANISMS INVOLVED IN COPULATORY BEHAVIOR. Frank Beach in *Physiological Review*, Vol. 47, No. 2, pp. 269–316, 1967.
CHARACTERISTICS OF MASCULINE "SEX DRIVE." Frank Beach in *Nebraska Symposium on Motivation*, M. R. Jones, ed., University of Nebraska Press, pp. 1–32, 1956.
COITAL BEHAVIOR IN DOGS. (1) PREFERENTIAL MATING IN THE BITCH. Frank Beach, Burney LeBoeuf in *Animal Behaviour*, Vol. 15, No. 4, pp. 546–558, 1967.
COMPARISONS OF THE EJACULATORY RESPONSE IN MEN AND ANIMALS. Frank Beach, W. H. Westbrook, L. G. Clemens in *Psychosomatic Medicine*, Vol. 28, No. 5, pp. 749–763, 1966.
THE DESCENT OF INSTINCT. Frank Beach in *Psychological Review*, Vol. 62, No. 6, pp. 401–410, 1955.
EXPERIMENTAL INVESTIGATIONS OF SPECIES-SPECIFIC BEHAVIOR. Frank Beach in *American Psychologist*, Vol. 15, No. 1, pp. 1–19, 1960.
"PSYCHOSOMATIC" PHENOMENA IN ANIMALS. Frank Beach in *Psychosomatic Medicine*, Vol. 14, No. 4, pp. 261–270, 1952.
A REVIEW OF PHYSIOLOGICAL AND PSYCHOLOGICAL STUDIES OF SEXUAL BEHAVIOR IN MAMMALS. Frank Beach in *Physiological Review*, Vol. 27, No. 2, pp. 240–305, 1947.
THE SNARK WAS A BOOJUM. Frank Beach in *American Psychologist*, Vol. 5, No. 4, pp. 115–124, 1950.

Overview of Stress

IN VIVO: THE CASE FOR SUPRAMOLECULAR BIOLOGY. Hans Selye. Liveright, 1967.
PSYCHOLOGICAL STRESS; PSYCHOANALYTIC AND BEHAVIORAL STUDIES OF SURGICAL PATIENTS. Irving L. Janis. Wiley, 1958.
PSYCHOLOGICAL STRESS AND THE COPING PROCESS. Richard S. Lazarus. McGraw-Hill, 1966.
THE STORY OF THE ADAPTATION SYNDROME. Hans Selye. Acta, 1952.
STRESS: SOURCES, MANAGEMENT, AND PREVENTION. Lennart L. Levi. Liveright, 1967.
THE STRESS OF LIFE. Hans Selye. McGraw-Hill, 1956.

The Psychopharmacological Revolution

DRUGS AND ANIMAL BEHAVIOUR. H. Steinberg in *British Medical Bulletin*, Vol. 20, pp. 75–80, 1964.
DRUGS USED IN THE TREATMENT OF PSYCHIATRIC DISORDERS. M. E. Jarvik in *The Pharmacological Basis of Therapeutics*, L. S. Goodman, A. Gilman, eds. Macmillan, 3rd ed., pp. 159–214, 1965.
THE HALLUCINOGENIC DRUGS. F. Barron, M. E. Jarvik, S. Bunnell, Jr. in *Scientific American*, Vol. 210, pp. 3–11, April, 1964.
THE INFLUENCE OF DRUGS UPON MEMORY. M. E. Jarvik in *Animal Behaviour and Drug Action*. Hannah Steinberg, A. V. S. de Reuck, Julie Knight, eds. Churchill, 1964.
THE RELATION OF PSYCHIATRY TO PHARMACOLOGY. A. Wikler. Williams & Wilkins, 1957.

Index

Picture Credits

Cover photograph by Steve McCarroll

Photographs by
John Conover: page 58
Steve McCarroll: pages 50, 80, 102, 116, 134, 144, 160
John Oldenkamp: pages 2, 5, 10, 18, 28, 74, 77, 78, 90, 108,
    124, 156
James A. Simmons: pages 56, 59
Tom Suzuki: page 150
John Waggaman: pages 52, 54
Robert Watts: page 60
Paul Weller: page 83 (prior publication in *Scientific American*)
Steve Wells: page 36

Illustrations by
Gerri Blake: page 96
Robert Hostick: page 13
Darrell Millsap: page 15
Karl Nicholason: pages 82, 86, 87, 99
George Price: page 152, 171–173

Photographs courtesy Stanford University: pages 13, 15
Photograph courtesy Bell Telephone Laboratories: page 15
Photographs courtesy Gordon M. Burghardt: pages 47, 48
Photographs and illustrations courtesy Vincent Dethier: pages
    124–132
Drawings courtesy Mercury Archives: page 7

Design by Tom Gould: page 36

Illustrations courtesy Bela Julesz: pages 41–48

Depiction of nerve cell redrawn from Anthony Ravielli
    illustration in *The Human Brain: Its Capacities and
    Functions* by Isaac Asimov, Houghton Mifflin Co., 1964:
    page 110

CRM BOOKS
David A. Dushkin, *President and Publisher*, CRM BOOKS

Richard L. Roe, *Vice-President, CRM BOOKS, and Director, College Department*
Sales Manager, College Department: Richard M. Connelly
Fulfillment Manager, College Department: Nancy Le Clere
College Department Staff: Elaine Kleiss, Carol A. Walnum, La Delle Willett

Jean Smith, *Vice-President and Managing Editor*, CRM BOOKS
Senior Editor: Arlyne Lazerson
Editors: Gloria Joyce, Cecie Starr, Betsy H. Wyckoff
Editorial Assistants: Jacquelyn Estrada, Cynthia MacDonald, Johanna Price, Ann Scales
Rights and Permissions: Donna L. Taylor

Jo Ann Gilberg, *Vice-President, CRM BOOKS, and Director, Manufacturing and Production*
Production Manager: Eugene G. Schwartz
Production Supervisors: Barbara Blum, E. Cecile Mayer, P. Douglas Armstrong
Production Assistants: Georgene Martina, Patricia Perkins, Toini Jaffee
Production Staff: Mona F. Drury, Margaret M. Mesec

Tom Suzuki, *Vice-President, CRM BOOKS, and Director of Design*

Art Director: Leon Bolognese
Promotion Art Director: John Isely
Designer: George Price
Associate Designers: Catherine Flanders, Reynold Hernandez
Assistant Designers: Robert Fountain, Pamela Morehouse
Assistant Promotion Designer: John Madison Hix
Art Staff: Jacqueline McLoughlin

Paul Lapolla, *Vice-President, CRM BOOKS, and Director, Psychology Today Book Club*
Assistant: Karen De Laria

Controller: Robert Geiserman

Assistant: Maryann Errichetti

Office Manager: Lynn D. Crosby

Assistant: Janie Fredericks

Officers of Communications/Research/Machines, Inc.
John J. Veronis, *President;* Nicolas H. Charney, *Chairman of the Board;*
David A. Dushkin, *Vice-President;* James B. Horton, *Vice-President*

This book was composed by American Book–Stratford Press, Inc., New York, New York.
It was printed and bound by Kingsport Press, Inc., Kingsport, Tennessee.